A People's History of Psychoanalysis

Psychoanalytic Studies: Clinical, Social, and Cultural Contexts

Series Editor:
Michael O'Loughlin, Adelphi University

Mission Statement

Psychoanalytic Studies seeks psychoanalytically informed works addressing the implications of the location of the individual in clinical, social, cultural, historical, and ideological contexts. Innovative theoretical and clinical works within psychoanalytic theory and in fields such as anthropology, education, and history are welcome. Projects addressing conflict, migrations, difference, ideology, subjectivity, memory, psychiatric suffering, physical and symbolic violence, power, and the future of psychoanalysis itself are welcome, as are works illustrating critical and activist applications of clinical work.

See https://rowman.com/Action/SERIES/LEX/LEXPS for a list of advisory board members.

Titles in the series

A People's History of Psychoanalysis: From Freud to Liberation Psychology, by Daniel Jose Gaztambide
Rethinking the Relation between Women and Psychoanalysis: Loss, Mourning, and the Feminine, edited by Hada Soria Escalante
Lives Interrupted: Psychiatric Narratives of Struggle and Resilience, edited by Michael O'Loughlin, Secil Arac-Orhun, and Montana Queler
Women and the Psychosocial Construction of Madness, edited by Marie Brown and Marilyn Charles
Revisioning War Trauma in Cinema: Uncoming Communities, by Jessica Datema and Manya Steinkoler
Women & Psychosis: Multidisciplinary Perspectives, by edited by Marie Brown and Marilyn Charles
Psychoanalysis from the Indian Terroir: Emerging Themes in Culture, Family, and Childhood in India, edited by Manasi Kumar, Anup Dhar, and Anurag Mishra
A Three-Factor Model of Couples Psychotherapy: Projective Identification, Level of Couple Object Relations, And Omnipotent Control, by Robert Mendelsohn

A People's History of Psychoanalysis

From Freud to Liberation Psychology

Daniel José Gaztambide

LEXINGTON BOOKS
Lanham • Boulder • New York • London

Published by Lexington Books
An imprint of The Rowman & Littlefield Publishing Group, Inc.
4501 Forbes Boulevard, Suite 200, Lanham, Maryland 20706
www.rowman.com

6 Tinworth Street, London SE11 5AL

British Library Cataloguing in Publication Information Available

Library of Congress Control Number: 2019950462
ISBN 9781498565745 (cloth)
ISBN 9781498565769 (pbk.)
ISBN 9781498565752 (electronic)

This is what the LORD says: Administer justice and righteousness. Rescue the victim of robbery from the hand of his oppressor. Do no wrong or violence to the stranger, the fatherless, or the widow. Do not shed innocent blood in this place.—Jeremiah 22: 3

You must not exploit or oppress a stranger, for you yourselves were strangers in the land of Egypt.—Exodus 22: 21

Quitate tu, pa ponerme yo. / Remove yourself, so I can place myself.—Puerto Rican saying

Contents

Preface

I was walking through the book stacks of Burke Library at Union Theological Seminary, balancing a leaning tower of books between my hands and my chin, looking for a copy of Jessica Benjamin's *The Bonds of Love: Psychoanalysis, Feminism, and the Problem of Domination* (1988) for my master's thesis. I was writing about the parallels I saw between her psychoanalytic theory of intersubjectivity and Paulo Freire's critical pedagogy, noting a resemblance that could provide an entry point for a dialogue between psychoanalysis and liberation psychology. Paulo Freire, after all, had been a major influence for Ignacio Martín-Baró, the founder of liberation psychology itself. Making this connection could provide me with a way of talking about psychoanalytic thinking as a participant in social justice activism. I was not too enamored with Freud back then. He seemed stuffy, cold, distant, and unrelatable. My undergraduate studies and much of what I was exposed to at the time impressed upon me the idea that Freudian psychoanalysis was outdated, irrelevant, and past its prime. Worse still, psychoanalysis and its founder were irredeemably White, bourgeois, and oppressive. Psychoanalysis did not address issues of culture, let alone inequality, colonialism, and oppression. It was part of the problem. But maybe, I thought, there was the possibility for *contemporary*, especially *relational* psychoanalysis to be part of the solution. What was old was bad and what was new, well, it had to be good.

Liberation theology and psychoanalysis were strange bedfellows at Union. Students and faculty looked askance at psychoanalysis with suspicion at its erasure of social and political forces in the life of the soul. Psychoanalytic faculty and students at times, too, recoiled as they defended why a focus on the inner life, the passions, and embodied aliveness was meaningful irrespective of politics, but also crucially important to them. As a master's student from Puerto Rico with a commitment to social justice and a desire to explore how psychoanalysis and clinical psychology could inform social liberation, I found myself trying to bridge worlds, communities, and discourses. Could psychoanalysis, despite its retrograde history with respect to race, gender, class, and sexuality still have something to say to me? Could it—

I trip over a small ladder; my fumbling grants the stack in my hands wings as books flew everywhere. I get absentminded sometimes when I'm deep in thought. I start to berate myself for not looking where I'm going when I spot a book out the corner of my eye. I scan the title a couple of times to make sure I'm reading it right and that it says what I think it says. *Freud's Free Clinics: Psychoanalysis and Social Justice—1918–1938*. Elizabeth Danto. Freud and . . . social justice? I did not know what to make of this book, but I was curious. I pulled it from the shelf and added it to my stack.

A year passed. I defended my thesis, and during this time I applied and was admitted into Rutgers University's Graduate School of Applied and Professional Psychology (GSAPP). I did not remember Danto's book until the day I was packing to move from New York City to New Brunswick to start doctoral school. In between filling boxes with books and clothes, I took a break and decided to leaf through the book. I was immediately enraptured and finished it within the day. My thoughts were racing as what felt like a hidden and forgotten history revealed itself through Danto's work. A different history from what I had been led to understand, one in which Freud and his colleagues were in thought and in deed engaged with expanding the contours of psychoanalysis to include issues of economic inequality, racial discrimination, and colonial exploitation. Danto's work led me to Sander Gilman, and his erudite volumes on Freud's racial identity as a Jew growing up in an anti-Semitic climate that treated him, and the rest of the first generation of psychoanalysts, as an other. Through Gilman's work as well as others, I became exposed to a different depiction of Freud and the early analysts, one in which they navigated a world brimming with far-right fascism, everyday racism and discrimination, and the ebb and flow of inequality that affects us all. For the first time, the story of psychoanalysis spoke to me.

It has been exactly ten years since that experience at Union. As a doctoral student in clinical psychology at GSAPP, I was exposed to multicultural psychology, a diverse field of scholars, researchers, and clinicians dedicated to social justice, and the empowerment of racial, ethnic, gender, and sexual minorities. Multicultural psychology, I was excited to learn, considered itself an intellectual descendant of Paulo Freire and Martín-Baró. At the same time, however, it harbored the same healthy cultural suspicion my peers at Union Theological Seminary had toward psychoanalysis. Over the course of that time my graduate studies and my scholarship continued to focus on race, social justice, psychoanalytic thinking, and liberation psychology. For the longest time it felt like I was still trying to bridge together disparate worlds, guided only by a feeling. An intuition that *something* bound these discourses together.

At first the parallels I originally studied between Benjamin and Freire seemed like a coincidence, a case of thinkers from totally different traditions coming to similar conclusions. Then I discovered that Paulo Freire and the psychoanalyst Erich Fromm had been friends and conversation partners. In fact, it had been Fromm who remarked to Freire that his work constituted a kind of "historico-sociocultural and political psychoanalysis." Reading Freire more closely, I realized he cited and drew on Fromm's works, especially *Escape from Freedom* (1941), also known as *The Fear of Freedom* outside of North America. But Freire also drew on the Black psychiatrist-revolutionary Frantz Fanon, as did his intellectual inheritor Martín-Baró. I was aware that Fanon had some relationship to psychoanalysis, with some scholars wishing to separate him from any association with Freud and his legacy. I started to think—if there is another story to be told about Freud, could there be another story to be told about Liberation psychology? Could there be more to this relationship?

The experience of writing this book has been somewhat like a process of discovery, akin to Freud's metaphor of the psychoanalyst as an archaeologist, digging deeper beneath layers of history. Each layer revealed new stories, new relationships, and new chains of influence between psychoanalysis and liberation psychology. Far from being two antithetical discourses—one regressive and oppressive, the other progressive and liberationist—they came to form part and parcel of a tradition that constantly reinvented itself while at the same time maintaining the essence of certain ideas which continue to inform social justice discourse, pedagogy, and training in multicultural psychology and cultural studies. Perhaps most surprising was the realization that a period of time existed in which psychoanalysts of Jewish and Iberian descent and psychiatrists, sociologists, and philosophers of color engaged in ongoing collaborations aimed at bringing psychoanalysis to bear on issues of racial and economic justice. This series of relationships allowed for the transmission of psychoanalytically informed ideas about race and class that actually connect psychoanalysis to liberation psychology.

The more I read, the more I wondered—could there be more *still*? And each time I asked that question I would happen upon another reference point, another connection, a liaison between discourses and peoples previously thought incommensurable. But for the thinkers reviewed in this book, especially thinkers of color, psychoanalysis was neither irreconcilable nor incompatible with racial and socio-economic justice. It was, in fact, essential to struggles for liberation then, just as much as it has bearing for us in our world today.

Portions of Chapter 2 were originally published as "A psychotherapy for the people: Freud, Ferenczi, and psychoanalytic work with the underprivileged" in *Contemporary Psychoanalysis*. They are shared here with permission from the editors. As my research led me to read certain primary sources in Spanish and Portuguese, I have provided my own translation where applicable and note as such in the text. Although I am thankful for the friends, peers, mentors, and conversation partners that have informed my thinking in this work, all errors and mistakes contained therein are my own.

This book is about a story not often told, because it needs to be told "from below." From the perspective of Black people fighting racism and the legacy of slavery in North America. From the perspective of Afro-Latinx and Latinx people fighting Whiteness and economic exploitation in Latin America. From the perspective of colonized people in Africa and the Caribbean fighting for their independence. From the perspective of workers and revolutionaries fighting the greed of the wealthy and the rise of fascism in mid-century Spain and Germany. A history *from* the people, from Freud to Fanon to Freire to Martín-Baró; from Vienna to Harlem to Algeria to Argentina to Brazil to Spain to El Salvador and back again. A history without borders that welcomes the other—a people's history of psychoanalysis.

Acknowledgments

This book is the culmination of over twelve years of thinking, researching, and synthesizing the complex history of psychoanalysis, liberation psychology, and social justice, a work that I started with my graduate degree at Union Theological Seminary, and continued past my doctoral training at the Graduate School of Applied and Professional Psychology at Rutgers University (GSAPP). It is the product of a voice and a perspective, an ethic and a set of principles, a history and a people. But it is also the culmination of a matrix of relationships that defy disciplinary, cultural, and theoretical boundaries. They are the roots of my thinking, and the routes through which I found my way to this book.

Prior to my beginning to put words to my questions around race, class, colonialism and the psyche, there was a whole world of meaning given birth to under a great big *palo de mango*, a mango tree in San Juan, Puerto Rico. This mighty mango tree stood in the backyard of my childhood home, the same house my father grew up in. It was the heart of my home—physically, psychologically, and spiritually. I would help my maternal grandfather collect the mangos once they fell from the tree, clean them, and present them to him and my mother, who would eat them with my father and grandmother. Although I would not partake of the fruits of the tree—my palette was rather finicky as a child—I derived joy from my family's enjoyment of their sweet fragrance. Our mango tree scraped the firmament with its long branches, mirrored by the winding roots that bound it to the soil of Puerto Rico, at times breaking through the paved ground if only to make its presence known. And isn't that the purpose of roots? To ground us to the earth, yet time and again remind us of where we come from?

Every now and then the head pastor and youth pastor of our church would come visit, sit with my grandfather and mother, eat mangos and drink fine coffee. Now and then I'd overhear their *tertulias* as a child, often ripe with politics and religion, but also psychology. Our head pastor at times mused about writing a psychoanalytic study of the personalities of different characters in the Bible, while our youth pastor encouraged my budding interest in the field of psychology through his mentorship, humor, and empathy. But I would not have developed such an interest—or at least so avidly and so early in my life—if not for my mother who worked as their secretary. As a psychologist, I am aware of the irony.

My mother read books on psychology in part from her exposure to it through our pastors, but also from her own curiosity and hunger for knowledge. She always wanted to be a forensic psychologist, but could not fulfill this dream due to the cost and barriers this presented. She would read excerpts from different books and articles to me, pages brimming with theories and ideas about the human condition. She psychoanalyzed herself, me, our family, our island, and our collective condition. As I grew older, I did not always agree with my my mother's theories, but I could never fail to recognize the impression her scholarship, humor, care, and love left on me. And so my interest in psychoanalysis was nourished under a mango tree in the Caribbean. Once I became an adult and attended doctoral school in the U.S. mainland, my father started coming up stateside to see me speak at academic conferences and professional engagements. His curiosity about my work led him to raise many questions. And so my mother pointed me in the direction of psychoanalysis, and my father was the first audience I spoke to about Freud and Ferenczi, Freire and Fanon, listening intently even as he and my mother wondered, often aloud—*Pero a ti te pagan por eso, vel'da?* "But you're going to get paid for this, right?" Their academic curiosity was tempered with a parent's concern that I make a living, as parents are wont to do.

Of special mention is my younger brother David, whose heartfelt demeanor, laughter, and resilience is an ever present inspiration to me—I am learning from you every day. I am eternally grateful to my family, my pastors, *nuestra gente y nuestra isla* for the love and care they gave me and continue to give despite the complexities of our world. And also, for instilling in me the desire to learn of this thing called psychoanalysis. I may not always agree with you or share all of your values, but at least know that I share all the important ones—because once a child is shown the right way, even in old age they will not stray from it.

The seeds were sown at home, yet watered and given light by a "village" of supervisors, colleagues, and mentors. My life as an undergraduate at Rutgers was quite literally saved by Mahlon Smith, Carlton James, George Atwood, and James W. Jones—they provided mentorship and support during a time in which I struggled to adjust to life in the U.S. mainland. I am thankful to them for setting me on the path that would bring me to Union Theological Seminary. Although I did not originally plan for an education in theology, the courses I took with James Cone, Gary Dorrien, Hal Taussig, Harry Fogarty, Hyun Kyung Chung, and Ann Ulanov became my pillar and my compass. It was my coursework that I happened to meet Claude Barbre of the Chicago School of Professional Psychology, who first made me aware of Ignacio Martín-Baró and Latin American liberation psychology. Jan Rehman and Willie Baptist from Union's Poverty Initiative always brought me back to the big picture—rampant wealth inequality and how it divides and conquers the oppressed. Samuel Cruz, Daisy Machado, and Ana María Diaz-Stevens created a space where Latinx students could come together and find fellowship, camaraderie, and *familia*. Dr. Diaz-Stevens's living room introduced me to friends and community in the Puerto Rican and Latinx Diaspora in New York City.

James Cone would transition in the same year as I had lost other mentors and figures in my academic life. I am forever thankful to him and all of Union's faculty for pushing me forward into doctoral school, for helping me find a tradition to stand on, and sharpen the voice that would inform this book.

Doctoral school would bring me back to Rutgers and GSAPP, where I would find a home for my passion and my mission. I am forever indebted to Nancy Boyd-Franklin as my advisor, supervisor, and mentor. Her care and belief in her students is unshakable, empowering them to reach beyond the firmament, grounding their voice in the soul of their communities, all the while teaching them how to do therapy "in the real world." I am equally indebted to Nancy McWilliams for allowing me to work as her research assistant, and for her teaching and supervision in psychoanalytic psychotherapy. Also an ecumenical and integrative scholar, she showed me how the whole of psychoanalysis from Freud to Luepnitz and beyond had something to contribute to questions of social justice. Similarly, the GSAPP faculty across theoretical orientations supported, challenged, and empowered me in my development—Shalonda Kelly, Brian Chu, Shireen Rizvi, Karen Riggs-Skean, Stan Messer, Louis Sass, and Monica Indart all contributed to my thinking, creating a space where students of color could play with theory, and in playing, make theory come alive.

It was in writing a piece on Ferenczi, short-term therapy, and social justice for Stan and Karen's class on short-term dynamic therapy that I on a whim wrote Lew Aron for resources on Ferenczi and his contributions to psychoanalysis. Lew showed interest in my paper, and invited me to present it at the Ferenczi Center at the New School for Social Research (one of the events my father came up to see). It was through Lew that I would meet Jeremy Safran, who mentored me as an early career professional and encouraged me to pursue my academic goals and interests. Throughout the years during and after graduate school Lew and Jeremy showed me there was no question in their mind that I and others like me belonged in the psychoanalytic world. Losing both within the span of a year was tragic and heartbreaking. I hope this book honors their memory and the spirit of their vision for an inclusive, progressive, and ecumenical psychoanalysis.

There are many mentors and dear friends without whom this book would not have been possible. Aileen Torres, Neil Altman, Mary Watkins, Ernesto Mujica, Frank Solano, Annie Lee Jones, Almas Merchant, Lisa Harris, Jen Sawaya, Regina Hund, Leora Heckelman, Cory Bennett, Liz Clark, Carlos Padron, Richard Ruth, Chris Christian, Praytusha Tummala-Narra, Cristalis Capielo, Milton Fuentes, Patricia Gherovici, Sumru Tufekcioglu, Alexandra Woods, Michael O'Loughlin, and many others form part of my extended professional family. Elizabeth Ann Danto and her book *Freud's Free Clinics* are also an inspiration to the present work, and I was lucky to have her as a supervisor when I was an adjunct faculty member at the Silberman School of Social Work at Hunter College, and as a dialogue partner while I brainstormed the first iterations of this book. Richard Ruth took me under his wing when I was a graduate student, becoming a role model and mentor to me as a Latinx psychoanalyst. He was the first psychoanalyst of color to look at me, and with incredible warmth and fortitude tell me unambiguously that despite the struggle, "*You belong here in this space*."

To my colleagues of color who are active in governance in the American Psychological Association, thank you for welcoming a psychoanalytic perspective in rendering service to our diverse communities, and for your curiosity about psychoanalysis and social justice. I hope this book helps answer some of your questions, as well as raise many more!

To my colleagues at the New School for Social Research—Richelle Allen, Miriam Steele, Donna Mulcahy, Wendy D'Andrea, Doris Chang, and the rest of the faculty—thank you for supporting my work and for trusting me with the care of our students. It was in fact talking about the book during lunch with Doris—a cognitive-behavioral practitioner and fellow multicultural researcher—that she said, "It's like you're writing a people's history of psychoanalysis!" I was consumed by the idea, which from then on guided my writing and formed the title of the present work. My friend and colleague Anthony Smith has, as a social worker and consultant, been in the back of my mind as I strive to write this book in a way that makes psychoanalytic thought and history intelligible and relevant to practitioners of color from a diversity of theoretical perspectives. I am ever so thankful for meeting you over a decade ago, and for believing in me even in those times when I doubted myself. And also, for being candid about that "psychoanalytic mumbo jumbo."

I am thankful to Dr. Mariano Plotkin for helping me procure a copy of his and Mariano Honorato's text *Estimado Doctor Freud*. I have never had to order something online from Argentina, but the text was well worth it and much needed.

A special thanks to series editor Michael O'Loughlin and editors Kasey Beduhn, Allison Keefner, and Megan DeLancey. Michael's invitation to submit my book to Lexington was life changing, and set me on the professional path I am in today. A special thanks to Kasey and Allison for their patience and flexibility (especially with deadlines!). I am also deeply honored by my anonymous reviewers, who were incredibly gracious in their feedback to the present work.

To my brothers and sisters in the Puerto Rican activist and art scene—thank you for welcoming me into the Diaspora, and giving me a home away from home. Our soul calls for *la isla*, our heart beats to the rhythm of *el tumbao*. With each step, each word, each breath we express gratitude to our ancestors and those who came before us.

A heartfelt thank you to graphic artist and community historian Albert "Taino Image" Areizaga, for designing and drawing the cover art for this book. It was awesome collaborating with you on this image that captures its spirit and its vision.

To my patients—thank you for trusting me with your truth. Your courage and the risks you take in "saying everything that comes to mind" move and inspire me every day.

Lastly, to my students at Rutgers, Hunter College, City College, St. Luke's, and the Icahn School of Medicine, and the New School for Social Research—you have been my heart for the better part of the last seven years. This book is written for you. It is an attempt to give you a history you can see yourself in. A history I wish I had as a graduate student. A history my mother and father can read under a mango tree.

Introduction

"A Recovery of Historical Memory": Old Questions and New Horizons

We live in a time of rampant socio-economic inequality, radical political polarization, and increasing de facto ideological, economic, racial, and cultural segregation. Dialogue across difference, to the extent it ever existed on a mass scale, seems an increasingly fraught project, a distant impossibility for communities across different worlds of experience to come together along some shared goal, some mutual problem against which to pivot and enact change for the good of all. We are unable to even agree on what the problems are. And so we drift farther and farther apart, talking and listening to each other less and less. Minor differences—the skin on our bodies, the place we were born, the organs between our legs, the language we speak, the god we pray to—roar to become unbridgeable chasms. And humming along underneath it all, haunting the contours of our war over difference, is the material, economic inequality that divides us into "haves" and "have-nots," and turn have-nots against one another in perpetual conflict. Because only then do the have-nots come to finally possess and have *something*—the injury of being a have-not. And so I come to have the fact that I have-not, and believe I am so because you, *you* have. Your having is the reason I do not! We are, however, not able to see that even this other-who-has (we are assured they have, because why wouldn't they? *Just look at them*), also lacks and has not. All the while, those who truly have continue to have the most, unperturbed by the "sibling rivalry" that plays out beneath them. Now and then they allow a crumb to fall from their table, if only to tempt the wish to have a seat alongside them. But *only* now and then, because who knows? The have-nots may get wise, wonder where these crumbs come from, and decide to flip the table upside down.

The study of how these dynamics of polarization and social control take hold in the psyche of individuals and communities, and how we can free ourselves from them through critical consciousness and political action in the world, is a central concern of Latin American liberation psychology (Alschuler, 2007; Martín-Baró, 1994; Watkins & Shulman, 2008). Liberation psychology is a movement in Latin American psychology developed by Jesuit priest and social psychologist Ignacio Martín-Baró (1994) in the midst of the social and political upheaval of the Salvadoran Civil War (1980–1992). A synthesis of liberation theology, Paulo Freire's (1972; 1973) critical pedagogy, and various social theories, Martín-Baró's liberation psychology emerged as a critique of Latin American psychology's conformity in the face of widespread repression and inequality, and its dependency on North American psychology's ahistorical and apolitical orientation. Drawing on liberation theology's "preferential option for the poor," Martín-Baró called on all of psychology—whether social, clinical, or educational—to stand on the side of the oppressed, and join with them in the struggle for social justice.

Inspired by Freire's critical pedagogy, Martín-Baró collaborated with marginalized communities in El Salvador to develop research projects that empowered them to articulate their experience of political dislocation, and develop a critical consciousness of how those experiences were related to oppressive power structures. These projects culminated in the development of the University Institute for Public Opinion in 1986, through which Martín-Baró studied public opinion about the civil war, U.S. military involvement, and the Salvadoran government. Martín-Baró in turn published this research not only in academic venues, but also made it available to the public, allowing previously disavowed and repressed opinions to see the light of day, stimulating open discourse, critical reflection, and a greater public resistance to socio-political repression. As a result of these efforts, Martín-Baró was targeted by the Salvadoran government, and on the night of November 16, 1989, he was killed along with five other liberation theologians and two employees on the campus of the Universidad Centroamericana of San Salvador by U.S.-trained Salvadoran troops. As his closest friends and colleagues were slain, Martín-Baró cried out over the gunfire: "Esto es una injusticia!" "This is an injustice!"

THE SCOPE OF THIS BOOK

The intellectual tributaries that flowed into Latin American liberation psychology and Martín-Baró's work are wide-ranging and diverse, including critical theory, theology, social psychology, and pedagogy, to name a few.

Yet one stream that is often under recognized in its canon is psychoanalysis—and not without reason. Psychoanalysis has an undeniable history of theoretical and political conservatism manifested in its adoption of colonial, racist ideologies (Brickman, 2003), class elitism (Altman, 2009), homophobia (Drescher, 1997; Herzog, 2017), and misogyny and heterosexism (Kim & Rutherford, 2015). Many of these tendencies can be traced back deep into the theoretical structures of psychoanalysis, which created a series of binaries that privileged Whiteness, maleness, heterosexuality and the rich, while denigrating Blackness, femaleness, homosexuality, and the poor (Aron & Starr, 2012). This history has led to much "healthy cultural suspicion" on behalf of North American multicultural psychology, a descendant of liberation psychology, whose adherents express understandable skepticism about the clinical and political relevance of psychoanalysis to historically marginalized communities (Sue & Sue, 1977; 2015; Sue & Zane, 1987; see also Tummala-Narra, 2016).

At the same time, recent historiographical research on the relationship of psychoanalysis to social justice invites us to explore another history, another vision of psychoanalysis with great relevance to the struggles of historically oppressed communities and peoples. This body of work articulates how psychoanalysis—from Freud and beyond—became involved in, and contributed to, social justice discourses and leftist politics from Europe and America to the "Global South," serving as a source of repression *and* liberation depending on whose hands held this tool (Ahad, 2010; Danto, 2005; Herzog, 2017; Makari, 2008; Zaretsky, 2004; 2015). As Jacoby (1986) maintains, these thinkers did not constitute a special case of "political Freudians," but rather represent a history that was heir to and representative of psychoanalysis itself. Sharing its fate, these thinkers "sank into the psychoanalytic unconscious. When they are remembered, they are only half-remembered" (p. x).

This book is an attempt to articulate that vision, by revisiting the history of psychoanalysis from a perspective "from below," and tracing its roots and "routes" into the birth of liberation psychology. This project is concerned not just with historiography, but with outlining a series of ideas critical to liberation psychology, as well as a series of *relationships* that served as conduits for those ideas. This two-pronged approach—outlining a series of ideas and relationships—is an attempt to rekindle a century-long dialogue between psychoanalysis and liberation psychology. I will engage in this dialogue through a combination of theoretical exploration and historical exegesis, looking at the text and the "world behind the text" of core theorists and thinkers in psychoanalysis and liberation psychology, from the turn of the century to the 1970s and 1980s, from Freud to Fanon to Freire, and finally, Martín-Baró. In so doing, I hope to articulate not just a psychotherapy (a clinical method for relieving individual suffering), but a psychoanalysis "from the people," a psychoanalysis for liberation which also includes pedagogical and political sites of reflection on social justice and social transformation. Hence the main title of this text, *A People's History of Psychoanalysis: From Freud to Liberation Psychology*.

Placing such seemingly odd fellows in contact with one another requires defining certain terms and ideas. To that end, I will first define multicultural psychology, and the relationship between it and liberation psychology. Then I will further unpack Martín-Baró's thinking, as well as some of the theological and philosophical movements that guided his work. These same movements, grounded in liberation philosophy and theology, in turn inform the perspective from which I read the history of psychoanalysis and liberation psychology.

Multicultural Psychology and Psychoanalytic Thought

Liberation psychology is widely recognized as an inspiration and foundation for North American multicultural psychology (Arredondo & Perez, 2003; Ivey, 1995; Ivey & Collins, 2003; Tate, Rivera, & Edwards, 2015; Vera & Speight, 2003). Multicultural psychology refers to a broad, interdisciplinary network of scholars, clinicians, and researchers committed to addressing the mental health needs and social conditions of historically marginalized and underserved communities, such as ethnic minority and immigrant communities, lesbian, gay, bisexual, transgender, and queer communities (LGBTQ), women, the poor, and the diverse communities who exist at the intersections of each of these. Hence, a social justice orientation has been stated to be a core value of multicultural psychology (Ivey & Collins, 2003; Sue, 2001). However, save for a handful of scholars (e.g., Ivey, 1995; Vera & Speight, 2003) there has been little articulation of the theoretical underpinnings of liberation psychology within a multicultural framework. Furthermore, there is an ambiguous relationship between the broader emancipatory goals of liberation psychology (social justice and systemic change, material and economic equality) and the values of multicultural psychology (diversity and inclusion, cultural competency). One of the goals of this book is to describe the theoretical edifice of liberation psychology in detail, in order to provide a stronger foundation to multicultural psychology.

As mentioned above, there is a general skepticism in multicultural psychology about the applicability or relevance of psychodynamic and psychoanalytically oriented treatments to diverse populations, in spite of the burgeoning literature on working relationally across race, class, gender, and sexual orientation (Altman, 2009; Perez-Foster, Moskowitz, & Javier, 1996). Within the cross-cultural counseling field, this can be traced back to Sue and Sue's (1977) landmark paper, which opened up initial dialogues on cultural competency and the provision of mental health services to non-white ethnic minorities, immigrants, and the poor. Sue and Sue (1977) argued that clinical processes central to psychoanalytic therapies—such as emotional expression and reflection, the attainment of insight, self-exploration, the discovery of underlying feelings, an emotional bond with the therapist—were "inappropriate" for poor patients of color (p. 424). For example, encouraging patients of color to reflect on their feelings may lead them to feel "confused, alienated, and frustrated" (p. 424), since this process reflects more Western, Eurocentric values. Sue and Sue argue that that many patients of color expect "[i]mmediate solutions and concrete tangible forms of treatment (advice, confession, consolation, and mediation)" (p. 425). As such, counselors and clinicians are encouraged to be more "action-oriented" and skills-focused in practice when working with diverse populations.

A general consensus operating almost at the level of "common sense" in mainstream multicultural psychology psychoanalytic treatments project cultural values that are incongruous with ethnic minorities, while other treatment orientations such as cognitive-behavioral therapy or family systems therapy are more culturally congruent (Inclan, 1985; Interian & Diaz-Martinez, 2007; Sue & Sue, 1977; 2008; Sue & Zane, 1987). Although a full survey of this literature, with attention to every ethnic minority group, is beyond the scope of this book, I wish to give an example in relation to Latinxs, who are my own community and the one which I have been most involved with clinically.

Writing from a family systems perspective, Inclan (1985) sought to describe the "value orientation" of first-generation, poor Puerto Rican migrants in the United States, and outline the most culturally congruent mode of treatment. In contradistinction to psychoanalysis' emphasis on the past, Inclan states that "poor Puerto Ricans tend to exhibit behaviors that are expressions of a present-time value orientation" (p. 326). Whereas White culture exudes values of self-assertion and of mastery over nature, poor Puerto Ricans "are governed more by a value of subjugation to nature" (p. 330). With this fatalistic value of self-subjugation and passivity, the universe of poor Puerto Ricans is described as "rigidly stratified," with God reigning at the top and boundaries keep everyone in their place at the bottom. Within this value universe, "people tend not to challenge but rather to accommodate to the existent hierarchies and conditions" (p. 331). Such values of fatalism, submissiveness, and a preference for hierarchical relationships make poor Puerto Ricans a poor fit for "nondirective" and "insight-oriented" therapies. Rather, therapies that emphasize the present, the concrete, and foster more hierarchical therapeutic relationships are argued to be more in line with the value orientation of poor Puerto Ricans.

My desire to question this narrative notwithstanding, it must be acknowledged that it did not arise in a vacuum, as psychoanalysis itself is at fault for this turn of events. It must be noted that multicultural psychology's aversion to psychoanalytic thinking is partly in response to a historical injustice. Inclan (1985) eloquently and incisively summarizes the crux of the problem,

> The revolutionary insights of Freud were received so enthusiastically that psychoanalytic theory became heralded as a methodology for understanding all spheres of life and all peoples. As with global expectations, the promise became tempered by reality. One area in which psychoanalytic practice proved limited was in reaching poor and minority group peoples. "They" were not verbal, motivated, insightful, or able to delay gratification. "They" tended to act-out, be concerned with material things, and project causality to external sources. (p. 330)

Inclan draws attention to the historical exclusion of ethnic minorities and the poor from psychoanalytic treatment based on the so-called criteria of analyzability. The criteria of analyzability emphasized an explicitly verbal mode of communication, the capacity for insight, and impulse control as necessary requirements for patients to be admitted into psychoanalysis or psychoanalytic treatment. Such criteria have gone in hand with negative stereotypes and reactions by white, middle-upper class therapists toward minority and lower-class patients (Siassi & Messer, 1976). There is a troubling history in North American psychoanalysis where these criteria, alongside ethno-racial stereotypes, have served to marginalize people of color and the poor from psychoanalytic treatment and even psychoanalytic training (Altman, 2009; Wachtel, 2002).

While multicultural scholars rightly point out the history of the "analyzability criteria" being used to discriminate against non-white populations, instead of critiquing and deconstructing such ideas as ethnic minorities "don't do insight," or "aren't verbal," they potentially *reify* them as a inherent cultural trait and accept it as a given reality. In contrast to this tendency, there is internal work in contemporary psychoanalysis breaking down these barriers and showing that cultural competency, social justice, and psychoanalytic thinking need not be seen as antagonistic (Altman, 2009; Gaztambide, 2012; Gherovici, 2003; Tummala-Narra, 2016). Also in need of deconstruction is the idea that psychoanalysis is at best indifferent and at worst hostile to issues of culture, race, and class. Part of the goal of this book is to show that psychoanalysis in its inception was neither unavailable, nor exclusive of the poor and racial "other," and that central psychoanalytic thinkers thought deeply and cogently about culture and society (Danto, 2005).

Liberation Theology and Philosophy as Hermeneutics

Liberation theology is a trans-national movement in Christian theology that synthesizes the message of the Christian faith with a devotion to social justice on behalf of the poorest and most vulnerable. Although originating in

Latin America, it has many different strands of thought worldwide, with different emphases with regard to the communities whose experience it centers in its analysis of social injustice. For my purposes here, I will focus on two different forms—Latin American liberation theology, which has specific relevance to Freire and Martín-Baró who were inspired by it, and Black liberation theology, which developed concurrently with the former, and emerged in the context of the African-American experience in the United States, and also informs my own thinking and analysis.

Latin American liberation theology arose in the Catholic Church during 1950s and 1960s as an attempt to integrate Marxist insights with the Christian gospel in response to the egregious wealth inequality and political violence ravaging Latin America. The term was first coined by the Peruvian priest Gustavo Gutierrez (1988) who wrote the foundational text *A Theology of Liberation*. In it, he declared liberation theology's primary epistemological and ethical tool—the "preferential option for the poor." Gutierrez, like other liberation theologians, argued that throughout the Judeo-Christian scriptures there is a recurring concern with the "the poor, the widow, and the stranger," in which God stands on the side of the vulnerable and enslaved against the injustice of the powerful and dominant. The Exodus, from this point of view, is the key biblical narrative for many liberation theologians. The "chosenness" of the enslaved Hebrews as an oppressed and exploited people is interpreted as "proof" of God's preferential option, joining with them in their struggle for liberation through the figure of Moses as both liberator and lawgiver. Indeed, Michael Walzer (1985) in *Exodus and Revolution* recognized how the story of the Exodus has served as the political symbol par excellence of revolution for a wide range of communities, including liberation theology, Marxist thought, and African-American civil rights leaders.

For Gutierrez, the preferential option for the poor is intricately tied with a concern for "the other," grounded in the Hebrew word for righteousness, *tsedaquah*. This term carries a number of meanings, among them committing an act of righteousness on behalf of the poor and downtrodden, as well as justice. It also involves, in the eyes of some Christian ethicists, a love for what is "alien" (Maguire, 2005). It is from the alien, the stranger, the poor and defenseless, that a site of truth may be found, a wisdom to be heard, a power to behold. Often misunderstood in the concept of the preferential option is that it somehow proclaims God's love for the poor not for the rich, affection for the oppressed and hatred for the oppressor. On the contrary, Gutierrez (1988) states that the preferential option emerges from the universality of God's love, which includes those who are excluded and marginalized from society.

Growing out of the Black civil rights struggle in the United States concurrently with Latin American liberation theology, Black liberation theology recognizes the historical relationship between Christianity, colonialism, and anti-Blackness, calling for a reading of the Judeo-Christian scriptures "from below," from the perspective of Black people suffering and struggling against racism and oppression. Originated by the late James Cone (d. 2018; 1970), Black Theology developed a framework in some respects similar to Latin American liberation theology, but with an emphasis on the problem of anti-Blackness and the problematics of the "color-line" (Latin American liberation theology would only later include an analysis of race and gender into its canon). For Cone, the primary object of theological scrutiny is the problem of "blackness" as an ontological category. In comparison with Gutierrez's focus on economic exploitation and post-colonialism, Cone wrote from two existential positions—(1) the lived experience of the historic Black community in the United States, and (2) the Black diaspora and other non-white peoples who suffered from the legacy of othering grounded in anti-Blackness.[1]

In this way, Blackness for Cone functions as a double-signifier. It refers most intimately to the historic Black community in the United States that struggled and continues to struggle with structural racism. But it also serves as an archetypal, symbolic, metaphoric symbol. Hence Cone (1970) writes, "Blackness . . . stands for all victims of oppression who realize that their humanity is inseparable from man's liberation from whiteness" (p. 28). It is in this theological vein that Cone makes the controversial statement "God is black." To state that God is Black is to maintain that

> God has made the oppressed condition his own condition. This is the essence of the biblical revelation. By electing the Israelite slaves as his people and by becoming the Oppressed One in Jesus Christ, God discloses to men that he is known where men experience humiliation and suffering. (p. 121)

Oppression, suffering, humiliation, and their transformation are salient topics in both liberation theology and liberation psychology. Related to this ontological and theological consideration of Blackness is Cone's interpretation of Jewishness—"Jesus *is* black because he *was* a Jew. The affirmation of the Black Christ can be understood when the significance of his past Jewishness is related dialectically to the significance of his present blackness" (Cone, 1975/1997, p. 123). As a Jewish prophet conducting his ministry under occupation by the Roman Empire, Jesus is interpreted from the perspective of the African-American experience and thus read as "Black." Jewishness and Blackness then represents an interesting dialectic. As I wrote in another context, "It is through God's identification with the blackness of the Jewish people that Israel operates as a light to the oppressed people of the world (cf. Isaiah 42: 6–7)" (Gaztambide, 2015).

Liberation theology in North and Latin America is then concerned with an ethics of justice and repair toward those rendered "other" in society. The preferential option for the poor, the oppressed, the Black person, women, the non-heterosexual and gender non-conforming, the differently abled, the immigrant and the stranger—these are all sites of theological, existential, and philosophical reflection. And as I will argue, a site for psychoanalysis. It is out of this concern for the other that Dussel (1985; 1996) articulates his philosophy of liberation, defining "exteriority" as that which falls outside the periphery of the self, beyond the totality of modernity. From his own positionality as a Latin American philosopher, he writes, "We were conscious of being the 'other face' of modernity" (1996, p. 21). It is from the exteriority of the other that the Levinasian *autrui* appeals, "[f]rom a 'beyond' of the horizon of the world, the Other irrupts 'into the world,' demanding justice. This is the ethical stance par excellence, the face-to-face stance" (p. 53). The other appeals, demands, pleads, *cries* for justice—"The cry paralyzes us, terrifies us, takes hold of our ego, beating at its doors like an enemy at the gates, 'I am naked, I am homeless, I am sick, I am a foreigner, I am in prison, I hunger and thirst for justice!'" (Gaztambide, 2015, p. 705).

A liberationist ethic, then, involves both the cry of the Other, and the self's reparative act. The ethical act lies in one's ability to attune and respond to this radical other. It involves a wrestling with the passions that can cause murder. Dussel (1985) writes that approaching the other in a spirit of repair involves "shortening the distance between someone who can accept or reject us, shake our hand or injure us, kiss or kill us. To approach in justice is always a risk because it is to shorten the distance toward a distinct freedom" (p. 17). This is a provocative but fundamental injunction to both my review of psychoanalysis and liberation psychology and the central thesis of this book—working toward social justice may necessarily involve an act of vulnerability (Freire would call it "risking an act of love") so radical, so destabilizing to the self and the social system, that it invites tangling with death itself, placing oneself at the mercy of a "murderous encounter." And yet by surrendering to this fact, this radical act of vulnerability, we may discover our own survival, and in surviving, be freed from our fears "toward a distinct freedom." This ethical act shifts from the radical to the revolutionary.

I go into length describing Latin American liberation theology, Black theology, and liberation theology for three reasons. Firstly, the preferential option for the oppressed informs my reading of the history of psychoanalysis and social justice. I will be attending explicitly and one-sidedly to a perspective "from below," examining often untold stories and unspoken actors in the history of psychoanalysis, social justice, and liberation psychology. Secondly, while Latin American liberation theology was clearly one of the inspirations for Martín-Baró's liberation psychology, my inclusion of Black Theology is meant to complement the former's emphasis on class and post-colonialism with a perspective grounded in race. So too, I will be reading the history of psychoanalysis with special attention to race, and how questions of race—especially the relationship between anti-Semitism and anti-Blackness—prove fundamental to our understanding of psychoanalysis. Lastly, my perspective also draws on Levinasian and Dusselian metaphysics, with the understand that while "the other" primarily refers to the "poor, the widow, and the orphan," it is not exclusive to those categories. In fact, an ethics for the other requires us to go beyond them, to consider not only "the other," but also "the other of the other." This last point will become clearer once we review what we learn from Freud, Fanon, and Freire.

LIBERATION PSYCHOLOGY: THEORY, EPISTEMOLOGY, AND PRAXIS

In the remainder of this introduction I will introduce liberation psychology proper, and in so doing highlight not only certain values which are profoundly psychoanalytic, but also raise a heretofore unexamined tension between liberation psychology and multicultural psychology. Ignacio Martín-Baró's (1994) call for a liberation psychology transcended the immediacy of his context as a social psychologist, demanding that *all* of psychology, including clinical psychology, be transformed in the interest of social justice (p. 19). Writing in the 1970s and 1980s in El Salvador, Martín-Baró criticized Latin American psychology's scientistic mimicry and dependent mirroring of North American psychology. He warned of "false dilemmas" imported from the North, such as the conflicts between humanistic, psychodynamic, and behavioral psychologies, or phenomenological and empirical approaches to psychology. He argued that a psychology of the people must concern itself with the *needs* and *experiences* of the people using a plurality of methodologies, not an allegiance to a theoretical orientation, a particular method of inquiry, or even one's own professional advancement.

In looking for a foundation for liberation psychology, Martín-Baró (1994) looked not to the behavioral sciences but to theology, specifically liberation theology. Martín-Baró drew upon liberation theology's "preferential option" for the poor and oppressed—that Truth is to be found among the destitute and brokenhearted—as the ethical bedrock of liberation psychology. Martín-Baró writes that "it is only the poor who offer the objective and subjective conditions for opening up to *the other*, and above all, to *the radical other*" (p. 26, my emphasis). Inspired by the preferential option, Martín-Baró argued that psychology required an epistemology that was both ethical and gnoseological. This new epistemology "has to be from below, from the same oppressed majorities whose truth is to be created" (pp. 27–28). Martín-Baró (1994) is quick to clarify that this perspective is "from" the oppressed, not "for" them. He draws on Paulo Freire's critical pedagogy in arguing that this "is not a matter of thinking for [the oppressed] or bringing them our ideas or solving their problems for them; it has to do with thinking and theorizing with them and from them" (p. 28). Just as in liberation theology it is from the poor that one finds the presence of God, "a psychology of liberation has to learn that only from the oppressed will it be possible to build and discover [their] existential truth" (p. 28). To take a perspective from below does not mean that the psychologist must discard all of their knowledge, tools, and research. Rather the psychologist relativizes and decenters that knowledge, placing it in dialogue with the experiences of oppressed people. It is "from below" that research questions are generated, that treatment options are chosen, and that theories are developed or rejected. Liberation psychology places a premium on the psychologist's investment and immersion in the experiences of the subaltern, the marginalized, and oppressed.

Having set forth the ethical and epistemological stance of liberation psychology, Martín-Baró (1994) stated three urgent tasks of any emancipatory psychological project. Firstly, liberation psychology promotes the "recovery of historical memory" as a primary goal. Recovering historical memory

> has to do with recovering not only the sense of one's own identity and the pride of belonging to a people but also a reliance on a tradition and a culture, and above all, with rescuing those aspects of identity which served yesterday, and will serve today, for liberation. Thus, the recovery of a historical memory supposes the reconstruction of models of identification that, instead of chaining and caging the people, open up the horizon for them, toward their liberation and fulfillment. (p. 30)

For Martín-Baró, one of the symptoms of oppressive conditions is fatalism, a passive accommodation to a seemingly God-given and unchangeable present. The first step toward overcoming fatalism is not only opening up the people's minds to an emancipatory future, but also recovering the memory of their individual and collective past. This is not a return to an over-idealized past which never was, or a retrieval of a fossilized culture which does not speak to one's present subjectivity, but a critical excavation of those elements which make up the individual, familial, and communal self's continued survival. Only by scrutinizing and reconnecting with one's roots can one take stock of where one comes from and on whom one depends, providing resources from which to construct a more robust, nuanced, and flexible identity (Alschuler, 2007). Hence, "[t]here is no true self-knowledge that is not an acknowledgement of one's origins, one's community identity, and one's own history" (Martín-Baró, 1994, p. 218).

Side by side with the recovery of historical memory is the de-ideologizing of everyday experience. For Martín-Baró (1994), knowledge is a social construction defined by what is "known" and what is "not-known." For all people, but especially for marginalized groups, life is "burdened by the lie of a prevailing discourse that denies, ignores, or disguises essential aspects of reality . . . a fictional common sense that nurtures the structures of exploitation and conformist attitudes" (p. 31). Ideology functions to structure subjectivity and mark the boundary between what is allowed to enter awareness and what is dissociated, unarticulated, or rendered verboten, maintaining the status quo. To de-ideologize consciousness is to establish a critical distance from that which appears to be "common sense," part of one's daily habits and ways of seeing the world, posing it as a problem to be discussed and explored. When what is previously seen as "natural" is recognized as something that is "not the whole story," a space is opened for reflection in which *other*—previously disavowed or unarticulated—stories come into focus. For many marginalized people and groups, this may include their own histories and experiences which have been covered over in order to maintain unjust conditions. In this very sense, "[t]o de-ideologize means to *retrieve* the original experience of groups and *return it to them* as objective data. People can then use the data to formally articulate a consciousness of their own reality" (Martín-Baró, 1994, p. 31, my emphasis). De-ideologizing lifts the veil of lies which clouds consciousness, and creates space for people's own subjectivity, for lost or dissociated experiences, to be brought to life by bringing them into contact with their lived reality. This "healing through consciousness" (Ricoeur, 1970) takes place in the context of a new relationship based in dialogue, a dialogue which recognizes the other as a subject.

Concientizacion: Critical Consciousness, Dialogue, and Relationship

Consciousness in all of its psychological and political dimensions is a key focus of inquiry in liberation psychology, just as it is in psychology in the broader sense. Martín-Baró (1994) defines consciousness as "the knowing or not knowing of self, through the world and through others, with praxis coming before mental knowledge" (p. 38). Consciousness is not some static substance existing in the individual subject, but an intentional process that is constantly revealed through relations with the world and with others, including "private" representations and feelings but also habits, behaviors, and social realities. More importantly, "the knowledge that counts most is not explicit and formalized knowledge, but rather the knowledge inherent in everyday praxis, usually implicit, structurally unconscious, and ideologically natural" (p. 29). What is "not known" (e.g., not conscious, inchoate, dissociated, repressed) is usually represented not in words but in the subtle, nonverbal behaviors through which we relate to the world around us. And that which operates outside of awareness has tremendous importance insofar as it aids or hinders the self-definition, humanization, and objective realities not only of individuals but also entire communities.

Given the importance of consciousness—and what is within or outside its boundaries—Martín-Baró (1994) asserts that "that the fundamental horizon for psychology as a field of knowledge is *concientizacion*" (p. 39). *Concientizacion* or *concientizacao* is a term Martín-Baró draws from Paulo Freire (I will discuss Freire and the origins of *concientizacao* in more detail in Chapter 5), referring to a critical consciousness which joins the psychological dimension of personal consciousness with the communal, social, and political. Used by Freire in the context of literacy education, concientizacion "involves more than the possibility of people reading and writing the alphabet; it opens the possibility of their being able to read about themselves and write their own history . . . achieving a critical understanding of themselves as well as of their world and where they stand in it" (Martín-Baró, 1994, pp. 18, 41). What is meant here is not a critique of "false consciousness" in the sense of consciousness itself being a lie. It is not the simple sentiment that *this* (overt, explicit) consciousness is "false" while what is outside of it is "true," but that what is false is the notion that what is readily conscious is "the whole story," whole and complete. Concientizacion appreciates the truth embedded in what is left out, and that reflecting on what is excluded transforms the self by broadening the horizons of consciousness.

By gradually decoding the implicit realities of one's world, one becomes aware of oppressive mechanisms operating in day-to-day life, and begins to deconstruct "the consciousness that mythifies that situation as natural, and opens up the horizon for new possibilities for action . . . which at the same time makes possible new forms of consciousness" (Martín-Baró, 1994, p. 40). A new experience of one's reality as open, malleable, and changeable leads to a new understanding of oneself. One begins "to discover themselves in their mastery of nature, in their actions that transform things, in their active role in relation to others" (p. 40). Interestingly, at this juncture Martín-Baró draws a parallel between the psychodynamic therapist's focus on addressing those defense mechanisms which block the patient's awareness of their inner life, and the liberation psychologist who draws attention to defense mechanisms which mutilate the consciousness of a marginalized person, internalizing social scripts which maintain their subjugation by alienating them from their own sense of personhood (p. 41).

A psychologist of liberation, then, is concerned with the various psychological, cultural, social, and political mechanisms which operate to distort consciousness and keep one's immediate experience from focus. It involves a concern for dissociated experience, the experience of the outcast. Exploring and articulating these experiences through dialogue, new material emerges which allows for new forms of consciousness. This process of *concientizacion* disrupts fatalistic thought processes and behavior, creating the possibility of a new, transformative experience.

The discussion of consciousness up to this point should not be taken to mean that concientizacion is a purely intrapsychic or individual process. Nor is it something that the Liberation Psychologist "installs" in the mind of an oppressed person or community, as one installs a program into a computer. This would be a relationship between a dominant subject and a controlled object. Liberation psychology addresses this dichotomy by questioning those mechanisms that block and distort "consciousness of an individual's social identity, causing him or her to act like a dominated being or a dominator, an oppressive exploiter or a person who is marginalized and oppressed." (Martín-Baró, 1994, p. 41). *Concientizacion* "assumes an escape from the reproductive machinery of the relationships of dominance and submission, *for it can be realized only through dialogue*" (p. 42, my emphasis). Individual self-knowledge and self-acceptance are only possible through changes in the type of relationships that make up the self, changes that subvert the subject-object, active-passive, oppressor-oppressed dichotomy. It is through a relationship that is grounded in dialogue, in negotiation and moment to moment responsiveness between subjects—not objects—that *concientizacion* can occur. For Martín-Baró this dialogical, intersubjective process of change is the same whether we are addressing the teacher-student relationship or the therapist-patient relationship. Just as oppressive relations between the self and the world lead to distortions in the self, so too do affirming, empowering relations lead to repair, rejuvenation, and new self-states. Using the specific case of victims of war trauma in Central America, Martín-Baró argues that the clinical encounter has to involve *concientizacion*, "a process that returns the word to these human beings, not only as individuals, but as part of a people," by addressing the way that identity is distorted by the enactment of oppressor-oppressed prototypes (p. 43). A psychotherapist influenced by liberation psychology would take care not to impinge their reality upon the patient, recycling a pattern of domination and submission, but seek to establish the relational conditions under which the patient can rediscover their experience by putting it into words, learn to "read" those words, and through this reading become the author of a new narrative.

The Problem of Fatalism: One Person's "Culture" is Another's "Oppression"?

Briefly touched on in this review of Martín-Baró's (1994) thinking was the concept of fatalism. Fatalism, or *fatalismo* as it is discussed in the multicultural literature on Latinos (see for example, the section on Latinos in McGoldrick et al., 2005) and Latin Americans, is a way of construing the world "in which everyone's fate is already predetermined and everything happens inescapably. Human beings have no choice but to defer to their destiny and submit to the lot that their fate prescribes for them" (Martín-Baró, 1994, p.

200). People with a fatalistic orientation feel they can do nothing to change their lot in life, as it is instituted by forces outside their control, such as God or the state. Negative emotions such as sadness or anger are seen as pointless and distracting, as one is to bear one's cross bravely and without complaint. "Fate" is accepted in order to avoid problems or conflicts with others. Passivity is encouraged not only as a virtue, but also as a way of surviving punishment from the authorities. One's life horizons are narrowed to the present, with the here and now being the only thing that counts; "Knowing the past or predicting the future serves only to confirm the inevitability of fate" (p. 201).

What is interesting about reading multicultural psychology's interpretation of fatalism or *fatalismo* side by side with liberation psychology is how strikingly they differ in interpreting this phenomena. For multicultural psychology, fatalism may be read as a cultural trait endemic to various ethnic minorities, Latinxs among them. As a cultural trait, it is to be respected, and psychotherapies are to respond in kind. Hence we see the call for psychotherapies which have an "active" therapeutic approach vis-à-vis the passive, fatalistic patient, with the assumption that to do otherwise is to be culturally incompetent. For liberation psychology, fatalism is a symptom of oppression and marginalization. It is the result of structural injustice and the ideological apparatus which serves to maintain inequality between the powerful and the powerless. Fatalism provides the oppressed with a way of making meaning of their surrounding misery, while installing in their psyches the very fears and distortions which serve the interests of the powerful. It would not be unfair to say that from a liberation psychology perspective, multicultural psychology's normalization, perhaps even elevation of fatalism to the level of common sense by seeing it as part of Latinx culture—culture as a kind of "second nature" divorced from economic, social, and political forces—represents a serious injustice. I read this normalization in light of Martín-Baró's indictment that "[i]n practice, ideological acceptance of fatalism amounts to acceptance of the oppressive social order" (p. 216).

Rather than become mired in discussions about the relative "passivity" or "activity" of different cultural groups, liberation psychology asks us to consider what kinds of psychotherapeutic and pedagogical relationships will foster a more holistic consciousness, a more integrated sense of self, a greater awareness of political dynamics, and a greater sense of freedom among historically marginalized communities. It asks us to place culture in a dialectical relationship with its immediate social, economic, and political context. This would be an important remedy to the danger of reducing issues of power and privilege to matters of "cultural difference." Liberation psychology also warns us against being complicit with oppressive forces by accepting fatalistic attitudes among underprivileged groups as somehow culturally natural. Martín-Baró (1994) asserts that in spite of behavioral signs of docility, oppressed people are never completely tamed, never completely convinced of their inferiority or powerlessness before "reality." From time to time, oppressed people make subtle, albeit emergent and tentative, challenges to the powers and authorities that dominate them. Rather than a desire for change being a foreign artifact outside of their culture, Martín-Baró writes that "There is no need to sow the seed of rebellion to throw off an unjust fate; it is already there in the spirit of the colonized and can sprout forth when circumstances are right" (p. 217).

Part of the task of this book is to explore, through different theorists and thinkers in the history of psychoanalysis and social justice, how oppressed communities and subjectivities overcome fatalism and develop this capacity for critical consciousness. And also, to identify what subjective, intersubjective, and systemic factors can derail its development.

PSYCHOANALYSIS AND LIBERATION PSYCHOLOGY: BEGINNINGS OF A DIALOGUE

Based on Martín-Baró's (1994) insights, the project of this book is primarily one of recovering historical memory—both the historical memory of psychoanalysis and that of liberation psychology. In recovering the historical memory of psychoanalysis, I also borrow Stuart Hall's distinction between identifying one's "roots" and one's "routes." I am not interested in identifying one unilateral root of liberation psychology in psychoanalysis. Martín-Baró's thinking is undoubtedly textured by a multiplicity of perspectives, of which psychoanalysis is only one. Rather, in the chapters that follow I wish to identify the routes by which psychoanalysis flowed into liberation psychology—the routes of its displacement, transmission, translation, and creative reinterpretation. These routes are themselves overdetermined, and subject to various socio-political and historical forces.

Given my emphasis on Latin American liberation psychology and how it informs North American multicultural psychology, I will necessarily ignore other tissues connecting psychoanalysis and liberation psychology, and focus on the period between 1888 and the 1970s, and a series of intellectual and affective relationships from Vienna to Berlin, from Harlem to Martinique, from Argentina to Brazil, Spain to Latin America, and finally the place of Martín-Baró's death, El Salvador. My focus then will of necessity leave out other stories that could be told, other relationships that could be narrativized (see Watkins & Shulman, 2008). It is also important to note that my purpose in this effort is not to contradict established scholarship on psychoanalysis' complicity in problematic discourses surrounding race, class, gender, and sexuality. The history of psychoanalysis' sins is well-established and documented, yet my reprising those arguments is not my primary goal. Rather, there is another story I want to tell, one that sits at the margins of psychoanalysis itself.

Engaging in this intellectual and historical excursus will accomplish a number of goals—(1) outline the historical and intellectual relationship between liberation psychology and psychoanalysis, (2) argue for the inclusion within the psychoanalytic canon of thinkers and intellectuals that historically have been excluded from it, (3) locate psychoanalysis as a emancipatory discourse within the diversity of perspectives found in liberation psychology, and (4) articulate a series of theories, ideas, and ethics about racial and economic inequality that *cut across* these discourses, and which speak to our current psycho-political struggles *today*. Hence, in the same way that liberation theology re-discovers the "Christ of faith" in order to speak to the experiences of marginalized communities and address contemporary political struggles and social antagonisms, so too am I not merely adopting a historiographical perspective for the sake of historical revisionism. Rather, I am "creating and finding" Freud and psychoanalysis through the lens of a liberationist perspective to shed light on contemporary clinical, pedagogical, and political problems. In this sense, I am following Badia Sahar Ahad (2010) in approaching psychoanalysis "with less critical suspicion and more attention to the ways in which articulations of race rely upon theories of interiority for their very existence, and conversely, recognizing how theories of interiority are entirely dependent on the subject of race" (p. 159).

This book is organized into three parts. Chapters 1 and 2 will situate the historical and sociological context of both psychoanalysis and liberation psychology, providing a backdrop against which the origin of core concepts in the latter emerge from the historical contingencies of the former. Chapters 3, 4, and 5 will focus on the intellectual and relational routes through which psychoanalysis influenced and informed liberation psychology, from Freud to Fanon to Freire. Chapter 6 and the conclusion will integrate the various theories of oppression and liberation reviewed, and show how these theories reflect a genealogy leading to Martín-Baró's work. In doing so, I will both complete the chains of relatedness that tie psychoanalysis to liberation psychology, and create and find ideas that have broad-ranging implications for contemporary clinical work, multicultural pedagogy, and social justice activism.

In Chapter 1, I will situate the sociological origins of psychoanalysis in the context of colonialism, anti-Blackness, and anti-Semitism. The fact that the majority of the first and second generation of psychoanalysts—Freud included—were left-leaning, progressive, socially active Jews will be explored against this backdrop. I will argue that Freud's positionality as a Jew, and as a Jew fully aware of the relationship between Jewishness and Blackness in the racial discourse of his times, had a fundamental impact on psychoanalysis as a body of theory and as an intellectual movement committed to social justice. In this historical review, I will also delineate important ways in which the history of psychoanalysis is reflected in our own today. As a psychologist of color in the United States writing in a post-2016 world, it is important to me that I make this trans-historical connection explicit in order to make the stakes of this book clear. Again, I am not interested in mere historiography, but in making the past present again, so that we might learn from it. And in learning, make sure not to repeat it.

Chapter 2 will circle "around Freud" by exploring the activism and leftist politics of the first and second generation of psychoanalysis. This chapter will reference Freud's relationship with other leftist Jewish members of the psychoanalytic movement, with special attention to the life and work of Sandor Ferenczi, Otto Fenichel, and Erich Fromm. I will provide an account of psychoanalysis' progressive origins, and unpack some of the clinical and political thought of this generation. In doing so, I will begin to identify a series of ideas that would become transmitted over time, following certain specific "routes" from Vienna to Harlem to the Caribbean to Latin America and back. These ideas include an analysis of how victims of trauma and oppression come to identify with their victimizers, how socioeconomic and racial antagonisms "take root" in the psyche, and how psychoanalysis can contribute to individual and political liberation. It is important for me to also provide an account as to what happened to this progressive history of psychoanalysis and how it died as analysis was displaced as a refugee world-wide, yet how its trajectories were kept alive under different circumstances, by people of color throughout the Americas. Although these emancipatory discourses will be shown to have occurred around Freud, it is still important to clarify whether Freud himself participated in these dialogues, and held these views himself.

Chapter 3 will focus on Freud and his thinking on culture, society, inequality, and politics. Through an in-depth review of his core "cultural texts" from *Totem and Taboo* through *Moses and Monotheism*, it will be shown that Freud developed a cogent, lucid, and radical theory of how the oppressed come to identify with and internalize their oppressors, and how this psychodynamic tension complicates movements for social justice. I will also describe Freud's psychoanalytic perspective on social justice, and how it is grounded in the recognition of one's own wounding by oppression, and the renunciation of an identification with the oppressor which then, mimetically, reproduces this violence upon others. In many respects, as I will argue in my conclusion, Freud develops not only a psychoanalysis of oppression, but also a fully realized psychoanalysis of right-wing populism, and the psychology of the European/White working class that becomes enthralled to it through the mutual exclusion and denigration of an other (e.g., non-Whites, Jews, etc). I will argue that these ideas from Freud's corpus sets in motion a conversation that goes beyond him, and continues to be elucidated in the words of psychoanalytically-informed thinkers throughout Latin America and the Caribbean.

Chapter 4 will trace a series of relationships from Harry Stack Sullivan to Frantz Fanon, each one a link in the chain connecting psychoanalysis to the Black struggle in North America during the Harlem Renaissance, and extending internationally into Fanon and Richard Wright's engagement with psychoanalytic-existential thinkers such as Jean Paul Sartre and Simone de Beauvoir. I will trace various psychoanalytic and socio-critical routes that inform Fanon's work, as well as provide an integrative reading of Fanon, from *Black Skin, White Masks* to *The Wretched of the Earth*. This reading will lean not only on Fanon's work as a pioneer of post-colonial thinking, but also as a performative thinker influenced by the poetics of Aimé Cesaire. I will argue that only by reading Fanon dialectically—proclaiming both a psychoanalysis of racial dialogue and a politics of conflict and revolution—can one truly grasp the genius of his work and the depths of his contribution to liberation psychology. Ultimately, he will be argued to be a critical transitional figure providing "connective tissue" between psychoanalysis and liberation psychology.

Chapter 5 will shift from Harlem and the Caribbean to Argentina and Brazil, painting a picture of progressive psychoanalysis in Latin America. Special attention will be paid to the pioneering work of Marie Langer and Juliano Moreira, each representing an integration of psychoanalysis with Marxism and the Afro-Latinx struggle, respectively. Argentina was to become a nerve center for psychoanalysis throughout Latin America, including Brazil. But as we shall see, Brazil had its own unique history with psychoanalysis, grounded in tensions surrounding the country's relationship to Blackness and Black consciousness as a redemptive, revolutionary force. All of these intellectual and cultural routes will come to influence the work of Brazilian educator Paulo Freire, who not only inherited the psychoanalytic sociology of his intellectual Afro-Brazilian ancestors, but also engaged psychoanalytic contemporaries such as Erich Fromm and Frantz Fanon in developing his groundbreaking opus *Pedagogy of the Oppressed*.

Chapter 6 will review and recontextualize psychoanalytic liberation psychology from Freud to Fanon to Freire, synthesizing their insights into a broader theory of oppression and liberation, while simultaneously re-contextualizing them within their respective historical and material contexts. This dialectical shift will further clarify not only the relationship between psychoanalysis and liberation psychology, but also a broader meta-theory that explains how oppression generates trauma, humiliation, and political polarization that maintains different groups entrenched in a reactionary politics that circumvents true liberation. Using contemporary attachment theory and epidemiological research on inequality, this chapter will maintain that a emancipatory psychology seeks to undermine the oppressor-oppressed dialectic itself through a radical ethic of dialogue. The premise of this book is that only dialogical methodologies that humanize all parties of a social antagonism are capable of reaching toward true liberation and transformation. It will be shown how these psychoanalytic sensibilities ultimately flow into and inform Martín-Baró's liberation psychology.

In my conclusion, I will review the insights gained from this history of liberation psychology and psychoanalysis, and draw out their implications for clinical practice, critical pedagogy, and political activism today. I will argue for the inclusion of Fanon, Freire, and other Black, Afro-Latinx, and third-world theorists within the canon of contemporary psychoanalysis, as well as the inclusion of psychoanalytic approach to political action. Beyond this plea for inclusion, I will argue for an emancipatory ethics which pushes for a praxis of solidarity which yearns for transformative change.

This book emerges from a particular philosophical and social vantage point, and carries with it a certain politics, inspired by Howard Zinn's (2005) own historiographic classic, *A People's History of the United States*. In a similar vein to Zinn's project, the purpose of the current work is not simply to idealize the victims of oppression and denounce their oppressors. As history shows and Zinn intuited—perhaps with his own psychoanalytic insight—"the lines are not always clear" (p. 10). The oppressor may also turn out to be a victim of the same destructive system, while the victim, "themselves desperate and tainted with the culture that oppresses them, turn on other victims . . . The cry of the poor is not always just, but if you don't listen to it, you will never know what justice is" (p. 10). Beyond history and psychology, the central drive of this book to discern what exactly justice is and can look like.

NOTE

1. Cone argued for this ontological definition of Blackness based on his experiences observing oppression in both national and inter-national contexts. For example, Cone (personal communication, 2009) related his experience of being invited to Japan to speak to a community of Korean Christians who were descendants of Korean women kidnapped and trafficked to Japan as "women of comfort." This community expressed how they resonated with Cone's description of ontological Blackness, based on their invisibility and othering by their surrounding Japanese world. This type of experience speaks to the complexity of Cone's concept of ontological Blackness, which includes but goes beyond skin-color in explaining how different peoples are "othered."

Chapter One

"A Tool to Achieve Power"

Colonialism, Anti-Blackness, and Anti-Semitism

The history of psychoanalysis and social justice is fraught, split, and complex—not unlike its founder's own identity. Freud (1925) believed it was not "entirely a matter of chance that the first advocate of psychoanalysis was a Jew," and that to advocate for a vision of the mind wracked by conflict and internal domination that operated outside of conscious awareness required "a certain degree of readiness to accept a situation of solitary opposition—a situation with which no one is more familiar than a Jew" (p. 222). Yet over the course of his life he would see himself as both Hannibal standing in valiant anti-colonial opposition to the Roman Empire, and his father, who suffered silently through public embarrassment and anti-Semitic violence if only to survive (Breger, 2000; Gay, 1988). Freud was aware of his social world, and cognizant of his position as a Jew in it. But he also fancied himself a *conquistador*, a gallant adventurer casting himself across the globe "with all the curiosity, daring, and tenacity characteristic of a man of this sort" (Freud, 1900). But the *conquistadores* of history were more interested in gold than adventure, land, wealth, and capital than romantics. Writing in his journal about his first encounter with the Arawak people—ancestors to Latinx-Caribbean peoples such as Dominicans, Cubans, and Puerto Ricans—Columbus reasoned, "They would make fine servants. . . . With fifty men we could subjugate them all and make them do whatever we want" (cited in Zinn, 2005, p. 1).

These two themes—Jewishness as a source of ambivalence for Freud, and marginality as central to psychoanalysis—will be a topic of this chapter. I will further argue that the social-historical context of colonialism and slavery which created discourses of anti-Blackness was fundamental in forging not only psychoanalysis, but the centrality of social justice to the psychoanalytic project. It is this tension I will argue laid the foundation to psychoanalysis' influence in liberation psychology. This chapter will lay out a common critique of Freud's relationship to race and culture, and complement that critique by laying out the broader cultural world in which Freud operated. It will be shown that this world is quite relevant to our own, and presents a key heuristic against which Freud and the early psychoanalytic movement must be read.

FREUD AND COLONIAL DISCOURSE: A CRITIQUE AND REAPPRAISAL

Brickman's (2003) classic, *Aboriginal Populations in the Mind: Race and Primitivity in Psychoanalysis*, identifies in Freud's work an intimate concern with race and with collapsing the illusory gap dividing White European and non-White subjectivities, laying bare the unconscious shared by all humanity. Freud's analysis of culture subverted "the supreme self-confidence of European self-understanding, contending that what had been consigned as 'primitive' actually lived on in the structures of modern European subjectivity and institutions" (p. 5). Brunner (1995) also notes how Freud in his theorizing broke with the "perversion-heredity-degeneracy" system which created arbitrary distinctions between men and women, White/Gentile and Black/Jew, heterosexual and non-heterosexual which privileged the former and damned the latter as primitive, biologically degenerate, and culturally decayed. This same system encoded differences resulting from oppression and social dislocation as being constitutional, biological, or cultural in nature, reinforcing hierarchies and inequality as intrinsic to each of the aforementioned denigrated groups. By rejecting the degeneracy model (setting a path his Afro-Latinx descendants would follow, see Chapter 5), Freud "eliminated all significant differences between Jews and gentiles, [which some] commentators have been tempted to depict . . . as part of his Jewish self-assertion in the face of rising anti-Semitism" (p. 22). Psychoanalysis as Freud envisioned it would "recognize no boundaries separating the normal from the pathological, suspect the respectable, place analysts on an equal footing with analysands and refuse to distinguish among ethnic groups" (p. 43).

At the same time, for Brickman (2003) Freud's universalizing project "shared with the project of modernity, of which it was a part, the problems of deep-seated connections to racism and colonization" (p. 11). The psychoanalytic vision of mature, healthy subjectivity risked continuing to enact "a rationalism whose unstated color was white, just as its unstated gender was male" (p. 72). In comparing the content of the unconscious to "aboriginal populations in the mind," Freud created a system in which what is earlier and past is irrational, "primitive," defunct, and must be superseded by more advanced, rational, and dominant subjectivities—ensuring that racial and cultural difference would be equated with pathology, "maturity . . . measured as a movement away from primitivity: a movement toward whiteness and away from the qualities held to characterize the cultural/psychological worlds of the 'darker races'" (Brickman, 2003, p. 89). As we will see, Freud's project is torn between a critique of a European culture that makes itself superior to non-White people, and a colonizing project that enacts that very denigration through a psychic developmentalism that frames non-Whites as non-beings that must be superseded by White, rational beings-for-themselves. Brickman argues that Freud's bipolar perspective "can be attributed to all these inflections of [his] situation as both outsider and insider, a situation that has yielded a unique 'kind of knowledge' that forces us to think together the differences of the universal and particular and to undermine the binarism of nature and culture" (p. 170). If, as Aron and Starr (2012) contend, "Being at the margins is what allows for reflexive self-awareness, the ability to look at oneself as both subject and object, without being caught up in one pole or the other" (p. 9), then Freud's insights must be seen as tentatively held, oscillating pre-reflexively between the position of subject and object, caught up yet rapidly shifting between identification with oppressor and oppressed. In this regard, Freud will present us with the very symptom we seek to understand, and through his symptom shine a light toward that very understanding.

Although Brickman (2003) herself does not argue that Freud is simply a racist colonialist who should be rejected wholesale, her work has contributed to a narrative in which Freud's work is seen as disinterested in matters of race and culture, or even as hostile to the struggles of people of color and other non-dominant groups. What I would like to do is complement Brickman with a different reading of Freud, along the lines of the late Edward Said's (2003) essay *Freud and the Non-European*. Said (2003), in his own reading of Freud through a Palestinian lens, argued that "it is imperative to read [him] as intrinsically worthwhile for today's non-European or non-Western reader, who is often either happy to dismiss [him] altogether as dehumanizing or . . . [left] in an archive labelled as the dead-end rubbish bin of racist thinking" (pp. 23–24). Said calls on non-White readers to fully engage Freud affectively, certainly critically, but also deeply. To do so for me is not so much, contra Said, to "vindicate" Freud so much as it is, following Said, to "illuminate situations that he himself might never have dreamed of" (p. 27).

A Proto-Postcolonial Freud?

I find a view resonant with my own in Jonte-Pace's (2006) review of Brickman's (2003) work. Jonte-Pace raises a critical question about Freud and his relationship to race, racism, and post-colonialism, while at the same time agreeing with the crux of Brickman's argument—Freud's privileging of "civilized" subjectivity as a progressive force that supersedes and devalues the "primitive" and non-white, religious, and the feminine. Jonte-Pace (2006) asks:

> could one argue, to phrase it simply, that Freud can be seen as a proto-postcolonialist thinker, rather than a racist thinker trapped in a colonialist ideology? Or, to rephrase the question, could one argue that the traces of colonialist ideology in Freud's work can be read as an analysis of racist discourse rather than as evidence of a straightforward reproduction of racist discourse? (p. 1)

Jonte-Pace identifies three different ways of reading Freud within post-colonialist (and I might add, liberationist) discourses. There are those who reject Freud outright as a White European bourgeoise thinker, without considering what contributions he might make to conversations on social justice. Then there are those who wish to include what Freud missed or left out in psychoanalysis, adding an additional layer of anti-racist, post-colonial discourse on top of an aged, superseded, defunct psychoanalytic project, recognizing Freud's insights as limited by his social context while calling for a progressive contemporary psychoanalysis. Lastly, there are those "postcolonialist analysts" who would argue, repurposing Juliet Mitchell's (1974/2000) feminist re-reading, that "psychoanalysis is not a recommendation for a colonialist society, but an analysis of one" (Jonte-Pace, 2006, p. 2). Jonte-Pace identifies Frantz Fanon and Anne Anlin Cheng as examples of this tradition, and I will similarly place Paulo Freire, Martín-Baró, and other ancestors within this "canon."

Jonte-Pace (2006) goes on to note that Brickman's reading of Freud identifies three ways of responding to racial difference—abhorrence and denigration, inferiority to the perceived superiority of the other, and recognition of difference without idealization or devaluation (one notes in passing the parallels with the three ways of responding to Freud discussed above). From this reading Jonte-Pace argues,

> Rather than concluding . . . that Freud tried to "subvert the imperialist arrogance of late nineteenth century European thought", but failed, could we not argue that he pointed toward a critique of western civilization; that he tried to develop a tripartite psychodynamic understanding of response to difference; that although he may have been limited by the ideas and ideologies of his day, he nevertheless aimed to develop a postcolonialist analysis and critique of

> culture and psyche? Could we argue, in other words, that he is a protopostcolonialist thinker? (p. 3)

The question of whether Freud can be considered a "protopostcolonial thinker" will comprise the majority of the present and subsequent chapters. Furthermore, in the following chapters focusing on Frantz Fanon and Paulo Freire as forerunners of liberation psychology, it will be argued that Freud's elaboration of a tripartite psychodynamic model of how human beings respond to racial difference laid the very foundations of liberation psychology.

In writing to Abram Kardiner regarding Jung's anti-Semitic remarks during their Wednesday meetings in Vienna, Freud said, "I think that we as Jews, if we wish to join in anywhere, must develop a bit of masochism, be ready to suffer some wrong. Otherwise there is no hitting it off. Rest assured that if my name were Oberhuber, in spite of everything my innovations would have met with far less resistance" (cited in Reijzer & Ringold, 2011, p. 33). Central to the present chapter is how Freud's own experience of marginality as a Jew informed psychoanalysis and his reflections on culture, race, and society. Although Freud's Jewishness and its relationship to the development of psychoanalysis has attracted much scholarly attention (Geller, 2007; Gilman, 1993a; 1993b; Aron & Starr, 2013), it often does appear at times as if psychoanalysis, and clinical psychology more broadly, did wish "Freud's last name had indeed been Oberhuber" (Reijzer & Ringold, 2011, p. xiii).

The Jewishness of Freud and the early analysts often led to them being "considered sexual perverts, compulsive and paranoid psychopaths, atheists, and political radicals who wanted to overthrow society" (Reijzer & Ringold, 2011, p. 30). When read through the lens of liberation psychology, Freud's Jewishness and that of the first generations of psychoanalysts provides a fascinating entry point to understanding the relationship between psychoanalysis and social justice. As contextualized by Zaretsky (2004),

> The fact that *all* of Freud's early associates were Jewish guaranteed that psychoanalysis would remain marginal. The Jews were the racialized "other" in European life of the period . . . Excluded from idealized correlations of masculinity with valor, supposedly imprisoned by the "hyper-trophy of the Jewish family," Jewish men were more likely to be cognizant of the passive, vulnerable, and "homosexual" qualities that lay behind the masculine ideal. Under these conditions, the Jewish composition of psychoanalysis guaranteed that all analysts regarded the dominant culture as hypocritical—an assumption shared by all oppressed or marginalized groups for obvious reasons. (p. 70)

The task of these first three chapters will be to identify this mindset among the early Jewish psychoanalysts as members of an oppressed community, and track how this mindset and the ideas they produced set the stage for later adoptions of psychoanalytic thinking among post-colonial people of color interested in addressing racial and economic inequality. To fully appreciate the historical arc of this relationship, it is important to start "at the beginning."

COLONIALISM, RACISM, AND PROTO-CAPITALISM

The history of the Jewish people in Europe is in tragic and important ways intricately tied to the history of the Indigenous people of the Americas and Black people kidnapped from Africa—each their subjectivities were distorted and rendered subhuman under the gaze of European Whiteness. The history of Jew qua Gentile/Aryan and Black qua White/European formed two sides of the same (racist) coin, a relationship of center and periphery, oppressor and oppressed, idealized self and degraded other, those deemed human and those who were not. This division can be traced in part to a wound in history that would have profound cultural, economic, and transhistorical repercussions—Columbus' "discovery" of the "New World," and the rapacious colonialism that followed. By the time Columbus first set forth on his voyage, two intertwined discourses of otherness had already been formulated in Europe—a "medieval/popular" discourse that cast outsiders to the European imaginary as "barbarians, wild men, and noble savages," and a "religious-legal" discourse arising out of the Crusades that framed a relationship to "infidels" as those who must be conquered, and whose lands are essentially "uninhabited" and needed to be brought within the fold of Christendom (Brickman, 2003, pp. 19–20). Classical exegesis of the biblical text defined those who were "wild" as cast out from the presence of God, an association that would reverberate in narrative defenses of slavery, "wildness as accursedness was long allied with notions of blackness and bondage through the story of Ham, son of Noah" (p. 20).

When Columbus landed in the Bahamas and encountered the Arawak people, he stumbled upon a society based on equality and the sharing of resources, which came across in their "hospitality" toward the foreign Europeans, who found this behavior "remarkable." Coupled with this material equality were gender and sexual practices which proved equally scandalous to the Europeans. The Dominican friar Bartolome de las Casas would later write, "Men and women alike choose their mates and leave them as they please, without offense, jealousy or anger . . . If they tire of their men, they give themselves abortions with herbs that force stillbirths" (cited in Zinn, 2005, p. 5). These traits of relative freedom in sexual practices and sharing of resources, Howard Zinn (2005) writes, "did not stand out in the Europe of the Renaissance, dominated as it was by the religion of popes, the government of kings, the frenzy for money that marked Western civilization and its first messenger to the Americas, Christopher Columbus" (p. 1). After the expulsion of the Jews and the end of the *Reconquista*, Spain had become a geographically and politically unified state. One which, like other nation-states of its time, included a highly stratified society of poor peasants in serfdom to the noble class, who made up two percent of the population yet owned 95 percent of the land (p. 2). Seeking a new route to India, Spain was on the lookout for gold and riches. Upon ascertaining the nature of the Arawak people, their society, and the potential for gold, Columbus realized he could make a killing.

Columbus established a fort on the island of *la Hispaniola* and returned to Spain. He exaggerated his report to the Spanish crown, spinning stories of rivers swimming with gold and a docile people ready for Christendom. His estimate that with fifteen men he could subjugate the entirety of the Arawaks, Columbus would undertake his second voyage with 17 ships and 1,200 men. Upon returning to the Caribbean, he found the fort in *la Hispaniola* destroyed. The men he left guarding it had started roaming the island looking for gold, enslaving children for labor and women for sexual exploitation. The Taino, realizing the grave threat there would be guests now posed, killed the Spaniards and razed their fort. Columbus was ruthless, instituting a system of virulent slavery in retaliation. The Taino people of Boriken, Hispaniola, and the Bahamas were to present gold to the Spaniards in exchange for a copper token, which would be hung around their neck. Those found without a token—who had not delivered gold to the Spaniards—had their hands cut off and bled to death. This abject brutality became the Spaniards' way of "educating" the Taino, and instilling in them an "ethic of work."

The Europeans saw it as their sacred mission to convert the primitive savages to Christianity through "the conquest of their lands and the appropriation of their wealth and labor" (Brickman, 2003, p. 23). Brickman (2003) cites David Brion Davis in pointing to the "curse of Ham" as serving as a central justification of slavery, with a pedigree dating back to Christian theologians ranging from Augustine to Aquinas. As for colonizing Spain, so too for the later American colonists—Whites would juxtapose themselves as "hardworking whites" to the Native people, who were seen as lazy and passive (Roediger, 2007, p. 21). The African people who would be brought in to replace the dwindling indigenous populations in particular were seen as "so deeply mired in the darkness and sin of their continent of origin that slavery was deemed by many Europeans to improve their condition" (Brickman, 2003, p. 28). Through slavery and brutality, the indigenous people of the Caribbean and Americas, and people from West Africa, would be "civilized" out of their primitivity.[1] As Roediger (2007) writes, "'Civilization' continued to define itself as a negation of 'savagery'—indeed, to invent savagery in order to define itself" (p. 22). This desire was not merely cultural in nature, but deeply bound to economics. Zinn (2005) writes that across its colonial enterprises,

> the frenzy in the early capitalist states of Europe for gold, for slaves, for products of the soil, to pay the bond holders and stockholders of the expeditions, to finance the monarchical bureaucracies rising out of feudalism, to participate in what Karl Marx would later call "the primitive accumulation of capital." These were the violent beginnings of an intricate system of technology, business, politics, and culture that would dominate the world for the next five centuries. (p. 12)

These piranha-like desires driven by the accumulation of wealth required theological and philosophical grounding, words, deeds, and feelings that both motivated and created a need to conquer, to consume, and in turn to destroy—the nascent embers of capitalism. Beyond that, it needed an ideology and a psychology that supported domination.

The theological reasoning for a racial caste system went in hand with clear economic interests, in turn supported by crypto-psychological fantasies. Depending on Aristotle's rationalizing of what kind of people made "natural slaves," Spanish and other European clerics and scholars argued that non-White people were essentially "born to be slaves" due to being "ruled by passion rather than reason" (Brickman, 2003, p. 28). Dark skin was synonymous with primitivity, savagery, "wild passions," and docility, associations that while concretized during the advent of colonialism, resonated with earlier Medieval narratives of wealthy nobles toward the poor multitudes. Brickman (2003) writes,

> In medieval Europe the peasantry were frequently associated with black skin color (because of their exposure to the sun or their nearness to the soil); and their servitude was justified by the same biblical narrative concerning the descendants of the sons of Ham as was used to justify the slave trade from Africa. As Hannah Arendt points out, such codings of the distinction between classes, and later between nation-states, formed the basis of later biologistic racist thinking in the nineteenth century. (p. 40)

Medieval notions of skin color then informed class distinctions and maintained wealth inequality, which in turn informed the evolution of racism over the centuries. Skin color informed class, and later textured race. We find then, an organizing principle of power and control that lasted centuries and generations—the "other," whether coded in terms of race or class (and we can add gender and sexuality as well), is "black," wild, dangerous, irrational, primitive, and in need of external control and domination. By contrast, the "self" is pure, white, rational, controlling, dominant, and civilized. Discourses around race become a tool for managing class antagonisms within the White European imaginary (e.g., the rulers versus the peasant class), yet curiously reconfigured in relation to the emergence and creation of a racial "other of the other." Those previously excluded from Whiteness—poor, landless, Europeans—come to be included within Whiteness in order to denigrate newly defined racial others. In making the poor White, the ruling classes simultaneously oppress another group of people defined as non-White (e.g., people of African and indigenous descent), while exerting psychological control over poor Europeans themselves.

The Contradictions of Race and Labor: The Demands of Capital

As this White Supremacist and Capitalist system evolved and matured, it began to create bizarre and at times contradictory socio-historical circumstances. Consider the curious case of Bartolome de las Casas, who in his *A History of the Indies* argued against the enslavement and exploitation of the Taino-Arawak people on the basis that they were human beings who "had a soul." On the one hand, the arguments he repeated and defended on Tainos and Europeans sharing a common humanity by way of arguing for a sacred sense of interiority were aimed at protecting indigenous people by bringing them under the Spanish crown "peacefully." However, this reasoning went in hand with economic pressures and continuing demand for labor to Spain and Europe to extract wealth from its new colonies. De las Casas complemented his appeal to the Tainos' soul with the position that they were not suited for hard labor. People from Africa, however, in keeping with religio-racial discourses described above, were deemed by him more suitable for enslavement due to their Blackness, "hardiness," and lack of a soul. The demands of forced labor, wealth accumulation, and social control almost seemed to require a scapegoat, as if the freedom of one group of people required competition with or subjugation of another.

Racial and economic contradictions textured other colonial contexts. During the early colonial era of North America there was a kind of *détente* between the newly arrived European colonists and the Native indigenous peoples. The indigenous people of the North knew how to live off the land, at times mocking the colonists for their inability to prosper. Once those among the colonists began deserting the colonies to live among the Native peoples—collapsing their own mythologies of "lazy Indians" and "hardworking Whites"—the colonists responded to this narcissistic injury with violence and fire (Zinn, 2005). During the 16th century, prior to the formal structuring of American slavery, there existed a system of indentured servitude that affected both White Europeans and Black Africans. However, this did not mean that they were treated "equally." Black people were punished harshly for intermingling with Whites or attempting to escape servitude (a prototypical form of slavery and anti-Blackness), while their White counterparts might get off with "making penance" for their offense at the local church. Feelings of envy, rage, and even affiliative bonds shifted between different positions and social structures.

Part of the reason for this legal discrimination in the 16th and 17th century American colonies had to do with the fact that "where whites and blacks found themselves with common problems, common work, common enemy in their master, they behaved toward one another as equals" (Zinn, 2005, p. 31). From time to time they would drink together, make connections, and even build romantic relationships, all the while also planning escapes and attacks on their joint masters, while leading riots and committing arson. The fear of these liaisons in the American colonies were at times even greater than Black rebellion—"the fear the discontented whites would join black slaves to overthrow the existing order" (p. 37). As a result, even harsher laws were enacted to keep White and Black indentured servants apart, leading to the institution of even more brutal forms of slavery, hand in hand with the exponential growth of the plantation system (p. 32). In early 1700s Virginia, for example, the general assembly proclaimed that *all* White men were superior to Blacks, offering their "social (but White) inferiors a number of benefits previously denied them."

White men who had completed their indentured servitude would be awarded ten bushels of corn, thirty shillings, fifty acres of land (effectively granting voting rights), and a gun. White women would receive fifteen bushels of corn and forty shillings in addition to the land. A greater distribution of wealth, with an almost egalitarian economic concern for women, occurred along racial lines and on the backs of Black people (a form of colonial red lining). The legal and social punishment for collaboration between Whites and Blacks then went hand in hand with the promise of superior status. Given the complicated Medieval and later colonial history of wealth, race, and Blackness—skin supporting wealth inequality, then racial subjugation—by becoming free and landed, European serfs turned indentured servants could then "un-black" themselves and become White. Such racial transubstantiation represented nothing less than the magic of Mammon.

This tendency toward both solidarity and division between enslaved and oppressed peoples was also notable in the Spanish colonies. As the first Black slaves were brought into Hispaniola in the 16th century, the Spaniard governor began complaining that "fugitive Negro slaves were teaching disobedience to the Indians" (Zinn, 2005, p. 32).[2] The paternalistic tone notwithstanding, the more likely case was Native and Black slaves banding together based on a shared cause for freedom. This led to revolts in Hispaniola, Puerto Rico, Santa Marta, and the territory now recognized as Panama. Following these rebellions, a "special police" for escaped slaves was instituted to eliminate solidarity among the enslaved. But even Black and indigenous solidarity were not left untainted by the power of capital. Cox (2018) brings to light the lost history of African American settlements on the frontier of America in the 1700s and 1800s. The Northwest Territorial Ordinance of 1787 had marked this region as free of slavery, offering equal voting rights to any man—regardless of race—who owned at least fifty acres of land. Some of the first African-descended people in the frontier already existed there prior to the American Revolution and lived with Native Americans, either as escaped slaves who fled their masters or as free men and women who had purchased their freedom with their labor. "[L]ater pioneers of African descent were sometimes different," Cox writes, "taking up arms during the War of 1812 to battle Native Americans in the Northwest Territory" (p. 4). Some African-American pioneers prior to the Civil War saw the Northwest Territory as "a place of fresh hope," despite the danger and violence they might suffer. But they also understood "how their settlement would displace Native peoples, with whom they might even come into conflict. But they sought success, and before the Civil War that meant owning good land and farming it well" (p. 4).

Although Cox (2018) documents this lost and fascinating history of Black resilience and ingenuity, she is also cognizant of its colonial implications, writing, "Pioneers and frontiers are not uncomplicated things in America" (p. 210). African-American freed men and women were intent on "fighting the Native peoples of the region to clear them from the land so that immigrants from the east could purchase and farm it" (p. 17). The First Nations of the Northwest Territory had already experienced 150 years of war, betrayal, and genocide, "And pioneers coming to the northwest frontier to clear lands and farm were not a welcome presence, no matter what the color of their skin . . . for they were a part of the same settlement movement that was destroying these First Nations' homes and livelihoods" (p. 74). In trying to create a new world of freedom and equality, pioneers of African descent became complicit in the destruction of indigenous people. In seeking land, wealth, and capital that would purchase citizenship, civil rights, and entry into the American body politic, these frontiersmen and women argued for equality between the White man and descendants from Africa, all the while "still hostile toward Native Americans, whom they . . . viewed as savages fit only to be killed or violently removed from the land" (p. 210).

These predominantly African-American, land owning settlements began a process of Black wealth accumulation, which at times resulted in the displacement of Native peoples. Of course, this was nowhere near the virulent nature of White colonization, but it did present the promise of capital, and with it, the possibility—albeit short-lived—of a Black land-owning class. Capital, again, promised entry into the socioeconomic system, in this case the (White) American project. And for a time, this capital *did* lead to increased political power, social integration, and the (temporary) dismantling of anti-Black discriminatory laws (Cox, 2018). But it was bought over the land and bodies of indigenous peoples. This presented a paradox—Black pioneers could internalize a rhetoric of Native Americans as savage and deserving destruction by identifying with, if not Whiteness itself, the possibility of creating space for themselves participating in colonial projects that supported wealth accumulation, and in turn, the very capitalism that supported White Supremacy. Or was it the very White Supremacy that supported capitalism?

Likewise, there is evidence of Cherokee and other First Nation peoples in North America owning slaves for their agricultural industry as a way to accumulate wealth, in the hopes of using that wealth to protect their lands from assimilation and encroachment. Some of them, too, had internalized the ideology of Black savagery, inferiority, and hardiness for labor as a way to justify this turn (Krauthamer, 2013). Perhaps by participating in slave economy, they reasoned, they could buy their freedom from interference by the White man—in a sense, by becoming like him. "No matter how 'civilized' the Cherokee had become," Cox (2018) writes, "with their big homes, fine farms, and slaves, President Andrew Jackson wanted them gone to make room for more whites and their enslaved people" (p. 91). Similarly, with the emancipation of slavery after the Civil War came renewed land disputes between Native sovereignty and the Union government. Freeing Black slaves in Native land would mean the sudden loss of the labor and wealth that supported their independence, facilitating the annexing of indigenous land by always encroaching Whites.

Divide, Conquer, and Assimilate

Groups who suffered different types and levels of marginalization, exploitation, and oppression fell at odds with one another throughout colonial history. The possibility that different peoples who suffered at the hands of wealthy White elites *would band together in solidarity against their masters* was one that needed to be not only discouraged, but outright destroyed with extreme (class and race) prejudice. Even as African-descended and Indigenous people became complicit in America's continued aggression against them, so too did a White working class, threatened by their advancements and wealth, commit incredible violence against them born out of envy, displaced class resentment, and the will of their masters. Laws were enacted that prevented Black landowners from seeking legal protection against Whites encroaching on their land. Poor Whites witnessed the accumulated capital of their Black neighbors with envy, eventually razing their settlements to the ground. Never mind the overwhelming majority of Black people still lived in bondage, or free and in fear from violence and discrimination. It was these land-owning communities of Black people who were "the problem"—*they* were the reason poor Whites could not find good work, stable housing, etc. Capital, the resentment of exclusion, the promise of inclusion, even of admission into Whiteness and a capitalist system, proved seductive as it would inevitably be destructive.

And so the violence of this "primitive accumulation of capital" wrought a wound upon the world, one which required an ideological and proto-psychological rationale to support it. This brief history brings a number of quandaries into focus. Colonialism was an economic, political, and *psychological* system aimed at creating a certain accumulation and distribution of wealth, and *protecting* that distribution through violence and psychological domination. But it is limiting to simply view this as domination between the colonizer and the colonized. Throughout this history, potential allegiances—against Whiteness, against economic domination, against slavery, etc.—between indentured or poor Whites and enslaved Africans, or Native peoples and escaped slaves, were also accounted for. In great part, to be sure, through the limited redistribution of capital. But also through the promise that in accessing this capital, *you could become like the powerful*—poor indentured servants from Europe could become White, freed or escaped Black people from Africa could become American, and even Native peoples could become "free" by mimicking a kind of racial entrepreneurship. A social system could be maintained, and all that was then needed was a third other upon whom violence could be visited. Violence that, perhaps, belonged to this system of distribution itself. Colonialism, anti-Blackness, and capital all co-textured and co-determined one another, spawning an intricate system of economic and psychological control. It is this system and this history that would spawn not just modernity, but its most pronounced medico-professional symptom—psychoanalysis.

One final point before shifting to consider psychoanalysis within this historical narrative—European racial ideologies drew on the denigration of Blackness and African peoples as a weapon to wield against other non-White groups, and my analysis will depend on an understanding of the psychological and socio-economic role of Blackness. However, it is important to clarify that I do not idealize Blackness as such any more than I idealize Black people or any other subaltern community. Black and indigenous peoples are not just passive victims of history—they are also active participants in it. And history teaches us that with the triangulating power of capital *and* identification, perpetrators create victims who can become perpetrators. There are no innocents. But to paraphrase Zinn (2005)—the cry of the oppressed is not always just, but if we do not listen to it, we will not know what justice looks like.

JEWISHNESS AND BLACKNESS

Argentinian philosopher Enrique Dussel (1985) reflects on this wound in history and the damage done by the White-European "ego cogito" which became center to the periphery of "savages." He inquired, "Are the Amerindians human beings?" Were they rational and civilized like the Europeans?

Did they have a soul or were they akin to animals? "The theoretical response was of little importance," Dussel writes, "We are still suffering from the practical response" (p. 3). The indigenous peoples of Latin America were seen as born to labor, "if not irrational, then at least they were brutish, wild, underdeveloped, uncultured because they did not have the culture of the center" (p. 3). Like Hannah Arendt, Dussel argued this theological and psychological system did not arise *ex nihilo*,

> It arose from a previous experience of domination over other persons, of cultural oppression over other worlds. Before the ego cogito there is an ego conquiro; "I conquer" is the practical foundation of "I think." The center has imposed itself on the periphery for more than five centuries. But for how much longer? (p. 3)

By centering itself upon the world by the sword, Europe positioned itself as the "archetypal foundational 'I,'" divinity as such, God on Earth. Dussel expands on the expression of this "I":

> From the "I conquer" applied to the Aztec and Inca world and all America, from the "I enslave" applied to Africans sold for the gold and silver acquired at the cost of the death of Amerindians working in the depths of the earth, from the "I vanquish" of the wars of India and China to the shameful "opium war": from this "I" appears the Cartesian ego cogito. (p. 8)

This violence in the periphery of the "New World" repeated prior centuries of violence contained within Europe—White-Christian versus Arab-Muslim, Gentile versus Jew, noble "Aryan" princes versus "black" poor peasants, men versus women, and so forth.

It is against this totality of the center that Dussel (1985) calls for a philosophy of liberation "rising from the periphery, from the oppressed, from the shadow that the light of Being has not been able to illumine. Our thought sets out from non-Being, nothingness, otherness, exteriority, the mystery of no-sense. It is, then, a 'barbarian' philosophy" (p. 14). Similarly we may ask, can a "barbarian" psychoanalysis rise from the periphery of the oppressed? Or has it already?

A large body of scholarship examining Freud's relationship to his Jewishness, and the relationship of that identity to psychoanalysis, has shown that embedded within the logic of psychoanalysis is an attempt to resolve the position of the (Black) Jew within White European society (Brickman, 2003; Geller, 2007; Gilman, 1993a; 1993b; Klein, 1981). Depending on the scholar in question, Freud accomplishes this with varying degrees of success or failure. What is of import in this chapter is to outline the relationship between the history of colonialism and racism to Freud's identity as a Jew in anti-Semitic, anti-Black Europe. To this end it becomes critical to describe how

Freud is embedded within his immediate cultural context. As Brickman (2003) point out:

> The rhetorics of colonialism and antisemitism converged: in Freud's Vienna, as elsewhere in Europe, the language of racial inferiority was used not only for dark-skinned peoples in such places as Africa, Australia, and the Americas but also for the Jews of Europe, who were variously described as "Oriental," "primitive," "barbarian," "white Negroes," "mulatto," and "a mongrel race." (p. 163)

Gilman (1993b) in his erudite scholarship on Freud and race, borrows Peter Horman's argument that "psychoanalysis emerged as the negative image, so to speak, of its Jewish surroundings" (cited in p. 4). I would add to this formulation that psychoanalysis emerges as "the negative image" of Europe's relationship with the non-White, Black, and dark-skinned other. It is against that backdrop that psychoanalysis can be re-contextualized as intimately relevant to communities of color.

In turn-of-the-century Europe, the Jew, "but very specifically the male Jew . . . is seen as different, diseased" (Gilman, 1991, p. 333). Being Jewish meant being placed in a denigrated category "with a status analogous to that of women . . . The Jew defined what the Aryan was *not* . . . The Jew became the projection of all the anxieties about control present within the Aryan" (Gilman, 1993b, p. 9). This projection equated the Jew as non-Aryan, and hence *non-White*, with the "male Jew and the male African [seen] as equivalent dangers to the 'white' races in the anti-Semitic literature of the late nineteenth century" (p. 19). This equation between Blackness and Jewishness was powerful and palpable in the racial thinking of the time. Gilman cites the example of the writer Jesenska, who wrote in 1938 about the persecution of the Jews, referring to them as the "Negroes of Europe" (cited in Gilman, 1993b, p. 20).

Blackness and illness marked the racial discourse of the late nineteenth century, such that Jews were seen as bearing a disease "written on the skin." The Jews "had 'black' skin . . . an inherent quality, but it was as much a sign of their illness as was their hair" (Gilman, 1993b, p. 20). Mythologies regarding the Jews' black skin and its origin abounded. "The Jews are black," writes Gilman (1991), "according to nineteenth-century racial science, because they are not a pure race, because they are a race which has come from Africa" (p. 99). Another line of racial theorizing saw Jews as a mongrel race who intermarried with Africans during the Alexandrian exile (1993b, p. 21). For the European imaginary, the Jew's Blackness and "origins" from Africa also held a special relationship to the transmission of syphilis as a disease that "darkens" the skin, leading to a moral panic "of the Jews as carriers of syphilis and the generalized fear that such disease would undermine the strength of the body politic" (1991, p. 96). Coincidentally, this racist association is first identified in Spain in 1492, at the advent of Columbus' first journey to the "New World." After Ferdinand and Isabel issued their Edict of Expulsion of the Jews—the Alhambra Decree—demanding either conversion to Catholicism or exile, approximately 200,000 Jews became refugees heading toward Northern Africa or Southern Europe. As some approached the city of Rome, they were not allowed to enter and so were forced to camp outside the gates. An outbreak of syphilis occurred which resulted in the deaths of 30,000 people. Chroniclers of the era blamed the Jews for this disease, despite it already being present in Italy (Tampa et al., 2014).

In the *scala naturae*, the "scale of perfection" of eighteenth-century biological science, the Jew was seen as distant from the Aryan/Christian as "the Hottentot, the 'lowest' rung" (1993a, p. 12). This was similarly paralleled by Count Gobineau's *An Essay on the Inequality of the Human Races* in 1853, which argued that the upper classes were a "race of princes" with higher levels of Aryan genetic traits, and so "destined to rule" over the masses—ironically seen as *less* White (Brickman, 2003, p. 40). Of note, Gobineau penned this essay in the aftermath of the revolutions of 1848, in which political liberals won against the aristocracy and the Church, leading to the emancipation of the Jews from social, economic, and political marginality, and the granting of civil rights. From this association of Jewishness and Blackness came other tortured ascriptions—the Jew as a violent criminal, a degenerate sociopath whose psychopathology "is closely linked to their intense sexuality" (Gilman, 1993a, p. 173). This racial discourse was a symptom of—and a support for—a racial caste system that marginalized Jews in the ghettoes of Europe, cast out into the periphery of country and polis.

Salberg (2007) reviewed how pre-emancipation anti-Semitic laws required distinct dress codes that made Jews hyper-visible and thus vulnerable to acts of violence. These codes restricted their mobility, and barred them from different forms of work. It was the Enlightenment movement, with its emphasis on reason, that was seen as a ray of hope for Jews. Drawing on Daniel Boyarin's work, Salberg explores how Jewish men who felt emasculated by their marginality engaged in an ambivalent relationship to European gender norms. They expressed contempt against gentile performances of masculinity, which valued strength, aggression, violence, and contempt for femininity. In response Jewish men attempted to construct alternate models of masculinity that prioritized scholarly study, creativity, and spiritual pursuits. At the same time, there was also a reactionary idealization of masculinity as emphasizing strength, leading to the performance of a "Jewry of Muscle," "a Jew who does not step aside but fights back" (Salberg, 2007, p. 205). Gilman (1993b) argues that Freud "commented on none of this," opting to move discussions of the deceased nature of the Jew away from race and emphasizing psychological universality. Salberg (2007) notes, however, how these tensions "hide in plain sight" in Freud's work, as the conflict between

Gentile and Jew, masculine and feminine, active and passive, textured his thinking and theorizing. As I will show in this and the subsequent chapter, Freud reflected on race, culture, and politics much more lucidly than he is given credit for.

Freud's Encounters with Jewishness

The electoral victories of Austrian liberals in 1848 reinforced a philosophy of the "rational man," who when exposed to a laissez-faire capitalist market would make rational, logical choices with their self-interest in mind (Schorske, 1981). Jewish advocates for civil rights and their liberal Gentile allies created the first freely elected Frankfurt Parliament in Germany, under the influence of Emperor Franz Josef the First, granted the Jews emancipation, freeing them from confinement to the ghetto and ratifying their civil rights. Later renewals of these laws would further ban discrimination against Jews, proclaim religious and cultural tolerance, and encourage interdenominational (in the eyes of some, interracial) marriage. Emancipation slowly spread to different European countries, going hand in hand with Jewish enthusiasm for the promises of the Enlightenment—a human brotherhood grounded in reason and science, freed from the prejudices of the past (Klein, 1981). By favoring Enlightenment ideals, Jews attempted to assimilate into the wider culture by upholding universal human rights (Klein, 1981). The 1848 statutes granting residential, property, and trade rights to Jews led to their increased migration from the eastern reaches of the Hapsburg Empire—Freud's Moravia in particular—allowing Jews to escape crushing poverty and persecution for the polis of Vienna (Geller, 2007). Eastern Jews including Freud's family became predominant in the district of Leopoldstadt, were they were increasingly seen as "intruders" destabilizing Gentile life (Klein, 1981, p. 9). Despite their poverty, Freud's parents sought to provide him with a bourgeois education beginning at the *Sperl Gymnasium*, where he first experienced anti-Semitic microaggressions from his peers (Geller, 2007; Gilman, 1993b).

Freud experienced what it was like to be poor and have unstable housing alongside the promises of a liberal education. The latter gave him the hopes of joining society as a man of science and learning, but this same education also exposed him firsthand to the racial discourse of his day, framing his Jewishness as not only different but also diseased (Gilman, 1993b). But the association of Jewishness and Blackness had made its way into Freud's associations with his identity much earlier. He remarked, for example, on how his being a "black haired Jew" was interpreted by his mother—"It appears that I came into the world with such a tangle of black hair that my young mother declared that I was a little Moor" (cited in Gilman, 1993a, p. 55). Race, blackness, and the discourse of disease were salient for Freud throughout his life and development. Nowhere was this clearer than upon his entrance to the university in the same year as the *Krach* of 1873.

Freud, like other liberal Jews of the 1860s, came of age in a time of great hope for civil rights and equality. He noted how in those days there were even Jewish members of the parliamentary *burgerministerium*, seen as symbols of society's progress and openness (Klein, 1985, p. 70). The emperor Franz Josef's social programme had "won many hearts by ensuring equal rights for minorities" (Makari, 2008, p. 138), a hope that collapsed following the stock market *krach* of 1873 (Geller, 2007). Economic anxiety and the perception of Jewish "intruders" moving from the periphery to the center of society led to a rise in reactionary anti-Semitism, leading to the election of the Christian Socialist Karl Lueger. In the 1860s and 1870s Freud would grow up in a world of contradictions, where heightened freedom and mobility existed side by side with a persistent fear of violence. In the economic instability that followed, liberal governance and policies fell into disfavor as anti-Semitic politics rose in the popular consciousness (Geller, 2007). The image of the "rational man" would collapse, giving way to the psychological subject as a symptom of political frustrations and social decay.

Many Germans, especially those of the artisanal and working class, blamed the crash on the Jews and the laws that had made them equal citizens within the empire. The Jew was seen as a competitor who was unfairly privileged by liberal elites, and a danger to the interests of the working class. A reactionary spirit swept through Austrian society. University fraternities, social clubs, and institutions began to again exclude non-Aryans from membership. Scientific discourse more forcefully elevated theories of degeneracy which pointed to Jews and other racial others as the cause of society's collapse. The anti-Semitic wave resulted in the election of Karl Lueger as Mayor of Vienna, who was elected five times, four of which Franz Josef declined to acknowledge. Freud was noted to celebrate this veto with a cigar, celebrating emperor Josef as the "savior of the Jews" (Schorske, 1981, p. 6). Political pressure from the Catholic Church, however, eventually forced the emperor to accept Lueger in 1897 (Makari, 2008). With his election the belief that reason and science would lead to social progress dissipated.

The Rise of Karl Lueger: Making Vienna Great Again

During the two decades of liberal rule in Vienna, their political base consisted of middle-class Germans and German Jews in the major cities. In order to maintain control of parliament, they used a restricted franchise system, which created a high threshold for voting rights based on wealth (Judson, 2016; Schorske, 1981). New social groups arose as a result of the discontent created by this political arrangement to challenge the liberal hegemony—urban artisans and workers, Slavic nationalists, as well as anti-Semitic Christian Socials and Pan-Germans. While many of the social programs enacted by the liberals were aimed at disempowering the aristocracy, they instead triggered a series of "explosions" among the working class. "The liberals succeeded in releasing the political energies of the masses," Schorske (1981) writes, "but against themselves rather than against their ancient foes. Every shot aimed at the enemy above produced a hostile salvo from below" (p. 117).

The combination of a *laissez faire* free market economy coupled with a multicultural, multi-ethnic coalition led to a number of cultural and economic crises. Perceived attacks against the aristocracy and the church summoned a rise in Austro-German nationalism that saw the liberals as cultural traitors. "Catholicism, routed from the school and the courthouse as the handmaiden of aristocratic oppression," Schorske (1981) explains, "returned as the ideology of peasant and artisan, for whom liberalism meant capitalism and capitalism meant Jew . . . The failure of liberalism left the Jew a victim" (pp. 117–118). Social groups that experienced exclusion from the electoral process due to wealth inequality and perceived the dissolution of their culture and identity rose up to challenge the liberal middle class. The liberal establishment believed that history, human psychology, and the functioning of the free market had a rational structure, and would naturally lead to the emancipation of the populace from the old ruling aristocracy and religious control. The rise of the masses who felt "neglected or rejected" by liberalism destroyed that vision. Leaders like Karl Lueger, who began as political liberals, would turn their back on liberalism to lead the Christian Social and pan-German coalition to dominance, with anti-Semitism as his weapon.

Karl Lueger is a complicated figure in fin-de-siecle Viennese history—recognized by some as an efficient statesman who erected monumental infrastructure projects and pro-worker policies during his tenure as councilman and later mayor, while infamously credited as having inspired Hitler's own diction and discourse on mass politics and anti-Semitism (Wistrich, 1983). Lueger's right-wing populist discourse empowered him into public office, which together with his public works earned him the moniker "King of Vienna." Some debate exists as to whether his anti-Semitism was "genuine," or whether, as Lueger is himself quoted as saying in private, it was "an excellent means of propaganda and of getting ahead in politics . . . the sport of the rabble" (cited in Wistrich, 1983, p. 254). Given corroborating information of the later, it is likely that beyond his political opportunism was "a hollow core without any real convictions or genuine substance" (p. 254). Leftists of the time regarded Lueger as a cynical demagogue who employed anti-Semitism to draw on the resentments of the displaced poor and artisanal classes to fight capitalist policies that had "left them behind." One social democrat of the era described him as "equally well equipped with wit and pathos, an almost amoral frivolity with regard to political principles, ruthless or pliable as the occasion demands" (cited in Wistrich, 1983, p. 255). If so, there is indeed nothing new under the sun. Nevertheless, Karl Lueger, his politics and background, and the impact he had on Freud's world, deserves further exploration. His story in the context of 19th century Viennese society reveals to us an oddly familiar world—one which Freud would respond to through psychoanalysis, as we will see.

These political trends reverberated throughout the German-Austrian world, becoming a model other Christian Socialists enthusiastically emulated—as the title of Buchen's (2012) paper on the influence of Karl Lueger on Cracovian clerics reads, "Leaning from Vienna means learning to win." So too, it cannot be denied, Lueger's discourse set the stage for, and directly influenced, the ideology and tactics of Adolf Hitler (Geehr, 1990; Wistrich, 1983). But part of what makes Karl Lueger and his mark on history so interesting is that he originally identified as a "liberal democrat," committed to fighting socioeconomic injustice and the plight of the poor. By the end of his life, he had not merely employed political anti-Semitism as a Machiavellian utilitarian, but enacted long-term policies denying Jews equal rights, remarking he would "only be happy after the last Jew has disappeared from Vienna" (cited in Geehr, 1990, p. 15). How did this turn from "progressive democrat" to "proto-fascist" happen? What could it tell us about the frustrations and politics of Freud's time? In discussing this history, I will in large part depend on Geehr's (1990) *Karl Lueger: Mayor of fin-de-siecle Vienna.*

Karl Lueger was born into abject poverty, the fourth of eight siblings, and among three who would live to adulthood despite harsh living conditions. Although he adored his mother Julianna, his father Leopold was an ambivalent figure in his life—the young Karl bore "lasting resentment" due to regular beatings received by his father. Yet the elder Lueger at the same time—not unlike Freud's parents—wished for him to achieve upper class status through education. He dressed his son in "fine clothes" when they went out for walks, leading strangers to express surprise that they were indeed father and son. Geehr (1990) writes, "Here began the 'subtle sense of social superiority despite his lowly origins' for which Karl became well known" (p. 22), a sense of superiority he would seek to recapture throughout his life.

Lueger was admitted in 1850 to the "School of the Three Doves." The role of education left a lasting impact on the young Karl Lueger, who came to see his school as "a paradise for poor people" (cited in Geehr, 1990, p. 24). Over the course of his higher education Lueger was impressed by Lorenz von Stein's vision of a classless society without inequality. He developed a sense of social justice and obligation toward the poor, later becoming a lawyer who provided free legal counsel to the underprivileged, earning him a reputation as a champion of the "little people." In 1872 Lueger joined the liberal club *Deutsch-Demokratische Verein*, where he met Ignaz Mandl, a radical Jewish physician who "inveighed against monopoly and corruption in the Liberal oligarchy that controlled the city" (Schorske, 1981, p. 137). They connected over common political grievances, and the impact of the depression on workers who migrated during the boom years of the 1860s—workers who "suddenly found themselves unemployed and without housing" (Geehr, 1990, p. 39). The dissatisfaction of the poor with the liberal status quo led to "a corresponding receptivity to novel political forms and expressions" (p. 40).

This created an opening for Lueger and Mandl's political aspirations. They fought for an extension of the suffrage that extended the ability for those in the lower tax brackets to vote. The resistance of the liberals, including the at the time mayor Cajetan Felder, led to increased anti-liberal blowback among the lower classes, making democracy and liberalism "contradictory terms" in the public imagination (Schorske, 1981, p. 138). In the run for a district council seat, Lueger, with Mandl's mentorship, defeated the liberal Felder by arguing that the latter governed as an elite disconnected from the common folk. Geehr (1990) writes that by contrast "Lueger held that he, as a true representative of the people, should have legal guarantees of that position, for without them there could be no government for the people and by the people" (p. 44). Under Mandl's mentorship, Lueger learned how "[the] 'people' would soon become his tool to achieve power" (p. 53).

As noted by Geehr (1990), Lueger did not necessarily believe the "common people" could rule themselves, only that their interests would be better served by "strong men" like himself. "The people" thus became a means to an end, as would his later anti-Semitism. He began to exploit the frustrations of the poor toward the liberal status quo, by pivoting to attacking inner city Jews as the source of these frustrations. This led to a rupture between him and Mandl, who started to realize that Lueger "would abandon anyone or any principle if they became political liabilities" (p. 63). This became especially apparent as Lueger took a more public anti-Semitic stance, which led to frictions with his supporters given his friendship with the Jewish Mandl (ironic given that Mandl himself experimented with anti-Semitism in one of his runs for office). This tension came to a head in the spring of 1883 during a political meeting in which Lueger and Mandl disagreed regarding a recent policy placing greater emphasis on religion in elementary education. Mandl opposed the measure, as he saw the emphasis on religion as a veiled imposition of Christianity, which would infringe on the religious freedom of Jewish children (Geehr, 1990, p. 64). Lueger, however, was enthusiastic about the measure, as it would oppose the minority liberals in Viennese parliament—and to *always* oppose the liberals was his political raison d'etre. Mandl and Lueger broke ties thereafter, consolidating the latter's allegiance to anti-Semitism in his populist coterie.

In his oratory rhetoric and in policy debates, Lueger "perfected" the use of aggression, intimidation, slander, emotionality, and theatrics, along with greater courting of anti-Semitic discourse. This emboldened his followers, who would later come to expand on his racial views, emphasizing a politics of "blood and soil" and the sacrifice of the self before the community (Geehr, 1990, p. 315). These developments were not exactly a far stretch from Lueger's own politics, however. He openly stated his belief that the ills of society result from "anti-Christianity," and that "Jews were the enemy and that only unified mass support by the Christians could defeat them" (p. 81). His election as mayor—finally ratified by Emperor Franz Josef in 1896 after rejecting it five times—was framed as "a part of the great struggle for the liberation of the Christian people" (cited in p. 95). Geehr (1990) noted that "[among] most Austrian Catholics, the Jew was the eternal alien" (p. 177), who despite being granted equal rights were seen as "unequal, a group apart, 'un-German,' even racially separate" (pp. 177–178). As mayor of Vienna, Lueger was vociferous in echoing these broader cultural norms, arguing that Jews should have their voting rights removed. He was likewise no stranger to inciting physical violence and lynchings against the Jewish populace. His pedagogical policies were largely aimed at ensuring that Viennese schools educated its children to be good Germans and good Christians, with a healthy dose of instruction on the ills of the Jews. He infamously exploited the Dreyfus affair and ritual murder hysteria to stoke aggression toward Jews, and supported anti-immigration bills focused on curtailing the entrance of Jewish migrants into the city. In short, Lueger framed the Jew as the source of all social ills, a plague to be removed.

Despite hagiographic accounts of Lueger's mayordom in the post-1940s arguing that the Jews were in fact well off under his tenure, Geehr (1990) documents how Lueger's demagoguery incited physical violence toward Jews, led to increased barriers in the universities, and—one of Lueger's major long-term goals—increased exclusionary policies that marginalized them in the medical professions. Lueger was no friend of the "liberal" press which condemned his wielding of anti-Semitism as a political weapon—he simply charged them as Jewish and hence biased against him. Lueger's use of anti-Semitism, even in its more cynical and opportunistic form, cemented it as a central feature of Christian Socialism throughout his mayoralty of Vienna, and was to have a profound influence in Hitler's later National Socialism—both by Hitler's own account and studies of the ideological relationship between these movements. In sum, Geehr (1990) writes, "Lueger made anti-Semitism respectable, and in so doing made it more dangerous" (p. 175).

Lueger's manipulation of anti-Semitism bears a striking resemblance to the forms of racial control and domination discussed earlier. Although initially grounded in an anti-capitalist critique, Lueger learned that drawing on anti-Semitic racism would propel him into the public consciousness, allowing him greater access to political power. This splitting of the populace would have a lasting impact on Freud, who would—along with his disciples—come to develop a psychoanalytic theory of right-wing populism, and of the racialized systems that maintain wealth inequality. These systems would shift economic antagonisms into cultural and identarian ones that would distract from class conflicts via a racial detour, instilling a conflict between Jews and White/Aryans in place of a confrontation between the rich few and the many poor. And just as a class conflict became a racial conflict, so too a racial conflict became a psychological one—this is the birth of psychoanalysis as such. And psychoanalysis in turn attempted, however flawed, to respond to the antagonisms and inequalities that gave rise to it.

Seeking Solace in the Jewish Community

Geller (2007) saw the rise of anti-Semitism as resulting from German Gentiles' struggle for recognition and self-definition—"the German individual desperately wants to become 'himself,' and the other, the Jew, is perceived as also wanting desperately to become that same German self" (p. 51). "Split and split off," Geller writes, "Jews became doubles to themselves" (2007, p. 52). In allying themselves to enlightenment ideals as the key to their liberation, Jews attempted to fulfill the assimilationist demand—"Be like us." However, the promise of this appeal was not to be, as German anxieties about purity and identity "slipped into the political discourse of everyday Vienna" (Geller, 2007, p. 61). Makari (2008) argued that the Jews who would go on to become members of the early psychoanalytic movement did so in order to find refuge from the authority of the church, the state, and the failed promises of the old liberal guard. Rose (2003), following Klein (1985), argued that Jews in general, and psychoanalysis in particular, "adopted universalism as a specifically Jewish dream of freedom and justice which was the task of Jews . . . to disseminate across the globe" (2003, p. 72). Freud sought refuge in this world in part through his membership to Jewish welfare organizations, such as the B'nai B'rith.

Freud's world was one of the "pre-Shoah double-bind"—the pressure for Jews to assimilate into Gentile-German society, along with that society's belief that they were incapable of doing so without "contaminating" the purity of German blood (Geller, 2007, p. 5). At the turn of the century, elements within the German-speaking world sought to find and create a unitary group identity, "a union of *Blut und Boden* (blood and soul [sic])" (p. 47). "*Judentum's* continuing function as exemplary other," Geller writes, "as the always already antitype of Austrian Catholicism, however, fomented a crisis" (p. 48). The dark side of the compulsion to assimilate, "You *cannot* be like us, you are alien and must be destroyed" showed itself time and again in the politics of the time. Freud saw the destructive nature of this pull toward cultural annihilation, recalling, "I considered myself German intellectually until I noticed the growth of anti-Semitic prejudice in Germany and German Austria. Since that time, I considered myself no longer a German" (cited in Klein, 1981, p. 55).

Freud rejected assimilation, as can be seen in his advice to Little Hans' father, Max Graf, to not deprive him of a Jewish identification by not circumcising him or raising him Jewish (Klein, 1981). When Freud was denied a professorship due to institutional pressures to curtail the number of Jews (Klein, 1981, pp. 69–70), he sought solace at the B'nai B'rith, a Jewish service organization devoted to providing aid to the poor, combating bigotry, and providing solidarity to its Jewish members. Klein (1981) argues that Freud's fellowship with the B'nai B'rith influenced the development of the psychoanalytic movement—the B'nai B'rith extolled values of universality and human rights, positioning the Jewish people as advocates for the transformation and reconciliation of Gentiles and Jews. These values of universality were to inform psychoanalysis, which itself attracted a predominantly Jewish following leading up to World War I. For example, until 1906 all 17 members of Freud's study circle were Jews—leftist, Marxist-Socialist, progressive Jews with humanitarian values and vocation (Danto, 2005; Klein, 1981). Given the particular positionality of the Jews as racially other, and their adoption of a Marxist-Socialist politics, could the reconciliation they yearned for be on just cultural, but political and economic grounds? There is an ethics here that would resonate throughout generations—to liberate themselves, the oppressed must liberate their oppressor as well.

In a letter to the B'nai B'rith, Freud extolled the "dark emotional powers" that drew him to his Jewishness, powers that defied being put into words. He recognized in this letter to his community that his Jewishness afforded him two "indispensable" qualities,

> Because I was a Jew, I found myself free of many prejudices which restrict others in the use of the intellect; as a Jew I was prepared to be in the opposition and to renounce agreement with the "compact majority." (cited in Frosh, 2008, p. 173)

Freud makes a link between his status as an outsider and being a participant in B'nai B'rith's humanitarian values, freeing himself from conventional inhibitions and opposing society's injustice toward the other. Frosh (2008), following a similar line, argues that these values flowed into psychoanalytic theory itself. Noting the anti-Semitic stereotypes of the Jews—especially the Jewish male—as being both sexually deviant and aggressive while also emasculated and psychosocially "castrated," Frosh outlines how psychoanalysis' claim that human subjectivity is constructed through lack and castration reflects a *universalization* of an anti-Semitic projection. "Freud's move is to remove the stain of deviance from 'the Jew,'" Frosh writes, "the Jew is rather the flag-bearer for the whole of humankind" (p. 169). As has been widely documented (Aron & Starr, 2012; Brickman, 2003; Geller, 2007; Gilman, 1993a; 1993b), Freud's theories are textured by anxieties regarding the status of Jews in *fin-de-siecle* European society, and by attempts to universalize—or "return to sender" (Gaztambide, 2015)—aggression and sexuality projected upon Jews. From this perspective, Freud attempts to show how these aggressive and sexual elements of the psyche are not inherently Jewish but in fact shared by all mankind, making us all—as Harry Stack Sullivan might say—more human than not. And if we can recognize one another's humanity, perhaps we can also recognize the social and economic antagonisms that impact our lives. And strive to challenge and transform them.

Did Freud Think About Race? Jews, Negroes, and "Negroes"

Freud's world was textured by culture, politics, race, and class in ways that he was painfully aware of. The relationship between Blackness and Jewishness occupied Freud's mind, and it would seem, that of the early psychoanalysts as well. This can be gleaned in his correspondence with Carl Jung and Sándor Ferenczi, for example. In the aftermath of their trip to America in 1909, Jung wrote to Freud:

> Just as the coloured man lives in your cities and even within your houses, so also he lives under your skin, subconsciously. Naturally it works both ways. Just as every Jew has a Christ complex, so every Negro has a white complex and every American a Negro complex. As a rule the coloured man would give anything to change his skin, and the white man hates to admit that he has been touched by the black. (*Collected Works* 10:508, par. 963, cited in Ahad, 2010, p. 1)

Within the psyche some other is implied, constructed through the categories of race and class. Similarly, Ferenczi wrote to Freud regarding his pessimism regarding humanity's proclivity to violence, making the following observation regarding race:

> The persecution of blacks in America reminds me of the case that Jung so sagely presented, according to which the blacks represent the "unconscious" of the Americans . . . Thus, the hate, the reaction formation against one's own vices. Along with the circumcision/castration complex, this could also be the basis for anti-Semitism . . . It is only since my analysis that I have understood the widespread Hungarian saying: "I hate him like my sins." (Brabant et al., 1993, pp. 186–187)

In this correspondence, Jung, Ferenczi, and Freud discussed the intersection of racism and the unconscious, making the argument that there is a relationship between the aspects of one's own psyche that have been disowned, and hatred of the racial other via projection. In Ferenczi's letter the relationship between disowned elements, Blackness, and Jewishness is even more explicit. But were these incidental thoughts put on paper and merely directed at Freud, or did Freud himself entertain these associations in his own mind?

A series of revealing papers by Ginsburg (1999) sheds much needed light on the subject. He draws attention to Smiley Blanton's memoir of his analysis with Freud, and a particular exchange they had about race. Ginsburg describes the anecdote:

> After his ninth session with Freud on September 9, 1929, Blanton recorded the following exchange: "At one point during the hour, Freud asked me if Jews were not put in the same category as Negroes. I said I had not met with this comparison. Freud said, 'I often have!'" (cited in p. 245)

This is a curious exchange between a White American Gentile analysand qua analyst-in-training and his Jewish-German analyst. Blanton, answering Freud's question within his own North American context, states he had never heard of the comparison between Jews and Negroes. Freud, speaking from his (non)European positionality, remarks with a tone of humor he "often" has. Ginsburg (1999) similarly notes that Blanton's observation, that Jews were not in the same category as Black people, "did not leaven Freud's later theorizing in *Moses and Monotheism* about the Pharonic origins of the Jewish faith" (1999, p. 247), an insight that will be critical in my reading of Freud's cultural writings in Chapter 3.

Another fascinating anecdote unearthed by Ginsburg (1999, 2015) relates to Freud's analysis of Clarence P. Oberndorf (1882–1954). An American Jew born in the South, Oberndorf suffered a head trauma during birth (his skull was crushed on both sides). In the year it took for his wounds to heal, he was cared for by an African-American wet nurse whose "devotion" aided in his survival. In his autobiography, Oberndorf remarked that memories of his early years "reside, or rest, or linger vividly in this Southern atmosphere, colored in both senses by the Negroes of the household, to whom one habitually resorted for solace and advice in childhood troubles" (cited in Ginsburg, 1999, pp. 243–244). Not fully registering the impact of his racial surround as an American Jew—racialized White in America—Oberndorf relates an interpretation Freud made of a dream during their analysis thirty years later. In the dream he was in the driver's seat of an old-fashioned wagon drawn by a white horse and a black horse. In Oberndorf's retelling of the interpretation, Freud

> made the inference that my life had unconsciously been under the influence of two fathers, a white father Joe, and a black father Joe, our Negro coachman who had been a slave but who taught me many things besides currying a horse and riding bareback. (cited in Ginsburg, 1999, p. 244)

Oberndorf seemingly dismissed Freud's interpretation that the two horses reflected a racialized conflict between his yearnings for his White, biological father, and his Black father in fantasy.

Interestingly, Ginsburg (1999) came across a different telling of Oberndorf's dream, reported by Abram Kardiner, as well as in an elegy to Oberndorf after his death by Lawrence Kubie (Ginsberg, 2015). In his own memoir of his analysis with Freud, Kardiner relates how "Oberndorf got to be on bad terms with Freud" after the latter interpreted a dream. In Kardiner's account,

> The dream was as follows: He was riding in a carriage pulled by two horses, one of which was white, and the other black. They were going to some unknown destination . . . this particular dream happened, rightly or wrongly, to hit upon one of Oberndorf's apparent weak spots, because it was Freud's interpretation that he, Oberndorf, could never marry because he didn't know whether to choose a white woman or a black woman, and so he was in a quandry. (cited in Ginsburg, 1999, p. 244)

In Kardiner's retelling, Freud's interpretation "infuriated" Oberndorf, and became a point of contention for months in the treatment. In his analysis of the account, Ginsburg (1999) stated that the "hierarchy of race relations, which let the white child drink milk from the nurturing black woman's breast at the same time as she was relegated to a subservient lot in life," (p. 247) possibly constituted an important component to Oberndorf's subjectivity. Similarly, in his elegy to Oberndorf, Kubie is cited as stating that "a method of treatment which was designed to help people rid themselves of emotional illness and psychic blind spots was refused by a worthy disciple, because of the interlocking forces of sex and race, American style" (cited in Ginsburg, 2015, pp. 14–15).

My interest here is not so much to examine Oberndorf's racialized object-relations, or to identify the "objective" or correct version of this clinical exchange with Freud—whether he focused on the father or the mother.[3] Rather, it is to note that both versions of this account show Freud actively engaging with and thinking about race and racialized unconscious conflict in the psychoanalytic encounter, suggesting that Freud did indeed mentalize about race and its impact on subjectivity in his clinical work. Putting together Blanton's and Oberndorf's vignettes, we can see that Freud (1) was cognizant of the association between Jewishness and Blackness in his European cultural milieu, and (2) was able to think clinically about how a Jewish patient struggled with the libidinal cathexis of a racially grounded ambivalence between Blackness and Whiteness. In Freud's interpretation of Oberndorf's dream, the latter as Jewish patient operates as a "excluded third" before the primal scene of Blackness and Whiteness itself. This is a tripartite, some might argue structurally Oedipal, interpretation. But these were not the only ways Freud explicitly positioned himself in relation to race and Blackness.

Tate (1996) brings to light an "old joke" that Freud often repeated his colleagues, hiding in plain sight in Jones's biography of Freud. The joke was initially based on his penchant for referring to an American patient as "his negro." After the publication of a cartoon in the journal *Fliegende Blatter* in 1886, in which a yawning lion was depicted muttering "twelve o'clock and no Negro," Freud, who started his consultations at twelve in the afternoon, would go on to periodically tell variations of this "joke" to his psychoanalytic colleagues—who would, ostensibly, "get" the joke. As an African-American, psychoanalytically informed critic, Tate employs psychoanalytic theory in her critique of Freud's joke, in order to show the utility it has for understanding and subverting racism.

In Tate's (1996) analysis, Freud, in identifying with the lion, establishes an equation between the analyst-patient dyad and the historic White master/Black slave relationship, revealing how the power imbalance of the analytic relationship can be belied by implicitly racialized terms (Brickman, 2003). But Tate also notes how in this identification, Freud shifts out of his own anxious position as the Black/Jewish other in his social context, and takes up the role of devouring White male subjectivity in relation to Blackness. In essence, he cleanses himself of his own racialized otherness and becomes White, his repetition of the "joke" an attempt to compulsively master his own racial trauma and humiliation. And "master" it in more ways than one, by through the mechanism of the joke becoming the White master to the Black man. So too also in Freud's othering of women's subjectivity as the "dark continent," as Africa as such.

Harper's (2012) reading of this joke is somewhat more generous, but picks up on a theme implicit in Tate's (1996) analysis. Harper notes Freud's bipolar identification with *both* the lion and the Negro, "with both the coloniser [sic] and the colonised [sic], European and non-European" (p. 101), which he interprets as the driver of Freud's enjoyment of the joke. Harper suggests that by "siding up with his superego" Freud can laugh at the persecuted *Ostjuden*/Negro and enjoy them being fed to the lion rather than an secular Jew suffering this fate. But even this suggests a tripartite structure, which gets to the core insight of Tate's (1996) critique:

> Freud's joke reconstitutes the polarized economy of power . . . by transforming this relationship into a tripartite one of relative social privilege among whites, Jews, and Negroes before collapsing the triangular formulation into the simple polarity of white and black. This reconstitution has the effect of whitening the metaphorical blackness of Jewishness in direct proportion to the prominence of actual black bodies. Such prominence erases the Semitic blackness presumed by Aryans because Jews under these circumstances become absorbed

> into the category of whiteness. No doubt, such an exchange would seem like scapegoating to African Americans. (p. 57)

The joke exploits, in words James Cone might use, "the ontological blackness of African Americans to erase the figurative blackness of the Jewish body" (Tate, 1996, p. 57). Here Tate gets precisely at what I will argue is not only Freud's enacted racism, but also Freud's very particular *analysis* of racism, and how racism is used to triangulate social relations and maintain wealth inequality.

FREUD IN COLONIAL, RACIAL, AND ECONOMIC CONTEXT

These vignettes from Freud's personal history, correspondence, clinical work, and humor evidence how in his 19th-century world he could take different positions in relation to the signifiers Whiteness, Jewishness, and Blackness. In his own discussion of his "Moorishness," the associations between Jewishness and Blackness, and discussions with colleagues over anti-Semitism and anti-Black racism, Freud evidenced his identification with Blackness as a Jew. In his clinical work, we can see his ability to interpret the triangulated relationship between a Jew and his struggle with an ambivalent conflict between Whiteness and Blackness structured by America's racial imaginary. And lastly, in Tate and Harper's analysis of his "joke," we can see Freud taking on an identification with Whiteness which repudiates his Jewishness and takes a position of a devouring, dominating power toward Blackness. In Chapter 3 we find will find each of these positions being worked through in his writings on culture, religion, and society. I will argue that an analysis of his work yields, reading Jonte-Pace with Brickman, *both* an enactment of racialized dynamics *and* an analysis of them. I will explain how Freud's model can not only be read to analyze Freud himself (as Tate has done), but how his struggles set in motion a series of antagonisms and dialogues that, through various routes, flowed into his descendants in Harlem, the Caribbean, and Latin America, ultimately setting the foundations to liberation psychology.

NOTES

1. Brickman (2003) rightly notes the survival and complete reproduction of this narrative in a 1914 volume of the psychoanalytic journal *Psychoanalytic Quarterly*. In that issue, numerous authors "arranged their clinical material to demonstrate that black peoples regressed more quickly and easily to psychosis because of their lower position on the sociocultural evolutionary scale" (p. 87). Slavery, in turn, was argued to have been "the most wonderful thing" for introducing Black people to Christianity and the "value" of work.

2. One cannot help but note the trans-historical irony of this paternalistic statement. In the 16th century Black slaves were "teaching disobedience" to the indigenous people of the Carib-

bean. In the 20th century, we find a curious echo of this ideology on the lips of Homer Loomis Jr., an American fascist—"the Negro would behave himself if it wasn't for the Jews. It's the Jews' fault that the Negroes are getting out of place" (cited in McWilliams, 1948, p. 214). Now it is the Jew who is "teaching disobedience" to African-Americans. In both cases the formula is the same—to discount two oppressed peoples engaging in solidarity over shared economic, cultural, and spiritual interests. As if one of these peoples did not already carry furor over their oppression, encrusted in their bodies (see my discussion of Fanon, Chapter 4).

3. It is interesting, however, that in the United States Oberndorf was an ardent advocate of de-segregation and integration of Black psychiatrists, nurses, and patients within psychiatric hospitals, and made contributions to debates on de-segregation (Ginsburg, 2015). At the same time, he never married (Ginsburg, 1999).

Chapter Two

"A Sort of Inner Revolution"

Freud, Ferenczi, Fenichel, and Fromm

Russel Jacoby (1986) in the preface to his book *The Repression of Psychoanalysis*, wrote that the first generation of analysts "embraced psychoanalysis with a missionary zeal . . . They were rebellious intellectuals with broad cultural and political commitments. The spirit and ethos that animated them and their psychoanalysis did not endure" (p. xii). I start with his morose and melancholic words in order to orient us to a sense of loss. The first generations of psychoanalysts were comprised of politically left-leaning Jews who formed part of a persecuted and marginalized minority community—Erich Fromm, Otto Fenichel, and Wilhelm and Annie Reich identified as Marxists, whereas Ernst Simmel, Bruno Bettelheim, Grete Bibring, Helene Deutsch, Siegfried Bernfeld, and Sandor Ferenczi were Socialists. Edith Jacobson and Marie Langer were communists, while Eduard Hitschmann, Paul Federn, Karen Horney, and Sigmund Freud were Social Democrats (Danto, 2005, pp. 18–19; 21). From these disparate left and center-left positions, they had regular, ongoing, and theoretically rich discussions about the relationship between psyche, culture, and society that deftly maneuvered between an analysis of class structure, socio-economic inequality, and racism, alongside an analysis of the construction of gender and sexuality. These theoretical and clinical labors went in hand with a period from 1918 to 1938 that not only expanded the scope of psychoanalysis to provide equitable mental health care, but also resulted in greater psychoanalytic participation in public policy, public interest, and social activism (Danto, 2005; 2016). These efforts encapsulated Freud's vision that for psychoanalysts to be effective agents of change they must recognize their therapeutic limitations and deepen "our determination to change other social factors so that men and women shall no longer be forced into hopeless situations" (Freud, 1909).

This chapter will trace the roots and routes of psychoanalysis' engagement with social justice, and how these pathways yielded a series of ideas and practices that would become central to liberation psychology. I will trace these routes through attention to two members of the first and second generation of psychoanalysis, Freud's friend and collaborator Sandor Ferenczi, and Otto Fenichel, respectively. Ferenczi articulated a brilliant set of insights around trauma, identification with the aggressor, and what makes relationships curative, that would either influence or resonate with later thinkers in the canon of liberation psychology. Likewise, Fenichel's oft-ignored posthumous analysis of race and class reveals a psychoanalytic sensibility for examining social hierarchies and how they produce inequality and emotional distress. Both Ferenczi and Fenichel would leave their mark on the younger Erich Fromm, who as we will see, served as a critical bridge between psychoanalysis and liberation psychology. By outlining the broader intellectual milieu of the first generation of psychoanalysts, this will provide further context within which to examine Freud's own thinking on inequality and how it structures the human psyche, which will form the core of the subsequent chapter. I will conclude this chapter by providing an account of how psychoanalysis lost touch with this tradition as the Jewish emigres became refugees in the United States.

EMPATHY, HYPOCRISY, AND JUSTICE: FERENCZI, FREUD, AND THE FIRST GENERATION OF PSYCHOANALYSTS

Sandor Ferenczi was born into a middle-class, liberal, multilingual, and multicultural Jewish-Hungarian family. Exposed to the liberal values of a post-emancipation family growing up, the young Ferenczi was "an open-minded and innovative person, with a high level of tolerance and a liberal attitude. All of these later played a role in the psychoanalytic movement" (Meszaros, 2012, p. 80). After meeting in 1908 he and Freud felt a kinship for one another as they collaborated on the development of psychoanalysis as a clinical and cultural project (Meyer, 2005). As second-generation Jewish migrants and sons of families from Galicia, this cultural affiliation informed their work as they navigated the turn-of-the-century world (Sziklai, 2016).

In Ferenczi's writings, one finds ongoing self-scrutiny and reflection on the challenges posed by the power difference between analyst and analysand, and how this inequality must be negotiated in cases of severe trauma. Arnold Rachman (2007), a psychoanalyst who pioneered the resurgence of interest in Ferenczi's life and work, notes that Ferenczi's clinical experiments with empathy and mutuality were based on meticulous observations of the therapeutic relationship, especially the patient's moment-to-moment reactions to the therapist. These experiments, ranging from "active" intervention to the provision of reparative emotional experiences, pioneered the psychoanalytic treatment of complex trauma, and "laid the foundation for a relational perspective in psychoanalysis" (p. 76). It should come as no surprise, then, that before joining the psychoanalytic movement Ferenczi's professional life involved clinical work with poor and marginalized populations who were victims of chronic trauma from the broader society (Rachman, 1993). Although Ferenczi, like Freud, was embedded in cultural streams of patriarchy and misogyny, and no less likely to repeat its ideologies wholesale (Meszaros, 1993), one can nevertheless discern that he struggled with these discourses. It is through this struggle that Ferenczi in turn challenged and critiqued them.

Ferenczi began his clinical work in hospitals devoted to the poor and marginalized members of Hungarian society at the time. The populations Ferenczi served often included men and women who were persecuted due to their sexual orientation, or were pushed into such destitution that prostitution became the only means for survival (Rachman, 1993). Perhaps the best known patient from Ferenczi's pre-analytic days is "Rosa K," a lesbian woman who was condemned as a "cross dresser." The publication of his therapeutic relationship with Rosa K in 1902 was the first article written in Hungarian calling on the medical community to recognize the humanity of male and female homosexuals, and to reject theories of degeneracy that pathologized and dehumanized them (Rachman, 1993). Ferenczi saw Rosa K during his clinical tenure at St. Elizabeth's Hospital for the poor in Budapest. Rachman's (1993) moving depiction of their encounter is suggestive of Ferenczi's later clinical developments:

> Ferenczi described the sad fate of Rosa K in an empathic way; it is clear from his description of her that he was attempting to understand her, not to judge, moralize about, or categorize her. Hunted, incarcerated, and oppressed by everyone, Rosa K, like most homosexuals at the turn of the century, was socially isolated and emotionally unstable when she met the young Ferenczi. The attitude of her family, the medical community, and society at large toward Rosa K was universally negative, rejecting, and condemning. But Ferenczi viewed this "cursed" woman as a person. (p. 82)

In order to better understand her experience of interpersonal and systemic trauma, Ferenczi encouraged her to write an autobiography, which they used therapeutically. Ostracized by her parents, mocked by her peers, unemployed and harassed by the police, forced into homelessness, poverty, and discriminated against, her relationship with Ferenczi may have been her first experience of recognition from an-other. Rachman (1993) states that "[t]his early perspective of 'the other in the treatment process' was to become a significant theme in Ferenczi's clinical work" (p. 84), work that would redefine psychoanalysis into a transformative relational encounter grounded in empathy.

Ferenczi's clinical and social concerns for those who were oppressed increased after he joined the psychoanalytic movement, when he reflected on the sociopolitical implications of psychoanalysis soon after his first meeting with Freud (Moreau-Ricaud, 1996). In 1908, Ferenczi openly advocated for the rights of homosexuals, urging his analytic colleagues to "take sides against the unfair penal sanctions which homosexuals are subjected to in many countries, especially in Germany, but also in our country" (cited in Rachman, 1993, p. 84).

Politics and society were also vibrant topics of conversation in Ferenczi's correspondence with Freud, in which social vision of psychoanalysis was present early in their thinking. As noted in Chapter 2, in a 1910 letter, Ferenczi reflected on an insight by Carl Jung, drawing attention to the parallels between anti-Semitic and anti-Black racism, based on the projection of disowned aspects of the self upon the other, which are the denigrated jointly. This racial projection of one's own unwanted thoughts and feelings smacked of hypocrisy for Ferenczi. Hypocrisy in politics, as well as in the therapeutic relationship, would become a prevalent theme in his work. In 1911, he published an article in the Hungarian progressive student periodical *Szabadgondolat* (Free Thought), in which he discussed the intersection of social consciousness, education, and the psyche. He argued that repression of the passions was both a psychological and societal problem brought about by oppression, one which would be undone only by "a radical reform of psychical education . . . this will bring the end of a period of humanity which is characterized by hypocrisy, by the blind worship of dogmas and authorities and by the absence of self-criticism" (cited in Sziklai, 2016, p. 6). In that same year he similarly wrote about alcoholism as a symptom of social stressors which could be cured by the discovery of their material sources through psychoanalysis.

Ferenczi's thinking on psychoanalysis and social change came across in an earlier letter to Freud in 1910,

> I would like to recommend to you another point for consideration (in case you haven't come upon it yourself). That is the sociological significance of our analyses in the sense that in our analyses we investigate the *real* conditions in the various levels of society, cleansed of all hypocrisy and conventionalism, just as they are mirrored in the individual. (Ferenczi, 1910, emphasis original)

Ferenczi proposes that psychoanalysis reveals how society, its hypocrisies and contradictions, is internalized within the psyche. In exposing these inner prohibitions, the analyst assists the individual in liberating their critical faculties, so that they may free themselves from their influence. This idea would later reverberate in Freud's thinking on how society restricts the intellect of the oppressed, and in turn their emancipatory energies (see next chapter).

As can be gleaned so far, Ferenczi's insights on psyche and society arose organically from his clinical work. For example, he wrote about patients whose loss of social and class status resulted in painful narcissistic injuries (Ferenczi, 1922a; 1923), while other patients who achieved some level of social mobility became wracked with feelings of guilt and of inferiority (1922b; see also Freud, 1916). In each of these, issues of class inequality, affect and empathy, and societal hypocrisy became key clinical questions for Ferenczi. He (1908) believed that psychoanalysis could serve as a source of enlightenment to free mankind from unnecessary internal and external repression. He referred to

> A sort of inner revolution which each one of us must have experienced whilst incorporating Freud's teachings. Liberation from unnecessary inner compulsion would be the first revolution to bring real relief to mankind, for political revolutions have achieved only that the external powers, i.e. the means of coercion, have changed hands, or that the number of the oppressed has risen or fallen. (p. 283)

Ferenczi was critical of political change which simply exchanged one form of oppression for another, and called for a kind of "inner revolution" that would in turn facilitate, and lead to genuine and not hypocritical social change. This was not a mere internalization of politics within the psyche, but a recontextualizing of politics as such—some sort of inner transformation is necessary in order to facilitate socio-political transformation, and not simply exchange one master for another (as Lacan would have said during the revolutions of 1968). This "ethics of truth and justice" (Borossa, 2007) present in Ferenczi's clinical and social thought were further nurtured by Freud's own social awakening, and the direction in which he would take psychoanalysis at the 1918 Budapest Congress.

The Meaning and Effect of Freud's 1918 Budapest Speech

Ferenczi and Freud's dialogues from 1908 through 1918 led to the latter's commitment to more overtly expand on psychoanalysis' social values, especially in light of the masses of people rendered destitute in the wake of World War I. The ideas that would later become part of his 1918 keynote at the Budapest Conference were first put to paper the prior summer during Freud's stay in the home of Anton von Freund. Von Freund, a friend and training analysand to both Freud and Ferenczi (Danto, 2005), spoke with Freud about donating part of his fortune to help create a psychoanalytic clinic for the poor in Budapest. Freud would later write that von Freund's vision would "sharpen in all directions the sense of social justice" within psychoanalysis (Freud, 1955b, p. 267). Freud's Budapest speech was influenced not only by von Freund's plans for a community-based clinic, but also by Ferenczi's experiments with time-limited therapy and "active" intervention during World War I. Based on these experiments with "active treatment," Freud envisioned new directions and challenges in psychoanalysis, and reflected on their implications for work with the underprivileged.

In "Lines of Advance in Psychoanalytic Therapy," Freud (1955a) referred to Ferenczi's "active technique" as a step forward in psychoanalysis's evolution as a treatment. These techniques encompassed interventions we would today recognize as pre-historic forms of exposure therapy. Freud remarked that "One can hardly master a phobia if one waits till the patient lets the analysis influence him to give it up" (p. 165). In cases of agoraphobia, he argued, "one succeeds only when one can induce them by the influence of the analysis to . . . go into the street and to struggle with their anxiety while they make the attempt" (p. 166). Only then can further associations, dreams, and energies by freed to be worked through in psychoanalysis itself. Ferenczi's active interventions presaged a more interactive, interpersonal approach in psychoanalysis, and one which Freud would come to encourage at least until the 1930s.

Turning from the clinical to the social, Freud (1955a) addressed "the vast amount of neurotic misery which there is in the world, and perhaps need not be" (p. 165). Freud foresaw a future in which "the conscience of society will awake," and compel it to take responsibility for the psychological as well as material well-being of the poor and marginalized. Probably as a result of Ferenczi and von Freund's influence, Freud proposed the creation of outpatient clinics staffed by psychoanalytic clinicians where "treatments will be free" (p. 165). At such clinics, analysts would "be faced by the task of adapting [psychoanalytic] technique to the new conditions" (p. 167). Freud suggested that clients who lacked formal education should be provided appropriate psychoeducation, demystifying psychoanalysis and making them active participants in treatment. He further intuited that for such treatments to be successful, it would be necessary to address the client's economic as well as psychological needs, "[combining] mental assistance with some material support, in the manner of the Emperor Joseph" (p. 167), who as noted in the earlier chapter, Freud revered as an advocate of Jewish minorities and the poor.

Speaking from the progressive spirit of post–World War I Viennese social democracy, Freud (1919/1959) declared that

> the conscience of society will awake and remind it that the poor man should have just as much right to assistance for his mind as he now has to the life-saving help offered by surgery; and that the neuroses threaten public health no less than tuberculosis, and can be left as little as the latter to the impotent care of individual members of the community. When this happens, institutions or out-patient clinics will be started, to which analytically-trained physicians will be appointed, so that men who would otherwise give way to drink, women

> who have nearly succumbed under their burden of privations, children for whom there is no choice but between running wild or neurosis, may be made capable, by analysis, of resistance and of efficient work . . . Some time or other, however, it must come to this. (p. 167)

Freud called for a socialized healthcare system in which the state would ensure equal access to mental health care for all, but especially those rendered poor and vulnerable in the aftermath of war and economic disruption. This social welfare of the psyche would in turn demand psychoanalysts to become even more involved in policy and public interest concerns. In the wake of World War I, Freud concluded his speech by making a critical prediction about the future of psychoanalysis, "whatever form this *psychotherapy for the people* may take, whatever the elements out of which it is compounded, its most effective and most important ingredients will assuredly remain those borrowed from strict and untendentious psycho-analysis" (pp. 167–168; emphasis added).

Social worker and historian Elizabeth Danto (2005) chronicled the remarkable effect of Freud's speech on the psychoanalytic movement. In the vibrant period between 1918 and 1938, the first generation of analysts responded to Freud's words "half as prophecy and half as challenge" (Eitington, 1923), leading to the creation of about twelve cooperative mental health clinics "from Zaghreb to London" (Danto, 2005, p. 12), including Berlin, Vienna, and Paris. Psychoanalysts across Europe offered pro bono or sliding-scale psychosocial relief for the poor, developed new treatment methods, and participated in various feminist, gay, and Socialist-Marxist movements seeking social change in post-World War I Europe (Danto, 2005). In order to meet the needs of a broader range of people, psychoanalytic practitioners such as Franz Alexander, Max Eitingon, Ernst Simmel, and Sándor Ferenczi experimented with time-limited treatment and "active" interventions that increased the use of overt behavioral change strategies and the role of the therapeutic relationship (Danto, 2005). Psychoanalysts contributed a portion of their income (about 4% at the Berlin Polyclinic for example, see Aron & Starr, 2012, p. 88) and dedicated at least one fifth of their clinical hours to treating poor and low-income clients, making analysis "accessible to students, artists, craftsmen, laborers, factory workers, office clerks, unemployed people, farmers, domestic servants, and public school teachers" (Danto, 2005, p. 12). Coincidentally, this would have included working class groups whose economies would have been devastated by World War I and felt left behind by past liberal regimes.

It is important to note that these developments, while privileging the creation of treatment methods responsive to the clinical and social exigencies of populations ravaged by war and inequality, especially the poorest and most vulnerable, they were not exclusive to them. As has been documented, active treatment and innovative relational approaches were not simply "for the poor," but were employed with middle-class patients as well (Danto, 2005). A "psychotherapy for the people" did not equal psychotherapy for the poor in a reductive sense. Rather, it signaled not only the development of new treatment methods, but also a system for wealth redistribution that ensured all would be taken care of and have access to equitable mental health care. Those who had more paid more, while those who had less, paid less.

Concurrent with these developments within psychoanalysis during the post-war period, there were feminist and gay rights activists within Europe who were drawn to psychoanalysis' concept of repression as a tool for understanding how society imposes a "double consciousness" on gender and sexual subjectivity, drawing attention to how "[c]ivilization made a pathological split between day and night, above and below, the socially sanctioned and the sexual" (Makari, 2008, p. 143). Psychoanalysis became part of progressive discourse in Freud's Vienna, informing public discussions of homosexual and abortion rights, gender double standards, homelessness, and poverty (Danto, 2005, p. 130). Makari (2008) and Zaretsky (2015) explore in depth how psychoanalysis became part of a discourse of liberation throughout diverse social and political movements throughout Europe, Africa, and the Americas. It was precisely during this period, 1918–1938, which Makari (2008) dubs the "great flowering" of psychoanalysis (p. 299) that Freud wrote his most political treatises, which we will cover in the next chapter.

Ferenczi's Development of a Psychotherapy for the People

It was during the 1918 Budapest Congress that Freud introduced Ferenczi to Otto Rank, taking the opportunity to charge the two with initiating further experiments on therapeutic activity and the role of the analyst in the healing process (Haynal, 1993; Rachman, 2007). In their joint work, *The Development of Psychoanalysis* (1925), Ferenczi and Rank expressed their concern that clinical technique remained frozen in time while psychoanalytic theory soared to new insights (p. 2). Seeking to correct the atrophy of technique, they revisited Freud's earlier technical paper, "Remembering, Repeating, and Working Through" (1914), and created a series of reversals in their understanding of analysis. Although Freud emphasized the role of remembering, Ferenczi and Rank (1925) attributed the primary mechanism of change to "repetition" (p. 4), the enactment of the patient's core conflicts within the analytic session. In order for true change to occur, we have no choice but to repeat.

"The creation of the analytic situation," Ferenczi and Rank (1925) write, "really *exposes* the patient a second time to his infantile trauma . . . [relived] in the relation of the patient to the analyst, in order to bring it, with the help of the patient's insight, to a new and more fortunate conclusion" (pp. 20, 54;

emphasis added). The patient's forbidden wishes, feelings, and thoughts were to be enacted in relation to the analyst, consciously reexperienced, and allowed a "partial gratification" (p. 19) through the analyst's empathic responsiveness. Bringing the core conflict to a "new and more fortunate conclusion" (p. 54) makes new emotional and historical material available to consciousness, allowing the transition from repetition to remembering. Prioritizing repetition in relation to the therapist placed "affective factors of experience" (p. 62) at the center of the change process. Not just insight, but a repetition that yields a new emotional experience in the context of a relationship, would be critical.

Ferenczi and Rank's *The Development of Psychoanalysis* (1925) can be read as "The Development of a Psychotherapy for the People." They make it clear that their technical recommendations were inspired by Freud's Budapest speech (see Ferenczi & Rank, 1925, p. 58), in which he highlights the increasing importance of the analyst's activity in treatment. This acknowledgment of the analyst's role is the result of applying the underlying principles of "active" intervention to the therapeutic relationship itself. What began as a series of techniques employed to expose patients to the avoided affect, anxiety, and pain elicited by objects in the world, was now influencing the way Ferenczi and Rank thought about the patient-therapist relationship. The therapeutic relationship *itself* would be the context in which patients re-experience and are re-exposed to disowned affect and desire through the person of the analyst, who provides a corrective experience through their empathic, nonretaliatory responsiveness. Hence, their monograph is a product of the progressive energies unleashed by Freud's own reflections on the future of analytic technique, and their application to a broad population across socioeconomic classes in post-World War I Europe.

At the same time, there is a kind of gloss that Ferenczi applies to Freud's that subtly subverts and reformulates psychoanalytic ideas. In responding to the critique that psychoanalysis' emphasis on infantile sexuality is reductionistic and cannot explain the traumatic impact of war, Ferenczi argued that psychoanalysis

> treats all sensual and affectionate relationships of the individual to the opposite and to the same gender, emotions toward friends, relatives, any fellow person, even the affect relationship to one's own Ego and to one's own body in the rubric of "eroticism" that is, sexuality. (quoted in Aron & Starr, 2012, p. 85)

As Aron and Starr (2012) note, Ferenczi here resolves a tension in Freud's thinking by repositioning his theory of sexuality as a theory of attachment and relationships, specifically, the embodied and somatic experience of affect in relationships. If psychoanalysis is a theory of how somatically derived affect is experienced and regulated in relationships, then this would also imply our relationships to culture, identity, the state, and power.

Ferenczi's work reveals itself as a theory of relationships, affect, and power—mediated through the body—which cuts across interpersonal, therapeutic, and socio-political contexts. His work with Rank also affected his view of therapeutic action as relational, empathic, and embodied in nature, as opposed to intellectual or purely cognitive. He (1930) shared the results of an intervention in which he asked a patient to "give up the noticeably stiff posture of all her muscles and allow herself more freedom and mobility." Upon becoming aware of how her trauma-related defenses manifested themselves physiologically in her body, the patient experienced a temporary heightening of tension, followed by what "may safely be called relaxation. We must admit, therefore, that psychoanalysis employs two opposite methods: it produces heightening of tension by the frustration it imposes and relaxation by the freedom it allows" (p. 115). He spoke of the need for *nachgiebigkeit*, which is often translated as "indulgence," but more accurately refers to the analyst's "willingness to give to the other" (Rachman, 1998). By "indulgence" Ferenczi meant creating a space of empathic responsiveness in which patient's body can literally relax instead of being primed for fight, flight, or freeze.

The role of the therapeutic relationship beyond mere transference was to become central in Ferenczi's work, and ultimately mark his legacy and the legacy of the psychoanalytic movement. In his seminal article, "Confusion of Tongues" (1933/1994), Ferenczi took a radical step forward in theory and practice. He reported how trying to follow standard technique as outlined by Freud, even with his own and later Rank's recommendations, became insufficient in the treatment of patients with histories of chronic trauma. He noted the disconnect between the patient being able to verbalize insights and even narrativize their trauma, while still experiencing nightmares, dissociation, and hypervigilance, even of Ferenczi himself! As was his tendency, he began to experiment anew—he opened himself up to his patient's feedback and point of view. When his patients became dysregulated and hypervigilant, he began to listen when they started to call him "insensitive, cold, even hard and cruel, when they reproached me with being selfish, heartless, conceited, when they shouted at me: 'Help! Quick! Don't let me perish helplessly!'" (p. 157). His patients' alternated between seen him as a persecutory attacker and as a bystander with the potential to rescue them. In passing, I cannot help but read here Enrique Dussel's (1996) interpretation of Levinas' (1989) *autrui*, the appeal of the suffering other crying out for justice—"I am hungry! Don't kill me! Have compassion for me!" (Dussel, 1996, p. 80). It is important to remember that for Dussel as for Levinas, the other here is also a marginal other—the poor and destitute one, the widow, the orphan, and the stranger. I argue there is, in essence, a politics underlying Ferenczi's clinical theorizing.

Ferenczi (1933/1994) concluded that his patients had "an exceedingly refined sensitivity for the wishes, tendencies, whims, sympathies and antipathies of their analyst" (p. 158), even if the latter is not conscious of these feelings. However, instead of confronting the analyst's errors or blind spots, the patients "identify themselves with him," only in rare moments of rage raising their protest. Here Ferenczi discovered not only the patient's resistance to expressing their true feelings (and perceptions of the analyst), but also the resistance of the analyst themselves to not be open to this feedback. Here Ferenczi (speaking of himself as well as others) calls on analysts to "recognize all our unpleasant external and internal character traits" so that they can be prepared to face these as they are reflected in the patients' associations (p. 158). Here Ferenczi draws attention to how therapists suppress their negative reactions to their patients, as well as a theme he is keen to point out both in psyche and society—the disavowed criticism of patients is directed toward the analyst's "professional hypocrisy":

> We greet the patient with politeness when he enters our room, ask him to start with his associations and promise him faithfully that we will listen attentively to him, give our undivided interest to his well-being and to the work needed for it. In reality, however, it may happen that we can only with difficulty tolerate certain external or internal features of the patient, or perhaps we feel unpleasantly disturbed in some professional or personal affair by the analytic session. (pp. 158–159)

The answer to this impasse, for Ferenczi, is for the analyst to acknowledge this personal disturbance and enter into a dialogue with the patient about their experience of it as a fact, not mere transference or projection—they must practice a "[r]enunciation of professional hypocrisy" (p. 159).

By admitting their mistakes and being receptive to the patient's negative feelings, the therapist restores a feeling of trust and confidence in the therapeutic relationship. "It is this confidence," Ferenczi (1933/1994) writes, "that establishes the contrast between the present and the unbearable traumatogenic past," (p. 160) allowing the patient to have their experience validated in the mind of another, and hence able to validate this experience for themselves. But from where did this—contemporary psychoanalysis would call it today—enactment originate from? "[T]he restrained coolness, the professional hypocrisy" along with a dislike of the patient reproduced a situation not unlike the patient's original traumatic situation in childhood. Theorizing about the patient's childhood experience, Ferenczi describes a context in which the child feels powerless and unable to protest, even silently, the power of the adult that "makes them dumb and can rob them of their senses." "The same anxiety," Ferenczi clarifies,

> compels them to subordinate themselves like automata to the will of the aggressor—to divine each one of his desires and to gratify these; completely oblivious of themselves they identify themselves with the aggressor. Through the identification, or let us say, introjection of the aggressor, he disappears as part of the external reality, and becomes intra- instead of extra-psychic; the intra-psychic is then subjected, in a dream-like state as is the traumatic trance. (p. 162)

Ferenczi's theorizing here is critical—the original traumatogenic object is internalized and housed within the psyche of the victimized. What the aggressor wants, the victim wants and fulfills. Such is the immersion of the victim in the psychology of the perpetrator that the latter's subjectivity comes to haunt the former, enthralling them as if within a dream, "dumbing" down their ability to resist. This necessarily results in a splitting of ego—the victim is both their perpetrator and themselves. This theoretical innovation is in many respects *foundational* for future psychoanalytic theorizing, including psychoanalytic theorizing around oppression and liberation.

Reinforcing this introjection and identification with the aggressor, the perpetrator behaves "as though nothing had happened" (Ferenczi, 1933/1994, pp. 162–163), in effect "gaslighting" and invalidating the victim's experience of trauma. If the perpetrator is one parent, the other parent may become a bystander to the violence—in some cases, a co-conspirator and co-perpetrator, in others a co-victim, and in yet others, both a co-victim and co-conspirator. It is the victim's identification with the aggressor which for Ferenczi is so critical, in that it distorts—as Jessica Benjamin (1988) might say—the bonds of love into chains of domination. At the same time, behind the submissiveness or idealization that children may feel toward their parent-victimizer "there lies hidden an ardent desire to get rid of this oppressive love" (p. 164). In ways that resonate with personal as well as social liberation (see the discussion of Freire in Chapter 5), Ferenczi writes that, "If we can help the child, the patient or the pupil to give up the reaction of identification . . . we may be said to have reached the goal of raising the personality to a higher level" (p. 164). There is something about generating a dialogue in which the analyst renounces their identification with the position of oppressive, enacted, hypocritical authority, and acknowledges their re-victimization of the patient, thus entering into the rupture that occurred *from the perspective of the patient*, that leads to a heightened consciousness in the patient which helps them renounce their identification with the aggressor, which is ultimately curative. It is precisely this process of rupture and repair that leads to the transformative power of the therapeutic relationship, influencing much relational thinking on enactments (Aron, 1996; Benjamin, 2004; Safran & Muran, 2000).

For Ferenczi it is *impossible* to avoid these moments of rupture as they are ubiquitous. It is similarly fruitless to try to provide a sterilized environment in which limitless empathy and compassion abounds. It is both important and *inevitable* to repeat. This is exactly what prompted Ferenczi (1932/1985) to write in his *Clinical Diary* that though the analyst "may take kindness and relaxation as far as he possibly can, the time will come when he will have to repeat with his own hands the act of murder previously perpetrated against the patient" (p. 52). This early on in psychoanalytic thinking, there is something about the relationship between patient and therapist, victim and perpetrator, oppressor and oppressed, that requires—almost *demands*—a murderous encounter. One in which the therapist/oppressor renounces their identification with the position of power, and in so doing, empowers the patient/oppressed to renounce their identification with the powerful. Given Ferenczi's relentless criticism of hypocrisy in politics *and* therapeutics, his clinical thinking not only resonates with a certain kind of politics and political action, it also *emerges*, as shown above, from political meditations on power, the role of the state, and the alienation of individuals and communities.

Ferenczi, the Relational Perspective, and Social Justice

Ferenczi's continued elucidation of a relational perspective after 1925 echoed an "ethics of truth and justice" (Borossa, 2007), demonstrating his ongoing focus on the power difference between the therapist who "is the representative of the whole of human society" and the patient whose symptomatology is the result of ruptured relationships with society (Ferenczi, 1922c, p. 376; cited in Eros, 2014, p. 370). Governmental bureaucracy, combined with the ravaging effects of World War I, prevented von Freund's dream of starting the first psychoanalytic free clinic in Budapest from becoming reality. Although Ferenczi was an aggressive advocate for a free clinic, one was not to be established in Hungary until the early 1930s. He blamed inadequate social services and economic destitution not only for the delay of the clinic's establishment, but also for the lives lost to hopelessness and poverty. In 1929, he published a case report, "From the Childhood of a Young Proletarian Girl," a clinical plea for social reform and increased awareness of the psychological effects of poverty.

The case report was the diary of a 19-year-old woman from an impoverished family, whose suicide Ferenczi was unable to prevent. The diary chronicled her first 10 years of life, describing the misery she experienced as a result of her social class. Rendered powerless as a clinician in the face of structural injustice, Ferenczi took the words of her diary to heart and tried to give her in death what she could not have in life: her voice, reminiscent of his work with Rosa K,

> Rich children are lucky . . . They can learn many things, and [learning] is a form of entertainment for them . . . and they are given chocolate if they know something. Their memory is not burdened with all the horrible things they cannot get rid of. The teacher treats them with artificial respect. It was like this in our school . . . I believe that many poor children learn poorly or only moderately for similar reasons and not because they are less talented. (quoted in Danto, 2005, p. 220)

Ferenczi's patient spoke truth from the margins of psychoanalysis. Freud, Ferenczi, and others struggled creatively to refine psychoanalysis to be more responsive to the needs of those who do not have the time or the money for long-term, open-ended, multiple-times-a-week analysis. These patients' limitations are not due to a lack of ego-strength, inability to tolerate frustration, or any such ideologically motivated notions. Ferenczi's "proletarian girl" exhibited none of these. She displayed a keen understanding of the forces that underlay her trauma, and composed a striking indictment of unjust conditions. Although economic and political changes prevented the opening of a free clinic in Hungary until much later, the first of these clinics would instead be built in Berlin. It was there that a second generation of analysts would continue extending psychoanalytic insights into questions of race, class inequality, and social change.

Before turning to discussing the second generation of progressive psychoanalysts, it is important to underscore that Ferenczi's introduction of empathy and concern for the therapist's hypocrisy in the face of trauma were not mere humanistic ascriptions. They emerged directly from his reflections on socioeconomic inequality, and from his clinical work with poor and marginalized populations. Although empathy, of course, is universally important, his contribution to psychoanalytic and later humanistic, client-centered, and process-experiential perspectives came out of specific social and political circumstances. Empathy is not something to be thought of "beyond" culture, race, and class. Empathy—or as will be discussed in Chapter 6, mentalization—includes thinking deeply about culture, race, and class.

Ferenczi's politics led to a theory of empathy, trauma, and relationality which circled back again and informed his politics. As another concrete example, later in life Ferenczi wrote a series of unpublished reflections on socialism, psychoanalysis, and inequality in which he conducted a psychoanalytic critique of the erotic attachment to the commodification of land and wealth, deriving an analytic rationale for a "land tax" to reduce economic inequality. Eros (2014) in translating these documents discovered the indirect influence in Ferenczi's thinking of American political economist Henry George (1839–1897), who argued that the land-owning classes were the main beneficiaries of the wealth produced by free market economies. George proposed a tax on the land itself as a remedy for wealth inequality through redistribution. The implementation of such a tax, for Ferenczi, would involve a resolution of the fixation with land and wealth accumulation, in turn a de-eroticizing of identification with the powerful.[1]

THE SECOND GENERATION: FENICHEL, FROMM, AND THE *KINDERSEMINAR*

Siegfried Bernfield was born in 1892 into a Jewish family from Galicia that later immigrated to Vienna (much like Freud and Ferenczi). Growing up in Vienna, Siegfried read Freud's *The Interpretation of Dreams* in 1907 as a 15-year-old attending the *gymnasium*. In 1910, he enrolled in the University of Vienna to study biology and psychology, during which time he became a figurehead in socialist and Zionist youth movements, all the while working as a secretary for Martin Buber. A later wunderkind of the psychoanalytic movement, at 21 Bernfeld published an article in the *International Journal of Psychoanalysis*. After serving in the army during World War I, he changed his major to pedagogy and psychology, graduating with his PhD in 1915, the same year he joined Freud's Vienna Psychoanalytic Society, eventually becoming a full member in 1919. That same year, in the shadow of World War I, inspired by Freud's Budapest speech Bernfeld founded the *Kinderheim Baumgarten*, a psychoanalytically informed orphanage for Jewish children orphaned and displaced from the war. Freud would later remark that, "He is an outstanding expert of psychoanalysis. I consider him perhaps the strongest head among my students and followers" (cited in Benveniste, 2012, p. 3).

Bernfield was fully committed to the application of psychoanalysis and socialism to the challenges of clinical work, pedagogy, and social change. He would write a series of articles exploring the intersections between each of these, such as "Socialism and Psychoanalysis" in 1926, "The problem of the masses in socialist pedagogics" in 1927, and "On the problem of psychoanalysis and Marxism" in 1928 (Holloway, 1978). His integration of psychoanalysis and socialist thought would clash with other Freudo-Marxists in the psychoanalytic movement such as Wilhelm Reich, but his personality and commitment to liberation in psyche and society proved magnetic. He drew the praise not only of Freud, but also of others in the youth Socialist movement in Vienna. Among those drawn to Bernfield, and ultimately to psychoanalysis, was Otto Fenichel.

Fenichel was a Viennese Jew born in 1897. Like Bernfield he had read Freud in his adolescence, and like other liberal-progressive Jews felt drawn to the promise of exploring the deep recesses of the psyche. His father, however, demanded that he choose a profession that would actually allow him to make a living. So the young Fenichel entered into the field of medicine, as Ernst Simmel (1946b) would recall, with every intention of studying psychoanalysis. Fenichel became involved in the youth Socialist movement during his studies, which is where he met its centerpiece Bernfeld. After his military service ended in 1915 he started attending Freud's lectures at the University of Vienna, then accompanying Bernfeld to the Vienna Psychoanalytic Society, where he would start giving talks in 1918 at 21 years old. Fenichel would later move to Berlin in 1922 to complete his medical studies and engage in intensive psychoanalytic training at the recently founded free clinic, the Berlin Poliklinik. Founded by Max Eitingon, Ernst Simmel, and other progressive psychoanalysts, the Poliklinik and its inpatient service, the Schloss Tegel Sanatorium, provided fertile ground for the next generation of analysts to pioneer treatment approaches still in use today (Danto, 2007). In line with Freud's call for a "psychotherapy for the people," patients of all socioeconomic backgrounds were provided with accessible care. It was here that Fenichel would train and later become faculty, having the opportunity to work alongside with or teach future analysts such as Franz Alexander, Karl Abraham, Edith Jacobson, Karen Horney, Wilhelm and Annie Reich, Melanie Klein, and—central to our purposes—Erich Fromm (Danto, 2007).

Psychoanalysts like Fenichel were free to associate in (or be founding members of) any number of activist groups, such as Ernst Simmel's Association for Socialist Physicians. Reflecting dialogues had at the Berlin Poliklinik, Fenichel would later write, "we recognize in Freud's Psychoanalysis the germ of the dialectical-materialist psychology of the future, and therefore we desperately need to protect and extend this knowledge" (cited in Danto, 2005, p. 17). Other young analysts like Reich and Fromm would be exposed to Fenichel's writing, drawn in by how he addressed women's struggle of agency over their own body, alongside the impact of the political economy on the psyche (Danto, 2005, p. 36). Sandor Rado and Franz Alexander would participate in these dialogues on occasion, whereas others like Simmel enjoyed discussing theory and praxis "day or night." Perhaps the clearest, and potentially most radical, of these discussions took place in Fenichel's class for the younger generation of analysts.

In what would later be called the *Kinderseminar* or Children's Seminar, Fenichel created a space where vibrant young candidates could explore topics outside of the Poliklinik's curriculum. More and more the course's focus of became political in nature (Danto, 2005, p. 138). Students in attendance included the Reichs, Jacobson, Francis Deri, Bertha Bornstein, Kate Friedlander, Alexander Mette, Barbara Lantos, and among others, Erich Fromm. Ernst Simmel (1946b), one of the founders and directors of the Berlin clinic, wrote a moving obituary after Fenichel's passing. The senior analyst recalled a pivotal movement in the *Kinderseminar*'s development:

> Among the lectures and seminars Fenichel gave in Berlin was one which—although the students attending were very enthusiastic—temporarily did not find approval by the Directors of the Institute. It seemed to us that Fenichel

> devoted *too many* evenings to the discussion of the relation of psychoanalysis to sociology and Marxism, instead of confining it to discussions on psychoanalytic matters. Fenichel did not yield to his "superiors"—his reaction was: "What of it? If you don't like the way we do it—let us be naughty children." From then on this seminar became famous under the official title, "The Children's Seminar." (p. 70)

I would like to imagine that the directors of the Berlin institute—including Simmel—responded in a manner akin to the contemporary vernacular, "Yeah, you right." That personal conjecture aside, one cannot object to the humor and warmth in display between Fenichel and his "superior" Simmel. In the end, the "Naughty Children's Seminar" would, as noted above, influence the thinking of future analysts of renown including Franz Alexander, Edith Jacobson, and Erich Fromm.

Debating Fenichel and Reading Ferenczi: Fromm's Psychoanalytic Social Psychology

One of the pupils inspired by Fenichel's act of resistance was none other than Erich Fromm, who took readily to the discussions of Marxism, politics, and psychoanalysis. As he developed his own voice, however, he would start clashing with Fenichel, in part due to Fromm's increasingly critical attitude toward Freud (Danto, 2005, p. 204). Although Fenichel and Fromm would continue a critical correspondence full of dialogue and debate in the years during and after World War II, Fenichel would go on to publish a series of responses critical of Fromm's work (Burston, 1991, pp. 159–160). Fromm would become critical of the authoritarianism that consumed psychoanalysis leading up to World War II, partly due to chaotic political circumstances but in great part also due to Freud's own personality and difficulty accepting critique and independent thought. Nowhere was this clearer than in Fromm's critique of Ferenczi's excommunication and blacklisting from the psychoanalytic canon after his death in 1933.

Although a rebellious pupil in Fenichel's *Kinderseminar*, Fromm was also heavily influenced by Ferenczi and his work (Bacciagaluppi, 1993). He referred to Ferenczi's work on empathy extensively, and favorably quoted Ferenczi's claim that a true cure results from the dissolution of the superego—both with renouncing repressive demands and one's identification with the one demanding repression (Bacciagaluppi, 1993, p. 187). After reading Ferenczi's *Confusion of Tongues*, he expressed that "anybody who reads it can convince himself that this is a paper of extraordinary profundity and brilliance—in fact, one of the most valuable papers in the whole psychoanalytic literature" (cited in p. 187).

Bacciagaluppi (1993) points out the direct and indirect influence of Ferenczi on Fromm's clinical and socio-political thinking. From Ferenczi,

Fromm drew on the idea that understanding, listening, and empathy, "feeling the patient within oneself" becomes indistinct from love. Practicing such love by acknowledging one's mistakes is itself dependent on a recognition of reciprocity and mutual influence in the patient-therapist relationship. In words that would echo both relational thinking and Freire's musings on the teacher-student relationship, Fromm wrote, "The analyst analyzes the patient, but the patient also analyzes the analyst, because the analyst, by sharing the unconscious of his patient, cannot help clarifying his own unconscious" (cited in Bacciagaluppi, 1993, p. 189). Ferenczi's clinical attitude reflected a philosophy of mutuality, cooperation, and recognition of difference that subverted power and authority, something Fromm would identify with a "biophilic" or life-affirming position (p. 190).

As evidenced above, Ferenczi's early clinical work focused on empathy toward "the other." His exposure to the progressive social ethos of his upbringing and his enthusiasm for the social implications of psychoanalysis all informed his analysis of how class and race take hold in the psyche, ethics which found their way into his clinical theorizing on how identification with the aggressor takes place in familial and therapeutic relationships, and how vulnerability is (clinically) emancipatory. Fromm's exposure to Ferenczi's relational clinical technique in turn informed his clinical and *political* thinking. As for Ferenczi so too for Fromm—progressive politics become technique which informs politics informing technique, and then through Fromm "in a peculiar way, technique becomes politics" (Eros, 1990, p. 7). In a curious and fascinating way, Ferenczi's proto-relational technique then becomes an influence for Fromm's psychoanalytic social psychology (Bacciagaluppi, 1993; Eros, 1990), and through Fromm, liberation psychology itself (we will also see a similar dynamic play out in Fanon's reading of Ferenczi in Chapter 4). Fromm would bring these sensibilities to his fieldwork in Mexico in the 1950s, where he would study changes in the psychological and political consciousness of the poor before and after the Mexican revolution (Millan, 2000).

"A Weapon of Class Warfare": Fenichel's Psychoanalysis of Racism

Although Fenichel would become renown in America for his encyclopedic contributions and "orthodox" defense of Freudian analysis, including his *The Psychoanalytic Theory of Neurosis* (1945), his Marxist beliefs were virtually unknown in "the land of the free" (Harris & Brock, 1991). As I will discuss below, there were socio-political reasons post-exile that Fenichel and other Jewish left-leaning psychoanalysts had for suppressing their views. In what follows, I want to review two pieces, both posthumously published, that shed light on the most mature forms of his thinking post-World War II.

In a piece which would later be published in Simmel's (1946a; Fenichel, 1946) post-war text, *Anti-Semitism: A Social Disease*, Fenichel (1940) develops a psychoanalytic theory of anti-Semitism. He addresses the stereotype that analysts favor the past and ignore current, material social conditions, outlining a dialectical-materialist psychoanalysis. Fenichel begins by identifying how the "general misery" suffered by the working class generates a "rebellious tendency directed against the ruling powers" (p. 26). The ruling class in response promotes propaganda blaming the Jew as the source of their poverty, leading the "revolutionary tendency" to be displaced toward the racial other. As the poor masses experience a conflict between the desire for freedom, they fear it (as Fromm would later say) out of their respect for the authority of the powerful. Anti-Semitism provides the marginalized poor with a kind of socio-systemic compromise formation, satisfying their rebellious impulses simultaneously by discharging their aggression against another, defenseless group of people, while maintaining a submissive attitude toward the upper classes whose wrath is not incurred.

But what exactly makes the Jew so "suitable" to this kind of projection? Fenichel (1940) outlines how

> when the social order, or rather, disorder, produces much misery then he whom this misery affects is seldom in a position to discover its origins, partly because the connections are too complicated and partly because the ruling class does everything it can to make the true connections unrecognizable. The point is then to find someone in his surroundings who appears to him to be the cause of his misery. (p. 27)

One group of oppressed—the White European working class—is unable to identify the systemic origins of their oppression and the web of connections that maintain it, including their identification with the powerful. The ruling class, in order to preserve their power, exploit this lack of consciousness by providing a "suitable" scapegoat—the Jew who is perpetually displaced and marginalized, framed as the always already religious and then racial other. Despite the Jews' actual condition of poverty, social exclusion, and persecution, the phantasy of the Jew operating exclusively within a commercial class, rising above the poverty of the ghetto, is meant to arouse a combination of hatred and envy—"How *dare* these 'others' make progress and rise up the socio-economic latter, but not *I*?"

Fenichel (1940) notes how these dynamics reflect an important systemic function of racism—a mechanism by which to control the fears and aggression of the working class—as well as its central psychological mechanism, while at the same time acknowledging the similarities and differences in how racism is expressed toward Jews and other marginalized groups, such as African-Americans in the United States. He draws the comparison thusly,

> The American negroes were slaves, and their ostracism is a result of the historical and social troubles which arose around the problems of slavery. But these negroes have another characteristic which makes them suitable as scapegoats: they are black. The Jews have also been viled by the antisemitism because of their cultural or physical "racial" peculiarities. *They, too, were black*, not their skins, but their hair, and are foreign in their customs and habits, in their language, their divine service, and their everyday life which is so interwoven into their divine service. (p. 28, emphasis added)

Reflecting the racial discourse of the time, Fenichel underscores how European racism made a phantasmatic connection between anti-Semitism and anti-Blackness—anti-Blackness serving as a vehicle through which to denigrate the Jews as an other, which cyclically reinforces the denigration of Black people, other people of color, and non-Whites. With Fenichel as with Freud, there was a clear awareness of this relationship within their anti-Semitic/anti-Black Viennese European culture. Alongside their linguistic, cultural, and religious difference, so too was there the fantasy of a specifically *Black* racial difference which re-contextualized and further heightened the "foreign-ness," the otherness of the Jew. The purpose of this fantasy, in turn, is to maintain a system of racial and economic inequality.

Part of what makes this system of displacement so effective is that for the White working-class, those "who are of the same kind as oneself, *and as the ruling powers are*, one does not suspect of evil, but people who look different and speak differently and behave so differently, they may be capable of anything" (Fenichel, 1940, p. 28, emphasis added). A synthesis across class lines occur between the poor and the powerful become housed within the contours of racial sameness (White, European, Aryan), while the racial other (who may also be poor and destitute) is identified as an object of hatred, an ambivalently experienced other who, "if the authorities said they were bad, then it was surely so, for one's own poverty was obvious" (p. 29). Of note, Fenichel identifies this as a kind of submerged, "primitive" thinking. As we will touch on in the next chapter, this implies a series of racialized associations and inversions, in turn originating in Freud's own work (Brickman, 2003). In this mindset the Jew is naturally framed as a murderer and a sexual deviant. In order to disrupt these corrupt projections, Fenichel (1940) argues, "we must search for the real sinner" (p. 30).

The "true culprit" for Fenichel (1940) lies in two domains—the ruling classes who manipulate the working class into redirecting their aggression, and the very repressed instincts of the working class. The Jew—and we might say also Black people and other people of color—is unconsciously transformed into everything "which brings him [the proletariat] misery, and not only his social oppressor but also his own unconscious instincts, which have gained a bloody-dirty-dreadful character from their socially caused repression" (pp. 37–38). It is this capacity that renders one's own unconscious "foreign." And it is "foreignness . . . which the Jews and one's own instincts have in common" (p. 31). This paints a picture of European working-class Whites who project upon the Jew their "social oppressor" whom they hate and fear, as well as the affect and aggression which is deemed a danger to the status quo (the ruling classes, the dominant socio-economic system, etc.).

With the projection of one's aggressive instincts, there is an ever-present fear of a "return of the repressed," both in psyche and society.

> The Jews as a racial minority were oppressed everywhere. It is clear that the ruling people must fear the possible revenge of the oppressed people, in particular where the oppression appears to be unsuccessful, when the oppressed people rise up again and again and, believing themselves to be a chosen people, refuse to give up their peculiarities under any torture. (Fenichel, 1940, p. 32)

The resilience of the Jews as an oppressed people and their belief in being chosen by a God who stands on the side of the marginalized instill fear among their working class and elite oppressors. No matter how much they are suppressed, crushed, and hunted, the Jews and the otherness they represent "appears to rise up again and again like a hydra, and they try to cut off its head. At the same time they despise it in the same way as they despise their own disavowed instincts" (p. 33). Of note, Fenichel cites the Roman practice of erecting statues and houses of worship to the gods of the people they conquered, as a way of warding off the wrath of the God of oppressed peoples. Fenichel similarly argues that the fear of the *revenge* of the oppressed and their God, the retaliation for injuries suffered, manifests in a manner akin to the sight of "a cripple" who evokes a sense of strangeness, "but also the special fear that he will want to make one a cripple like himself" (p. 36).

Fenichel (1940) argued that the perceived and fantasized peculiarities of the Jew, "the strangeness of their mental culture, the bodily (black) and religious (God of the oppressed peoples) peculiarities" (p. 38) make them targets for this kind of projection, to the extent that each of these traits are defined as *defiled* and *defiling*. He recognizes this sentiment in Hitler's *Mein Kampf* when the latter writes, "One often says . . . that the Jews are human, too. But if someone violated your mother, would you then say that he, too, was human?' Fenichel adds the following gloss, "And the Jew, it is maintained, violates the mother Germany" (p. 38). He similarly criticizes Hitler terming the spread of syphilis among Germans as a "judaisation of their soul" (p. 39). But Hitler's racism, it is important to remember, did not arise in a vacuum. It was itself spurned on by the racist science of turn-of-century Europe, in which Jews were not only stigmatized as diseased people contaminating the Aryan body with syphilis, but in many respects were seen as inherently syphilitic to European body-class politics (Gilman, 1991, p. 219).

The Jew then corrupts, "it" (reduced to the status of an object and source of humiliation) infects; the Jew *violates* the integrity of the White-Aryan body, bringing upon the European project a sense of humiliation that must then be expunged, even if this humiliation initially arose from the inequality and exploitation imposed by the ruling classes (the dynamics of shame, oppression, and humiliation will be discussed further in Chapter 6). This psychoanalysis of anti-Semitism and racism leads Fenichel to conclude that these complicated "isms" serve a very simple, but deadly purpose—they are "A weapon in the class-warfare dominating the present civilized world" (p. 39).

A Dialectical-Materialistic Psychology: Fenichel's Unfulfilled Legacy

Another posthumously published paper sheds light on Fenichel's vision for psychoanalysis as a force for social justice. His (1967) "Psychoanalysis as the Nucleus of a Future Dialectical-Materialistic Psychology" was likely written in the early 1940s during World War II, but was only published in the journal *American Imago* in the 1960s, after it was obtained from Olga Barsis, the sister of Fenichel's training analyst Hanns Sach. In it Fenichel criticizes the splitting that takes place between psychology and a materialist perspective, acknowledging that while there are Marxists and Socialists suspicious of psychoanalysis, this suspicion is unmerited. To resolve this contradiction, he argues that a truly materialistic psychology contextualizes the psyche within the "realm of nature," explaining the different forms the psyche can take based on their material reality—"his body as well as the concrete environment which affect him by their stimulations" (p. 292). By this Fenichel refers to the dialectic between "the needs arising from the body and originating in the course of biological ontogeny—the so-called drives—and of their modifications by external environmental influences" (p. 295). Hence, instincts, affects, and the passions, experienced and arising in the body within specific socio-economic relations, becomes central for Fenichel. Somatically experienced drives and their derivatives are thus shaped by "the real material conditions which influence the organism" (p. 296). Psychoanalysis, then, is no mere abstract, idealistic exercise, but parallel to Ferenczi's own thinking, a method for revealing the imprint of the realistic conditions of society upon individuals, their relationships, and their communities inscribed upon the body.

Fenichel (1967) argued that an account of how society is "taken inside" is missing in Marx and Marxist-Socialist thinking in general. "There is a danger," he argued, "in their repeated assertions that the ruling classes control the schools, religion and the press, and that the revolutionary party is weak and powerless" (p. 298). The lack of theorizing on how economic forces directly and indirectly influence the individual through "the detour produced in his changing psychic structure" becomes a source of "great impediment" for progressive causes (p. 298). He also condemns the argument that ideology simply dulls the intellect of the oppressed as superficial and lacking nuance. Ideology, transmitted by the means of production, economic conditions, interpersonal relations, and education does not just "give rise to ideas" in people's minds. Rather, they fundamentally change "the structure of the drives in these men in a way which *turns the energies withdrawn from the impulses* in question *against these very impulses and hampers their further development*" (p. 297, my emphasis).

The repression and control that results from ideology, then, operates by constricting and regulating affect and in turn the very bodies of oppressed and marginalized people. Racist, capitalist, and cisheterosexist ideologies in fact weaponize the minds, emotions, and bodies of oppressed people against themselves. This is why, Fenichel (1940) states, "Ideological influence always produces obfuscation of the intellectual functions. An enthusiast cannot be influenced by argument" (p. 298). Ideology impairs the ability to think critically. Hence, attempts at persuasion based on appeal to rationality or logic become limited. Let us remember again that Fenichel's dialectical-materialist psychoanalytic approach is no appeal to idealism or an abstract idealistic construct. Rather, by grounding the psyche in Freud's concept of drives, he is embedding political liberation in the body and the passions. Not mere ideas, but our embodied experience is manipulated by ideology and ideological apparatuses, as we will see more clearly in my discussion of Fanon in Chapter 4.

Fenichel (1940) asserts that socialism and psychoanalysis are both "unmasking sciences, which means that they are distrustful of what appears on the surface and view it as the result of hidden forces" (p. 301). Part of what they reveal is the psychological and material function of ideology as such. In talking about sexuality, drives, and somatically embodied affect, we are indelibly talking about libido which, as Ferenczi, Fenichel, and others in the psychoanalytic movement were wont to clarify, refers to our capacity for attachment and relationships. Fenichel believed a palimpsest for relating to power and communal belonging was first set in place in childhood, molding the child's psyche through the *promise* of love, and the *fear* of *loss* of love. He writes,

> The oldest form of love . . . had as its aim the complete incorporation of the object in order to become like it, to eat it up, so to speak, in order to have it always within oneself. In this way, the child to whom the parents have forbidden sexual wishes takes the parents into himself, as it were, and a part of his ego which has been altered by this incorporation now speaks within him as his parents formerly spoke outside. This is how it comes about that the energies of the original sexual impulses afterwards serve to intensify the parental prohibitions and lend their force to repressing rather than satisfying the drive. (p. 304)

This internalization of an other who is both feared and desired, and who instills prohibitions against the fulfillment of somatically experienced drives, trapping them within the body, can be molded and structured by the environment, which for Fenichel in the final analysis refers to economic conditions, referring favorably to Reich and Fromm's work on the application of psychoanalysis to socio-systemic analysis (pp. 307, 309).

Interestingly, then, by grounding his Dialectical-Materialist psychoanalysis in the drives and the body, Fenichel (1940) arrives at a position similar to that of Ferenczi (1933). Identification with the one in the position of power, whether the parent, the perpetrator, the therapist, the ruling class, etc., turns us against ourselves as well as others. The process of identification and internalization that begins in childhood—we may call it *mentalization* using contemporary jargon (see Chapter 6)—may be further employed by ideology and the means of production, or instead become *corrupted* by it. The body, then, becomes a site of both pleasurable affects that reward intersubjectively and societally desired behavior, and negative, aversive affects that punish their opposite. Whether discussing attachments between a child and their parent, analysand to analyst, or oppressed to their oppressor, we witness here a series of phenomena that will continue to shift and evolve across time, place, and politic.

But in discussing Ferenczi's ideas on identification with the aggressor or Fenichel's thinking on anti-Semitism and anti-Blackness as tools of class and racial domination, we must inquire as to whether these were errant thoughts of "rogue agents," a "distinct subspecies" of political Freudians (as Jacoby, 1986 might quip), or whether their intellectual father, Freud, shared in them. The former hypothesis is doubtful—Fenichel was renown as a staunch defender of Freudian psychoanalysis, and Ferenczi, his eventual rupture with Freud notwithstanding, was a close collaborator of Freud on matters both social and theoretical. We will address these questions in the next chapter. For now it is important to answer a crucial question—if psychoanalysis was comprised of a predominantly Jewish, progressive cadre of Marxists, Socialists, and Social Democrats committed to social justice, then what happened after World War II? How did it become so conservative, so restrictive, so *White* once it arrived in America?

THE END OF PSYCHOANALYSIS: DISPLACED REFUGEES AND IMMIGRANTS POST–WORLD WAR I

Leading up to World War II with the rise of Hitler's Nazi party the International Psychoanalytic Association (IPA) became increasingly conservative, and so began to clamp down on its progressive members. "Faced with censoring rejection from within the IPA and with surveillance and penalty (or worse) from outside," Danto (2005) writes, "Fenichel called all left analysts in Berlin together in order to discuss, in a take on Lenin's famously pragmatic question, 'what was to be done'" (Danto, 2005, p. 207). The IPA, in fear of the Nazi threat, sought to "moderate" the more radical members of the psychoanalytic movement, removing Fenichel as editor of the journal *Zeitschrift*, rejecting Wilhelm Reich's work without explanation, and threatening censure upon others. The *Kinderseminar* continued to be naughty, however, continuing their meetings in Reich's house. Fenichel's group refocused itself on caucusing against the rising conservatism of the psychoanalytic movement, and resist the "Aryanization" (replacing of Jewish analysts with German-Gentiles) of the free clinics, and the Nazification of the German Psychoanalytic Association (Harris & Brock, 1991).

Once Hitler came to power in 1933, "it was over" (Jacoby, 1986, p. 27). As Jacoby put it, "Jewish Marxist psychoanalysts were thrice marked—as Jews, Marxists, and psychoanalysts—and were eager to exit" (p. 27). The paths of flight were numerous, each marked by persecution, fear, and trauma:

> Martin Grotjahn recalls helping Ernst Simmel out his back window when Simmel received a message that the Nazis were en route to arrest him. Fenichel fled to Oslo, Prague, and then to the United States. Gero departed first for Copenhagen and later America. Annie Reich moved to Prague and afterward New York. Friedlander and Lantos first settled in Paris and later London. Gymoroi spent some years in Budapest before immigrating to Ceylon. Jacobson lingered in Germany and was arrested; she later escaped to New York. A chapter in psychoanalysis closed. (p. 27)

It was in the last meeting of the Children's Seminar that Fenichel would give his final paper before escaping Nazi Germany—"Psycho-Analysis, Socialism, and our Task for the Future." Simmel (1946b) recalled, "His own task was clearly defined—his sole aim was to remain the custodian of psychoanalysis, to see to it that psycho-analysis should not perish in the catastrophic events to come" (p. 70). The group disbanded and became a loose network of "psychoanalysts in exile unified by their belief in psychoanalysis as dialectical materialism" (Danto, 2005, pp. 207–208). They would be bound together in paper and phantasy by Fenichel's pen in the form of the *Rundbriefe*, or "round papers" that were circled among its members as a way of continuing their dialogue even in unknown lands.

Fenichel would initially flee to Oslo, then Prague for two years where he would continue some of his work, until finally establishing himself in California within the United States. Simmel (1946b) shares that Fenichel was never fully comfortable with his American peers, especially given their allergies to a Marxist, dialectical-materialist reading of psychoanalysis. He found that his colleagues reified Freud, reducing him to a monadic biologist instead of placing his theory of somatically derived affects—the drives—in a dialectical relationship to one's relational and material conditions. Simmel could only agree with his old friend, "There is no psychology of man in a vacuum . . . only a psychology of man in a certain concrete society and in a certain social setting within this concrete society" (cited in Simmel, 1946b, p. 71).

Recovering the history of how this trauma reconfigured psychoanalysis, Aron and Starr (2012) write that what came to be understood as "Freudian" in the United States "was in fact not identical with Freud's own theories and practices, nor was it an inevitable development of what he started. Rather, psychoanalysis in America was twisted and reshaped into a traumatic symptom" (p. xviii). As the Jewish analysts fled Europe, some were received as "stars" who were yet to be assimilated into a rising new Freudian orthodoxy. Whereas in Europe psychoanalysis emerged from "a more relaxed, coffeehouse salon culture of discussion and debate" (p. 104), in America psychoanalysis underwent intensive medicalization and institutionalization. As early as Freud's first (and last) visit to the United States in 1909, the American Medical Association had already engaged in an aggressive program leading to more restrictive licensing laws and medical education which imposed severe quotas on admissions for women, African-Americans, and Jews (Danto, 2009). This system privileged White, middle-to-upper class men, each a series of signifiers that would exert assimilative pressure upon the refugee analysts.

With the death of Freud in 1939, the vacuum left by the progenitor of psychoanalysis was filled by a rigid over-idealized facsimile, an idol erected to posthumously endorse the changes psychoanalysis would undergo. When the refugees turned "superstars" resisted assimilation to this new standard, scorning, punishment, and marginality followed. There was the case, for example, of Paul Schilder, a member of the Vienna Psychoanalytic Society who immigrated to New York due to anti-Semitism stalling his career in Vienna. His application to the New York Psychoanalytic Society was rejected due to being "too unorthodox"—giving his patients advice and seeing them less than five times a week on the couch. Just a year after Freud's death in 1940, William Menninger "reprimanded" Eduardo Weiss due to others at the Topeka Psychoanalytic Institute accusing him of "departing from Freudian procedure" by seeing patients only three times a week, and face-to-face to boot! Others objected that their American colleagues "barely knew what Freudian analysis was," and found it bizarre to condemn Weiss as insufficiently Freudian when he was a friend and colleague of Freud, a member of the Vienna society, and endorsed by Freud to organize the psychoanalytic movement in Italy (Aron & Starr, 2012, pp. 104–105). Those who learned psychoanalysis from Freud himself, or who took part of the second generation of analysts, were suddenly deemed not Freudian or psychoanalytic enough!

Aside from questions of clinical "orthodoxy," there were cultural, racial, and political pressures as well. As a Holocaust survivor (Aron & Starr, 2012, p. 111), psychoanalysis navigated its original European context where racial discourses around Jewishness, Blackness, and Aryanness dominated, finally erupting in the rise of Nazi Germany. Now refugees in America, they had to contend with the racial binary of Whiteness and Blackness which repositioned Jews as "White but not quite" yet able to choose assimilation into Whiteness as such. "Embracing whiteness came with certain costs to Jewish culture and identity," Aron and Starr write, "but how could these losses be mourned when what was given up was associated with Blackness, femininity, and primitivity—with the abject?" (p. 112). The walling off of their Jewish identity, and in turn the progressive values that emerged from identification with the oppressed community, in turn created walls between psychoanalysis and people of color and other marginalized communities. It is the task of this book to tear these walls down. With the free clinics in Europe "Aryanized," psychoanalysis in Europe was destroyed, paving the way for America to become "the world center of psychoanalysis" (p. 114). In this context of trauma, struggling with new concrete situations, many prominent psychoanalysts "switched sides," transforming "even brilliant maverick psychoanalysts such as Otto Fenichel, among others, into conservative conformists too afraid to make trouble in their newly adopted country" (p. 116), suppressing their identity or values. Or both.

Danto (2012) adds another dimension to this history of American suppression in the context of the "red scare" and anti-Semitism, anti-Socialist currents post-World War II. Otto Fenichel actually continued writing to his *Rundbriefe* group in America, maintaining written communication with other leftist analysts, continuing their reflections on psyche, society, class, and race. However, Fenichel also gave strict instructions for their members to read and then immediately destroy the letters (Jacoby, 1986). This was done with the intention of protecting the group from two threats—their American colleagues, and the authorities. Danto (2012) documents the involvement of the Federal Bureau of Investigation in the Jewish emigres lives—"many of the emigres had histories of left-wing engagement that, to [FBI director Herbert] Hoover, warranted investigation with variable degrees of intrusiveness" (p. 216). In the 1940s and 1950s Hoover's program became increasingly aggressive, merging "'communism' with 'homosexuality' as the quintessential un-American duality" (pp. 220–221).

American psychoanalysis was in charge. Many of those who knew and worked with Freud found themselves either submitting to the new order, or being excommunicated from the analytic establishment. This conservatism, along with the governmental intrusion of Hoover and later McCarthy "effectively diverted the psychoanalysts and their colleagues away from their commitment to social justice and directed them toward the kind of individual treatment for which they have become known in the United States" (Danto, 2012, p. 228). At the end of his career Clarence Obendorf, who had entered into a training analysis with Freud in the 1920s, reflected with disappointment how psychoanalysis had turned "legitimate and respectable . . . sluggish and smug" (cited in Jacoby, 1986, p. ix). "Once incorporated into medical schools," Jacoby writes, "psychoanalysis came to attract those who 'find security in conformity and propriety'" (p. ix).

Close to the end of his life, Fenichel gave up continuing the *Rundbrief*, finding the nature of the beast too unassailable, instead shifting his energies to trying to protect his vision of Freud's psychoanalytic practice. Erich Fromm no longer received the letters from his once mentor turned colleague turned critic. Soon after, when Fenichel died in 1946, his old friend Simmel (1946) remarked, "with Fenichel's death, Freud has died once more" (p. 67). "For the first time since 1902," Danto (2005) declared, "when Freud had convened a few friends for Wednesday evening discussions, the entire apparatus of progressive psychoanalytic activity in Vienna had been eliminated" (p. 264). Throughout Europe, Jewish analysts fled the Nazi menace for America, only to find the same interpellation that had threatened them most of their adult life—"turn white . . . or disappear." But for a moment, putting pen to paper in Berlin prior to his own flight, Fenichel urged his peers to continue fighting for the cause of psychoanalysis for social justice. "Where there is still truth," he wrote, "it will be preserved, even if it must flee far . . . The fate of psychoanalysis depends on the fate of the world" (cited in Danto, 2005, p. 265). And flee far it did, carried out across the world in the winds of war, change, and possibility.

"And other seeds fell into good soil and produced grain"

Meanwhile, in 1953, Fromm, the prodigal son of psychoanalysis living in exile in Mexico since 1950, discovered that he had been "dropped" from membership to the International Psychoanalytic Association (Rudnytsky, 2016). He was informed by letter he would have to apply in order to be reinstated as a member, and then go in front of a "screening committee" before he could be considered for re-admission. Fromm asked if the fact his clinical and political views were different from the current orthodoxy would be a factor for denying him membership. The snark-ridden reply from the IPA was that anyone who did not adhere to the "basic principles" of psychoanalysis "would anyway not be interested in becoming a member." And so psychoanalysis completed its identification with the aggressor by marginalizing a Marxist socialist Jew who was now equal parts freed and excluded to pursue his work outside the walls of the new hegemony. But Fromm and the progressive spirit of psychoanalysis would find itself in good company outside these walls. It would be here, in Latin America, that Fromm would later meet an educator from the favelas of Brazil who developed his own kind of "historical-socio-critical psychoanalysis" (Gaztambide, 2017). But that is a story for a later chapter (Chapter 5). For now, we turn to Freud's own thinking on culture and society, and mark the influence of Ferenczi and Fenichel's theorizing.

NOTE

1. Translations of these unpublished manuscripts can be found in Eros (2014).

Chapter Three

"For Justice, for Equal Treatment of All"

Freud as Proto-Postcolonial Theorist

As covered thus far, Freud was fond of jokes, especially risqué and politically inappropriate ones. A joke that bears mentioning by way of introduction is one he shared with Theodor Reik,

> The boy Itzig is asked in grammar school: "Who was Moses?" and answers, "Moses was the son of an Egyptian princess." "That's not true," says the teacher. "Moses was the son of a Hebrew mother. The Egyptian princess found the baby in a casket." But Itzig answers: "Says she!" (cited in Yerushalmi, 1991, p. 1)

Freud found this hilarious, apparently. But as he (1905) also observed, jokes are a way of expressing what is verboten and finding a way to process it. In that sense this joke belied Freud's anxieties as a Jew facing ever increasing persecutions, and the threat of catastrophic violence leading up to World War II. In a letter to Arnold Zweig, Freud writes, "Faced with the new persecutions, one asks oneself again how the Jews have come to be what they are and why they have attracted this undying hatred. I soon discovered the formula: Moses created the Jews" (Freud, 1968, p. 102). There was something almost relieving for Freud in making this seemingly bizarre conclusion, as if his mythology in *Moses and Monotheism* that Moses had really been an Egyptian prince and had really "created" the Jews resolved something within himself. What I will show in this chapter is that his thinking on psychoanalysis, race, culture, and oppression evolved to resolve a tension inherent in his relationship to Jewishness and Blackness. The evolution of his thinking both informed and was informed by the lucid reflections of his disciples (e.g., Ferenczi, Fenichel, Fromm) on these very issues.

I will focus here mostly on Freud's "cultural texts"—*Totem and Taboo* (1913), *Group Psychology and the Analysis of the Ego* (1921), *The Future of an Illusion* (1927), *Civilization and its Discontents* (1930), and *Moses and Monotheism* (1939). By focusing intimately on Freud's psychoanalytic exploration of society, oppression, and power, we will reveal the outlines of a psychoanalytic psychology of liberation that would reverberate throughout the genealogy of psychoanalysis and liberation psychology. Tracing Ferenczi, Fenichel, and even Fromm's thinking back to Freud will propel us forward toward Fanon, Freire, and ultimately Martín-Baró. After describing the ideas within these texts, I will then use Freud's ideas to analyze Freud himself, and show how he comes to us as an ambivalent figure that is both haunting ghost and feared ancestor. Only by wrestling with Freud can we appreciate the groundwork he laid for liberation psychology, as well as the limitations that restricted this rich tradition.

FREUD, TOTEM, AND TABOO

In *Totem and Taboo* Freud (1913) lays the foundation for his understanding of the distinctly ambivalent relationships underlying communal and social belonging. Taking the meaning of the "taboo" in indigenous societies as his stepping stone, he notes how a taboo functions as a bipolar signifier to what is sacred, consecrated, and holy while also dangerous, forbidden, and unclean (p. 18). Depending on the colonialist, racist discourses of 19th century anthropology, Freud sees the taboo as a "primaeval prohibition forcibly imposed (by some authority) from outside, and directed against the most powerful longings to which human beings are subject" (pp. 34–35). Its dominated subjects experience the ambivalent desire to violate the taboo, while also being beholden and fearful of the "magical power" it is believed to wield. He argued that "long before a table of laws was handed down by any god, these savages were in possession of a living commandment: 'Thou shalt not kill', a violation of which would not go unpunished" (p. 39). A more specific and related injunction was the taboo against harming one's ruler, who "must not only be guarded, he must also be guarded against" (p. 41). It is out of these reflections on 19th-century anthropology that Freud develops a theory—which I'll refer to as a mythology—of how human beings came to acquire taboos as an internalized mechanism of control. I will review Freud's mythology not to derive an understanding of actual historical events, but rather to understand his thinking on culture, power, and society.

Freud (1913) envisioned a pre-historic, patriarchal society led by a primal father who held control over all the women in his tribe, and denied his sons access to them. His sons became "a youthful band of brothers living together in forced celibacy," driven out from their society and excluded from their objects of desire (e.g., women), until they finally rise up to kill and eat their tyrannical father. Freud's mythologizing of the aftermath of this violent revolt is fascinating,

> After they had got rid of him, had *satisfied their hatred* and had put into effect their *wish to identify themselves with him*, the affection which had all this time been pushed under was bound to make itself felt. It did so in the form of remorse. A sense of guilt made its appearance, which in this instance coincided with the remorse felt by the whole group. (p. 143, my emphasis)

The brothers not only hated but *identified* with their father, the very tyrant who dominated his offspring and enjoyed the women under his control. Identification in this sense refers to a form of love, affection, and subjection to the father's authority. However, they each also wanted to *become* like him, and dominate others in turn while having all the women for themselves. Identification in this second sense meant identification with the position of tyrannical power and dominance they themselves wanted to achieve. However, once their lust for blood and power was sated, the band of brothers realized they not only hated their father, but also loved him. "The dead father," Freud writes, "became stronger than the living one had been" (p. 143). What had been prevented by the father himself—sexual access to the women of their tribe—was now prohibited by the sons themselves, who internalized it as a law in their hearts, "They revoked their deed by forbidding the killing of the totem, the substitute for their father; and they renounced its fruits by resigning their claim to the women who had now been set free" (p. 143).

The taboo, in Freud's (1913) eyes, was instituted out of the brothers' guilt in recognizing their love for the father they had murdered. But it was also meant to prevent the potential bloodshed that would ensue by the power vacuum left by the father's removal from power. Although the brothers had united to overthrow him, their identification with him as the dominant, powerful one—and hence their desire to each *become* the father—made them rivals and enemies to one another. Each one desired total dominion over the women as objects, as their father before them. Freud reasoned that

> [t]he new organization would have collapsed in a struggle of all against all, for none of them was of such overmastering strength as to be able to take on his father's part with success. Thus the brothers had no alternative, if they were to live together, but—not, perhaps, until they had passed through many dangerous crises—to institute the law against incest, by which they all alike renounced the women whom they desired and who had been their chief motive for despatching their father. (p. 143)

Out of the sense of guilt and love toward the father, to appease him via "deferred obedience" to him, and to prevent violence from spiraling out of control, the brothers instituted the totemic taboo against the murder of the totem animal (representing the father), which over time spread as a libidinal, affective tie to the other members of the tribe in the injunction "thou shalt not kill." In declaring this solidarity among members of the same clan, Freud wrote "the brothers were declaring that no one of them must be treated by another as their father was treated by them all jointly. They were precluding the possibility of a repetition of their father's fate" (p. 146). The brothers were *not* to treat one another as their father did before them; they prevented the repetition of a cycle of domination, violence, and rebellion. Rather, they were to treat one another as *equals*. This formation in Freud's eyes contributed to the development of culture and civilization, forming the backbone of the social contract.

Freud's story of the brothers' revolution is at the same time the story of a failed revolution—the brothers internalize the very prohibition and power structure they rebelled against. To paraphrase what Freud wrote in *The Future of an Illusion*, they went from being enemies of the father's will to being its vehicles (Freud, 1927, p. 11). In addition, their fragile alliance threatened to collapse at any moment into horizontal violence *between* the "oppressed" siblings. To avoid this violence, Freud depicts the brothers as engaging in an *ethical act*. They *renounce* the position of "the father," to prevent *repeating* their father's violence against one another, and treat one another (does this include the "freed" women?) as equals. These three dynamics, how the oppressed internalize their oppression, the threat of the oppressed engaging in violence against one another due to seeking to become oppressors themselves, and the renunciation of brute violence and domination run a course throughout Freud's thinking on culture and society. But there is another, more implicit theme in Freud's work which sheds light on problems encountered in liberation psychology.

Psychoanalytically informed feminist scholars such as Gayle Rubin have argued that psychoanalysis presents a detailed account of the damaging effects of acquiring a "normal" feminine position on women's subjectivity. In her essay "The Traffic in Women," Rubin (1997) employs a Marxist, psychoanalytically-informed, feminist lens to discuss how men in patriarchal societies exchange women's bodies in order to establish relationship. In Freud's text women serve precisely this role—that of commodified objects to be dominated, "owned," and warred over between men. Although he states in passing that the brothers murdering the father, and then renouncing his power, set the women "free" from bondage to either party, he does not spend any time elucidating their subjectivity or experience. In Freud's fantasy about men's liberation from paternal oppression, women take the role of passive objects—commodities—that are battled over. This sets up two interlocking dynamics. One is the implicitly triangulated relationship between the oppressing father, the rebelling sons, and women as a passive "excluded other." But as we will see in Freud and later Fanon's work, there is also a pattern in which one group (e.g., Jews, women, LGBT communities, African peoples) becomes an object for another's emancipation (e.g., White/cisheterosexual/men).

Similarly, there is the question of his dependence on colonialist narratives in anthropology, as critically examined by Brickman (2003). I agree that Freud positions himself very much as another colonizing gaze upon the indigenous Asian, Latin American, and African people deemed primitive and savage by the culture of his time. But over the course of *Totem and Taboo*, especially with the conclusion to his myth of the primal horde, he adds an interesting, and perhaps ambivalent, twist. In describing so-called primitives and savages as having a complex inner life, torn and bound by love, hate, and the ambivalence that textures all human relationships, Freud (1913) wrote,

> I am under no illusion that in putting forward these attempted explanations I am not laying myself open to the charge of endowing modern savages with a subtlety in their mental activities which exceeds all probability. It seems to me quite possible, however, that *the same may be true of our attitude towards the psychology of those races that have remained at the animistic level* as is true of our attitude towards the mental life of children, which we adults no longer understand and whose fullness and delicacy of feeling we have in consequence so greatly underestimated. (pp. 98–99, my emphasis)

He argued that the anthropological discourse of his time greatly underestimated the complexity and inner life of indigenous people, and that he was describing psychological principles shared by all human beings, a premise later shared by Franz Boas and his students who argued there was "no higher or lower in civilization" (Brickman, 2003). Similarly, it must be remembered that it was Freud who argued that there is a continuum, especially with regard to sexuality, between child and adult life. Freud noted this same bias can be found toward "those races that have remained at the animistic level," a bias similarly leveled against Jews like himself (as discussed in the previous chapter). Brickman (2003) and more recently Geller (2007) document the ascription that Jews had "animal-like status" in the European society of Freud's time, subject to signifiers that evoked the feminine, the primitive, and the bestial.

In this way, Freud positions himself as a white colonizer gazing upon "primitive," indigenous subjects, alongside moments in which he *tepidly* associates himself, perhaps even empathized with, those very same nonwhite others equated with the status of the degraded, dangerous, and unclean. The way that Freud identifies with the position of the powerful, the position of the oppressed, and with those who are excluded from this dyad, *and how he shifts between each of these positions*, forms a theme in his work. Per Brickman (2003), Freud developed "a theory of the political production of primitivity: primitivity is the psychology of domination and subordination" (p. 101). At the same time, primitivity in Freud's writing "is the psychology of those who are positioned as objects of exchange—within a society (women) or between societies (colonized or subaltern others)" (p. 103). Freud's model, as will be elaborated, is then an analysis of the triadic relationship between White/Patriarchal oppression, those unable to participate in the fullness of White/Patriarchal performativity, and those excluded from the terms of White dominance as such.

GROUP PSYCHOLOGY AND THE ANALYSIS OF THE EGO

Reading Freud's *Group Psychology and the Analysis of the Ego* (1921) in the wake of the 2016 U.S. election is like traveling back in time to a world very much like our own. Writing in the shadow of European anti-Semitism, and with Karl Lueger's rise to prominence in Vienna still fresh in his mind, Freud intuited that individual psychology is always already social psychology—"In the individual's mental life someone else is invariably involved, as a model, as an object, as a helper, as an opponent" (p. 1). His study of human beings as social creatures centered on group or "mass" psychology, and was concerned with one's identity "as a member of a race, of a nation, of a case, of a profession, of an institution, or as a component part of a crowd of people . . . organized into a group at some particular time for some definite purpose" (p. 2). Freud's "group book" is explicitly concerned with race, and specifically with racist, right-wing, anti-Semitic mass movements in turn of the century Europe. As we will see, he continues a line of thinking started in *Totem and Taboo*, and which continues to be developed throughout his writing.

Freud follows Le Bon's original work on "the crowd," which described the transformation in feeling, thinking, and behavior individuals go through when they form part of a mass movement. Le Bon thought that the individual's subjectivity becomes "obliterated" when submerged in a mass movement, exposing unconscious fears and rage shared by the group. This brings the individual into a "hypnotic," "mesmerizing" state where the aura of the group reigns. In this state the group "mind" becomes vulnerable to manipulation, lacking the ability to think critically about the ideology imposed on them. The group is moved by impressionistic images, whose feelings become both simple and exaggerated. Hence, the group is prone to emotional extremes, takes falsehoods to be "incontrovertible certainty," and turns dislike and disagreement into "furious hatred." Freud (1921) writes that the group,

> is as intolerant as it is obedient to Authority. It respects force and can only be slightly influenced by kindness, which it regards merely as a form of weak-

> ness. What it demands of its Heroes is strength, or even violence. It wants to be ruled and oppressed and to fear its Masters. Fundamentally it is entirely conservative, and it has a deep aversion to all innovations and advances and an unbounded respect for tradition. (pp. 10–11)

Freud reasons that individuals in populist movements turn to violence when "all their individual inhibitions fall away and all the cruel, brutal and destructive instincts" (p. 11) rise to the surface. In a sense, he argues that mass crowds lead people to lose their humanity, becoming enthralled by the "truly magical power of words" (p. 11) capable of evoking a raging tempest as much as silencing them.

The sense of truth and what is real similarly become distorted in the mass crowd, who demand illusions. Fact and fiction become blurred and indistinguishable, turning to a great leader to define their reality, one who is self-certain and self-assured (Freud, 1921, p. 12). In order to garner the group's faith in him, "he must possess a strong and imposing will, which the group, which has no will of its own, can accept from him" (p. 13). The leader, who promises a return to a glorious and prestigious past, grounded in the virtues of tradition, offers access to the glory and prestige to salve the wounds of humiliation and deprivation. This prestige "is a sort of domination exercised Over Us . . . It entirely paralyzes our critical faculty, and fills us with wonderment and respect. It would seem to arouse a feeling like that of 'fascination' in hypnosis" (p. 13). We are drowned with wonderment and awe as the leader or group promises to bring the good old days back and make the country great again. To partake in this majesty, and the love offered by the group and its leader, the individual surrenders their subjectivity.

Love for those like the self goes in hand with hatred for the projected others. Here Freud (1921) analyzes group dynamics in the armed forces and the Christian church. A group—whether a racial group, social class, religion, or nation—exudes love toward its members, while being "hard and unloving to those who do not belong to it" and seething with "cruelty and intolerance towards those who do not belong to it" (p. 30). This splitting of hatred toward "the other" supports love between members of the group, and in that way, the group can manage its own ambivalence toward its members. Freud argued that hostile feelings between closely related races—here he gives the example of various European culture and nations—can then be momentarily dispersed through the use of the racial other, allowing loving ties between these now in-groups to form. "We are no longer astonished," Freud writes, "that greater differences should lead to an almost insufferable repugnance, such as the Gaelic people feel for the German, the Aryan for the semite, and the white races for the colored" (p. 33).

Freud (1921) recognized that this love for one's socio-cultural group and identity and hatred for the "other" quells any criticism of what one's love object demands—"everything that the object does and asks for is right and blameless," he writes, "in the blindness of love remorse-lessness is carried to the pitch of crime" (p. 113). He summarizes his argument thusly, "*The object has been put in the place of the ego ideal* . . . such extreme developments of being in love as may be described as 'fascination' or 'bondage'" (p. 113, my emphasis). Citing Ferenczi's work, Freud argues that the object of identification becomes introjected as a force that dominates the mind's ability to think critically about that object—is the "other" truly an enemy? Should they really be crushed and repressed? Is what the group/leader/god wants just?

The lack of autonomy, independence of thought, and the fear of not "stepping out of line" from the group—lest one be rejected and abandoned—leads to a lack of critical thought, emotional restraint, delayed gratification, and the inclination to brutality and violence. This, Freud (1921) argues, shows "a regression of mental activity to an earlier age such as we are not surprised to find among Savages or children" (p. 49). Freud (1921) argued that this mindset leads the individual to be "ruled by those attitudes of the group mind which exhibit themselves and such forms as racial characteristics, class prejudices, public opinion, etc." (p. 34). We see here again a tension between Freud criticizing right-wing authoritarian racist movements, while depending on racist discourses of primitivity in doing so. This merits further unpacking. Brickman (2003) reminds us that Le Bon himself was a racist demagogue who wrote about mass crowds to condemn popular uprisings for social justice, while uplifting and advocating for the role of the "strong man" in authoritarian groups. Le Bon saw religious and state institutions "as necessary constraints against the power of the masses who threatened to overwhelm the status quo and rise up against it" (Brickman, 2003, p. 91). For Freud, however, it was these very social structures—the army and the church—that fed and supported the anti-Semitic mobs that brought Karl Lueger to power, and terrified subalterns like himself who did not fit into their vision of the body politic (Klein, 1985).

While in *Totem and Taboo* Freud tepidly questions racist, colonialist discourses, in *Group Psychology and the Analysis of the Ego* he reverses the logic of racism by arguing that it is the anti-Semitic masses and the racist social structures that support them that are savage and primitive. Brickman (2003) argues that Freud's critique of racist, totalitarian movements and the societies that give rise to them represents an incomplete revolt—he reverses colonialist discourses on primitivity, while also depending on them. It is important to note two things: (1) Freud's reversal of terms so that White Europeans are the primitive, uncivilized savages prone to brutality relative to Jewish/non-white subalterns, and (2) Freud's *identification* with the role of the civilized other before a mass of savage anti-Semitic masses. One might say—following his reasoning in *Totem and Taboo*—that while Freud revolts against his racist, anti-Semitic master, he could not renounce his identification with his master's tools. This dual role of reversal as revolt and identification with power will prove critical in understanding Freud's corpus, as well as later writers in liberation psychology.

Freud's (1921) analysis of the idealization of one's group membership, and the hatred projected unto the "out group," suggests there is one element that can break through this rigid splitting. For Freud, this element is love (p. 34). Freud argues that in the development of human society, just as for individuals, it is love—and specifically love for the other—that curbs the tendency toward violence (p. 35). The development of love for an-other—outside the self, outside of one's group—is for Freud an adaptive reaction-formation, and one whose first demand "is for justice, for equal treatment for all" (p. 52).

FREUD'S CONCEPTION OF SOCIAL JUSTICE

Freud had a particular vision of how societies form, give rise to inequality and hatred, and to demands for reparation and restitution. To gain a better picture of his social ethics, we must first turn to his (1914) analysis of Michelangelo's statue of Moses. Freud critiqued the traditional, biblical image of Moses as a rageful patriarch who, confronted by the idolatry of his people, smashes the tablets of the law upon the ground. He saw in Michelangelo's depiction of Moses a different model of subjectivity—as Brickman (2003) writes, he saw "a civilizing advance over primitive patriarchal power" (p. 99). Freud (1914) argued that rather than give in to his rageful impulses, Michelangelo's Moses *restrains* himself from acting them out. Freud interprets that in this depiction Moses renounces his drive for violence, reaching "the highest mental achievement that is possible in a man, that of struggling successfully against an inward passion for the sake of a cause to which he has devoted himself" (p. 233). Klein (1981) recounts Freud's identification with the figure of Moses as part of broader Jewish desires to serve as a "light unto the nations" before the Gentile world that persecuted and oppressed them, seeking an even greater ethical purpose and universal mission—one in turn grounded in the cause of social justice for all.

The relationship between violence, oppression, renunciation, and social justice in Freud's thinking becomes clearer in *Civilization and its Discontents* (1930). In this text Freud argues that one of the functions of society is to regulate the relationships between human beings. Without this regulation, society would be subject to the "arbitrary will" of the powerful, who would govern based on their own needs and impulses. In the case of a "strong man," nothing would prevent an even stronger man to appear to take his place. Only by drawing on the power of community to condemn the power of brute force could some semblance of equality be achieved—through members of the community agreeing to restrict their own desires and violent impulses for the sake of justice, and by overpowering would-be strong men from amassing wealth and power. "The first requisite of civilization," Freud writes, "is that of justice—that is, the assurance that a law once made will not be broken in favour of an individual" (p. 95). This implies nothing about the rightness of a given law, as Freud is aware that even the law itself can be structured to privilege certain racial groups. Thus, he writes,

> The further course of cultural development seems to tend towards making the law no longer an expression of the will of a small community—a caste or a stratum of the population or a racial group—which, in its turn, behaves like a violent individual towards other, and perhaps more numerous, collections of people. The final outcome should be a rule of law to which all—except those who are not capable of entering a community—have contributed by a sacrifice of their instincts, and which leaves no one—again with the same exception—at the mercy of brute force. (p. 95)

For this reason, Freud argues that what some express "as a desire for freedom may be their revolt against some existing injustice, and so may prove favorable to a further development of civilization" (p. 96). Freud outlines a central tension in culture and society, in which individuals and groups negotiate their impulses, desires, and civil rights, with love and affective bonds acting as a bulwark against violence, oppression, and the rule of the powerful.

This tension extends into the realm of sexuality. Freud (1930) points out how culture relates to sexuality "as a people or a stratum of its population does which has subjected another one to its exploitation. Fear of a revolt by the suppressed elements drives it to stricter precautionary measures" (p. 104), a phenomenon he argues has reached new extremes in "Western European civilization" (p. 104). Balance is necessary in Freud's eyes. He believed it justifiable to manage the sexual development of children in ways that were appropriate, yet without *disavowing* infantile sexuality as such. In regard to the sexuality of adults, however, he noted how sexual desire is restricted to heterosexual, monogamous relationships. "The requirement . . . that there shall be a single kind of sexual life for everyone," Freud wrote, "disregards the dissimilarities . . . in the sexual constitution of human beings; it cuts off a fair number of them from sexual enjoyment, and so becomes the source of serious injustice" (p. 104). Freud believed that *all* must sacrifice through a renunciation of their instincts through an equitable distribution of restriction. However, he also believed that whether in terms of sexuality, wealth, or power, those who were excluded from enjoyment so that the few could benefit from its excess have every right to call for change and struggle for social justice.

Returning to *Group Psychology and the Analysis of the Ego*, Freud (1921) reiterated that the first demand of civilization is social justice—that all regardless of race or caste be treated with equality. "Social justice," Freud wrote, "means that we deny ourselves many things so that others may have to do without them as well . . . This demand for equality is the root of social conscience and the sense of duty" (p. 53). In elucidating his understanding of social justice, Freud draws on rather striking imagery. He argued that the unconscious wish that drives or is sublimated into social justice "reveals itself unexpectedly" in the dread of those who contracted syphilis have toward infecting others:

> The dread exhibited by these poor wretches corresponds to their violent struggles against the unconscious wish to spread their infection on to other people; For why should they alone be infected and cut off from so much? Why not other people as well? . . . Thus social feeling is based upon the reversal of what was first a hostile feeling into a positively-toned tie in the nature of an identification. So far as we have hitherto been able to follow the course of events, *this reversal seems to occur under the influence of a common affectionate tie with a person outside the group.* (p. 53, emphasis added)

I find this analogy fascinating, as it suggests that when one is marginalized from the social order, it is as if one has contracted a disease. Once infected, there is an unconscious desire—filled with rage and identification with the one who first "infected" us—to infect others so they too experience the affliction. In struggling with this wish, Freud reasons, the syphilitic exerts an ethical choice—"I will *not* infect you with this disease, I will not make you feel my pain, I renounce my identification with the one who infected me—I *renounce* this violence and recognize your humanity." Freud makes a passing, but similar analogy when he references the story of Solomon and the two women who claimed to be the true mother of a child. According to Freud's view, *both* women would have felt the aggressive instinct to deny the other the child by having them cut in two, but one of them—the child's real mother—renounced this instinct, and her rights to the child in order to save him.

It is similarly striking that Freud draws on the syphilitic as a metaphor in talking about the unconscious wishes behind calls for social justice. As discussed in the previous two chapters, syphilis was a sexually transmitted disease associated with Jews in the racist discourse of Freud's world. The Jew expelled from society is framed as being diseased, carrying an illness which merits exclusion from the social contract and human existence as such. As with the syphilitic as with marginalized people, Freud argued that the excluded other wishes, *desires* to infect others with their affliction so that they too feel what it is like to be marginalized. But it is an ethical act for Freud to struggle against one's aggressive desires in favor of a cause to which one has committed oneself—in this case, the cause of social justice. Social justice for Freud is an ethical stance resulting from a psychological sublimation in which one renounces their destructive and violent impulses in favor of an affective bond with the other (outside the group). By recognizing this affective bond, we recognize the other as a human being and in turn restore our own humanity. This conception of justice, however, is ruptured when human beings split off into groups which hoard both their wealth and their affection from one another, while discharging their violence toward other groups now seen as objects for their exploitation.

THE FUTURE OF AN ILLUSION AS PROTO-POSTCOLONIAL TREATISE

It is curious to note that Freud's (1927) "religion book," *The Future of an Illusion*, carries his most lucid psycho-political thinking on culture and society. In it, Freud defines culture as all of the knowledge and skills humans deploy to accumulate wealth to meet their needs, and "the regulations necessary in order to adjust the relations of men to one another and *especially the distribution of the available wealth*" (p. 6, my emphasis). He remarked that human relationships are directly impacted by the distribution of wealth, as when a person "[comes] to function as wealth in relation to another one, in so far as the other person makes use of his capacity for work, or chooses him as a sexual object" (p. 6). Due to this trend toward domination and exploitation, every individual is "virtually an enemy of civilization," hence, the potential to lust for power and dominance over others needed to be curtailed.

At the same time, Freud (1927) reasoned that culture and society aims "not only at effecting a certain distribution of wealth but at maintaining that distribution" (p. 6). "One thus gets an impression," Freud writes, "that civilization is something which was imposed on a resisting majority by a minority which understood how to obtain possession of the means to power and coercion" (p. 6). This includes control of the distribution of wealth and restricting the populace's proclivity to violence to safeguard this distribution, while rewarding them for accepting a certain level of "privation." For Freud it is imperative to distinguish "between privations which affect everyone and privations which do not affect everyone but only groups, classes or even single individuals" (p. 10). As stated above, Freud believed that *all* had to sacrifice their aggressive impulses in order to live in community, and observe common laws that would not privilege one racial group over another (as was the case in his anti-Semitic, anti-Black milieu). He was concerned with the *inequality* of these restrictions, and inequality in the distribution of wealth. Freud theorized that the external coercion that supports systems of inequality over time becomes internalized by oppressed people in the form of the super-ego—literally, the *over I* that looks over the ego's, the *I*'s shoulder. By internalizing the commandments of the powerful, the oppressed "are turned from being opponents of civilization into being its vehicles" (p. 11). The internalization of oppression maintains the status quo, and resolves an expectable problem of inequality, one which Freud began theorizing about in *Totem and Taboo*.

In looking at the restrictions that only apply to certain socioeconomic classes or groups, Freud (1927) recognized that the oppressed will envy the privileges of the dominant and strive to free themselves from their "surplus of privation." An underlying discontent persists that "can lead to dangerous revolts." Freud argued that a society that does not address egregious inequality runs the risk "that the suppressed people should develop an intense hostility towards a culture whose existence they make possible by their work, but in whose wealth they have too small a share" (p. 12). It is here that Freud states his oft-cited remark, "It goes without saying that a civilization which leaves so large a number of its participants unsatisfied and drives them into revolt neither has nor deserves the prospect of a lasting existence" (p. 12). In order to maintain control and redirect the hostility of the oppressed toward their oppressor, the oppresed are offered alternative, compensatory satisfactions for their deprivation through an ego ideal.

For example, the ego ideal that although they are rich and we are poor, we are both part of a common "culture [that] claims the right to look down on the rest" (Freud, 1927, p. 13), as was the case of white landowners and poor white workers in the days of American slavery—poor whites were poor but at least they were *white*, and so could partake in identification with the landowning rich whites who sought to control them, and in turn Black slaves. The narcissistic satisfaction offered by this cultural ideal "can be shared in not only by the favoured classes, which enjoy the benefits of the culture, but also by the suppressed ones, since the right to despise the people outside it compensates them for the wrongs they suffer within their own unit" (p. 13). Using a curious parallel that would echo Marx, Freud states that one might be part of the poor masses of the Roman Empire, "harassed by debts and military service; but, to make up for it, one is a Roman citizen, one has one's share in the task of ruling other nations and dictating their laws" (p. 13).

Freud (1927) outlines a complex, nuanced, proto-postcolonial psychoanalysis of oppressor and oppressed, in ways that presaged—and I argue laid the foundations for—liberation psychology. At his most candid, Freud wrote,

> This identification of the suppressed classes with the class who rules and exploits them is, however, only part of a larger whole. For, on the other hand, the suppressed classes can be emotionally attached to their masters; in spite of their hostility to them they may see in them their ideals. (p. 13)

We find Freud's mythology of the brothers banded by their hatred of the father, and their unconscious identification with his power and privilege, now fully elucidated in terms of the structural powers of his day. He maintains that such relations of identification and subjugation explain how unequal societies endure despite the understandable hostility of the hosts of disenfranchised people.

Freud (1927) goes further to add that this identification with the power and privilege of the oppressor, the belief that "I too can have this power and be like them," is completely illusory. It is here that Freud introduces what he sees as religion's psycho-political function, to "compensate [the oppressed] for the sufferings and privations which a civilized life in common has imposed on them" (p. 18). Here Freud is clearly critical of religion, culture, and society in general, but he names and calls out the specific phenomenon he is critiquing—White, European, Christian, and capitalistic nations (p. 20, 38). White Christianity in Freud's eyes, especially the kind that empowered Karl Lueger's Christian Social Party, promised illusions to fulfill the wishes of the oppressed in the afterlife, compensating for their struggles here on earth, while also offering them others to hate in this life (e.g., Jews, unbelievers, non-white others, etc.).

Freud (1927) argued that from Columbus' illusion that he discovered a new route to India, to the illusion that the White/Aryan race is the only true and civilized culture (pp. 30–31), such illusions are fueled by the wish for power which drives acts of barbarity and violence upon the non-White people of the world. But Freud also noticed that Christian religion failed to provide the compensation it promised, "an appallingly large number of people are dissatisfied with civilization and unhappy in it, and feel it as a yoke which must be shaken off" (p. 37). People still desired to change society, or else go so far in their hostility that they would seek to destroy it. So long as religion could keep the people submissive with the belief that God is all good and humans are weak and sinful, it could exert power over them. Freud expected a protest from the perspective of the powerful: but what if the oppressed reject religion, its illusory satisfactions, and God's injunction not to kill your neighbor? Would they not enact tremendous violence to upend society without hesitation? Faced with that objection, Freud reasons that either the masses "must be held down most severely and kept most carefully away from any chance of intellectual awakening, or else the relationship between civilization and religion must undergo a fundamental revision" (p. 39).

As we have already seen, Freud (1927) was fond of making analogies between different social groups, and here he makes another no less interesting analogy between the position of the oppressed masses and that of women. He critiques the notion that women constitutionally have "a lesser intelligence" than men, and sees this as a result of the oppression women face of their thoughts, freedom of expression, and ability to experience the full range of sexual experiencing. "So long as a person's early years are influenced not only by a sexual inhibition of thought but also by a religious inhibition and by a loyal inhibition derived from this," he concludes "we cannot really tell what in fact he is like" (p. 48). Freud's counterargument, then, to the idea that without constant oppression the masses will rise up to destroy society in a whirlwind of violence is that *oppression itself distorts and restricts the subjectivity of the oppressed.* He reasoned that you cannot tell what a person is really like when they are subjected to constant oppression.

Freud (1927) favored a different view, that if the oppressed free themselves from the illusions of religion, racism, and inequality, they would naturally take hold of their critical intellect to change society for the better. His vision of this transformation is striking,

> As honest smallholders on this earth they [the oppressed] will know how to cultivate their plot in such a way that it supports them. By withdrawing their expectations from the other world and concentrating all their liberated energies into their life on earth, they will probably succeed in achieving a state of things in which *life will become tolerable for everyone and civilization no longer oppressive to anyone.* (p. 50, my emphasis)

Freud ends this proclamation for liberation by citing Heine: "We leave Heaven to the angels and the sparrows." He saw the possibility that an advance in critical faculties which scrutinizes the illusions of society would lead the oppressed to not only liberate themselves, but also create conditions under which the social order did not need to be oppressive to anyone, regardless of their group membership—whether in terms of race, gender, sexuality, class, or otherwise. This vision, however, did not temper Freud's cynicism regarding human nature, nor negate the reality of humanity's proneness to hatred and aggression.

SOCIETY BETWEEN LIFE AND DEATH

Freud developed a psychoanalytically grounded theory of how ruling classes and groups achieve and maintain their power through the psychological subjection of marginalized groups. He articulated how the oppressed internalize their aggression through an identification with the values and ideals of the oppressor. At the same time, he showed insight into how the oppressed can also identify with the position of the oppressor and fetishize the will to power. This tendency toward reversal through violence and aggression deeply concerned Freud, and gave him pause when considering, for example, the rise of communism in Soviet Russia.

Freud may have held a vision of social justice and social change, but this was hardly a utopian one. In *Civilization and Its Discontents* (1930) he outright rejected the idea that if economic inequality is resolved, this will *by itself* quell humanity's inclination toward aggression. He argued that our capacity for hatred, aggression, social division, and haves and have-nots would simply go elsewhere. Whatever direction even a more egalitarian society might take, "this indestructible feature of human nature will follow it there" (p. 114). Freud again argued it "is always possible to bind together a considerable number of people in love, so long as there are other people left over to receive the manifestations of their aggressiveness " (p. 114). He saw how easily it came to people in a given society to select a "small cultural group" as an outlet for their "hostility against intruders," a phenomenon he referred to as "the narcissism of minor differences" (p. 114).

The problem with this displacement of hostility is that it was itself brittle and transient. He noted with some sarcasm the "most useful services" Jews fulfilled as Other to White Christians' aggression, and how this hatred did little to bring peace and security to their societies. It was similarly not a coincidence for Freud (1930) that the illusion of "Germanic world-dominion called for anti-semitism as its complement" (p. 115), nor that the rise of Stalinist communism in Russia "should find its psychological support in the persecution of the bourgeois. One only wonders, with concern, what the Soviets will do after they have wiped out their bourgeois" (p. 115). There is for Freud something cyclical about a culture's need for an Other, of their desire for aggression that is never quelled, as well as the aggression that can accompany even movements for equality. In his gloss on the rise of communism in Russia, it is as if Freud intimates the following question: once those seeking economic equality have "wiped out" the rich and wealthy, where will the aggression go next? We are not far from Freud's mythology of the band of brothers who, after vanquishing the dictatorial father, risk turning on one another with the same violence and desire for power. At the same time, there is an egregious blind spot here that both reveals Freud's genius and his limitations in thinking triadically about socio-economic antagonisms.

Freud reckons that people are not able to reconcile the perception of their own goodness with the hostility they are prone to much like they struggle with the existence of evil, if they were to equally believe in the existence of an all-powerful, benevolent God. The Devil provides psychologically "the best way out as an excuse for God; in that way he would be playing the same part as an agent of economic discharge as the Jew does in the world of the Aryan ideal" (Freud, 1930, p. 120). Freud elaborates that just as one can hold God responsible for the Devil, so too should one hold anti-Semitism accountable for the wickedness projected upon the Jew—the Jew as a creation of the need for an Other (p. 120). We create monsters out of our own projections and desires, the excess of hatred left over when we consummate bonds of love with our kin. This was not a process devoid of love, but for Freud resulted from it. Human relationships—including intimate, affectionate ones—are in essence a struggle of life and death.

Human culture and society at its best for Freud "is a process in the service of Eros, whose purpose is to combine single human individuals, and after that families, then races, peoples and nations, into one great unity, the unity of mankind" (1930, p. 122). Love, sensuality, and life binds us together in our attachments to our loved ones, to our group memberships, and ideally also to others who are outside of us. But our aggressive instincts, "the hostility of each against all and of all against each" (p. 122) stand in a dialectical tension with this process. In an interesting existential turn, Freud sees this struggle of life and death (Eros and Thanatos) as humanity's a priori struggle for existence and community. Culture and society attempt to tame the rage and hatred of individuals and groups by setting up the super-ego within them. Freud returns to his mythology in *Totem and Taboo*, explaining how the love the brothers felt toward their slain father was internalized as a sense of guilt, whose aim it was to prevent the repetition of violence. The sense of guilt itself "is an expression of the conflict due to ambivalence, of the eternal struggle between Eros and the instinct of destruction or death" (p. 132). Guilt then serves a pro-social function, in that it helps stay the hand of violence through the recognition that the Other is also a human being—like the self—deserving of love and should not be killed. In the advent of World War II, Freud ends *Civilization and its Discontents* by recognizing the fear of human being's ability to oppress and murder one another to the end. "And now it is to be expected that the other of the two 'Heavenly Powers', eternal Eros," Freud writes, "will make an effort to assert himself in the struggle with his equally immortal adversary [Thanatos]. But who can foresee with what success and with what result?" (p. 145).

At this point in our review of Freud's psychoanalytic thinking on culture, society, and inequality, there is not only a model of the dynamics of oppressor and oppressed, but also a tacit, implicit model of the triangulated nature of social antagonisms. While Freud addresses explicit social contradictions between the ruling wealthy classes, the "masses" excluded from the distribution of wealth, and the relationship between this economic inequality and Whiteness, he does not fully unpack the role of the "excluded third." In *Totem and Taboo*, he discussed the father and the band of brothers, but left the role of women as passive objects observing the patriarchal drama play out before them. And although Freud names the role of the Jew-as-non-White as an excluded other before the dyad of Aryan ruling class and Aryan masses, he does not at this point expand on the subjectivity or psychology of Jews turned scapegoat in this drama. It is almost as if Freud, in leaving the Jew as this empty recipient of projection and hatred, allows himself to shift in his identifications between the "twosome" of wealthy Whites and suppressed, marginalized Whites. Hence, the position of the Jew in turn of the century society exists as an empty signifier for Freud. That is, until *Moses and Monotheism*.

MOSES AND MONOTHEISM: FREUD'S REDEMPTIVE VISION

Having started this review of Freud's thinking on race, culture, and politics with his mythology of the band of brothers in *Totem and Taboo*, it is fitting that we conclude it with his mythology of Moses and the Jewish people in *Moses and Monotheism* (1939). In a similar vein, I am not interested in this text as reflecting a historical exegesis, and more once again in how it reflects Freud's thinking on race, culture, and social justice. It is important to note Freud's motivation in writing this book in the shadow of the Nazis' rise to power in Germany, which only highlighted racial anxieties he faced throughout his life. As he confessed in a letter to Lou Andreas-Salome, the question of why the Jews have been so persecuted "has pursued me throughout the whole of my life" (cited in Bernstein, 1998, p. 25). It was to Moses, Freud argued, that Jews owed both the resilience that survived all persecution, and the source of so much hostility from the world around them.

Given the racial science and ideologies of Freud's time equating Blackness and Jewishness, his own associations toward *his* Jewishness and Blackness, and how these relationships textured his experience of discrimination and the discussions of race which took place within the psychoanalytic movement (see the previous chapter), Freud hit upon the following conclusion, also carrying the imprint of 19th-century racism and anti-Semitism: Moses was a prince from Africa, and it was he who created the Jews. He liberated the Hebrews from bondage and imposed upon them the tradition of monotheism. The first part of Freud's assertion—that Moses was Egyptian—has received much attention in the literature on psychoanalysis and Jewishness. I will follow a particular line of argumentation from this literature, and draw forth its implications for Freud's thinking on identity and social justice.

Frosh (2005), writing from his own positionality as a Jewish psychoanalyst, recognized that Freud making Moses an Egyptian "has the effect of asserting a brokenness within Jewish communal identity: at its source is an outsider" (Frosh, 2005, p. 51). Notions of racial, national, and cultural purity perpetually break down into veins of identification that are varied, multiple, rendered "impure" by the presence of an "outsider" who first set identity development in motion. Similarly Said (2003), in his lecture *Freud and the Non-European*, reads Freud's *Moses* through his own lens as a Palestinian man who identifies with the problem of the Non-European, the "non-White." He remarks on Freud's "casual assumption . . . that semites were most certainly *not* Europeans . . . and, *at the same time*, were somehow assimilable to its culture as former outsiders" (pp. 15–16, my emphasis). Said similarly provides a more generous reading of Freud's *Totem and Taboo*, citing Freud's "implicit refusal, in the end, to erect an insurmountable barrier between non-European primitives and European civilization" (p. 19). Said's enthusiasm notwithstanding, it must be acknowledged that Freud's identification with the colonizer *maintains* a barrier, albeit a porous and rather ambivalent one. So too with Freud's claim of the Jew's non-European origin—for example, Freud challenged the assertion that Jews were wholly different racially from their "hosts" in Europe, as they were "not a foreign Asiatic race, but mostly consist of the remnants of Mediterranean peoples" (Freud, 1939, p. 39). At the same time, Said (2003) points out, Freud *zealously insisted* on Moses being the "founder of Judaism, but an unreconstructed non-Jewish Egyptian none the less," while also pointing out that "Jahveh derived from Arabia, which was also non-Jewish and non-European" (p. 42). Freud, then, asserts that there is no fundamental difference racially and culturally between Jews and their White-Gentile hosts, while strongly claiming a non-European origin for Jewish culture and identity. More specifically, an origin that centers Africa and an African prince.

Said's (2003) recognition of Freud's insistence that Jewish identity "did not begin with itself but, rather, with other [non-White] identities" (p. 44) points to the latter's struggle with the position of Jewishness within anti-Semitic, anti-Black European discourses. This reading suggests that Freud's positioning of Moses as a non-White, non-European, non-Jewish Other who constitutes Jewishness as such is also an attempt to reconcile a theme that has been noted in earlier chapters—the equation of Jewishness with Blackness, of being "White-but-not-quite." Freud's focus on Moses being an Egyptian is no mere distortion, or a coincidence resulting from the particularities of the Biblical story (e.g., taking place in Egypt). Given how Egypt itself was *the geographical tissue that connected Africa, the Mediterranean, and Europe*, I argue this reflects Freud's ambivalent attempt to rework his own relationship to Blackness, and the association embedded in his racist European culture between Blackness and Jewishness.

In Said's (2003) point of view, Freud declares that "identity cannot be thought or worked through itself alone; it cannot constitute or even imagine itself without that radical originary break or flaw which will not be repressed" (p. 54). In this, his final text, Freud wrestles with a wound upon history which will not be forgotten, and which, in his eyes, impacted the Jewish people—the wound of anti-Blackness, anti-Semitism, and the quandary of the non-White. It is this insight Said believed can speak to other "besieged identities," by speaking to the experience of identity as something always already broken and in a state of disrepair, a soul wound "from which there can be no recovery, no state of resolved or Stoic calm, and no Utopian reconciliation even within itself" (p. 54). Rose (2003) in commenting on Said's lecture expands upon this very possibility, stating, "We could almost remove the 'and' from the title of this lecture, 'Freud and the Non-European,' and read it instead as 'Freud the Non-European'" (p. 70). This lens will frame my reading of Freud's final text.

After establishing the centrality of Moses' non-Whiteness, Freud (1939) states that to the liberated Jewish people he gave a "more spiritual conception of God, a single God who embraces the whole world, one as all-loving as he was all-powerful, who, averse to all ceremonial and magic, set humanity as its highest aim a life of truth and justice" (p. 75). This "Mosaic Legacy" called on the renunciation of "magic" (note the resonance with his psychology of the masses drawn to magical words and superstition) and demanded a "life of truth and justice" (note how Freud centers justice as a core ethic of this legacy). However, due to this demand and its renunciations being too great, Moses is murdered by the Jewish people (a la *Totem and Taboo*). Both his legacy and the act of murder itself are repressed in their collective memory. It continued to grow in strength over time, however, slowly exerting its influence on the character of the Jews through continued returns. It was this Mosaic Legacy "that enabled the people of Israel to surmount all their hardships and to survive until our time" (pp. 75–76). Freud writes,

> There arose from the midst of the people an unending succession of men . . . seized by the great and powerful tradition which had gradually grown in darkness, and it was these men, the Prophets, who sedulously preached the old Mosaic doctrine: the Deity spurns sacrifice and ceremonial; he demands only belief and a life of truth and justice (Maat). (p. 76)

The prophets re-established the Mosaic doctrine, which became central to the Jewish religion. Freud saw this as an "honour" for the Jews, who "kept alive such a tradition and produced men who lent it their voice, even if the stimulus had first come from outside, from a great stranger" (p. 77). The voice of this stranger from Africa, and the vision of a God of justice he instilled in the Jewish people lent them an enduring ability to survive the brutality of empires young and old. Even as the Assyrians, Babylonians, and Persians rose and subjected the Jews to oppression, the power of the Mosaic God "was recognized in that all those wicked empires were defeated in their turn and their empires destroyed" (p. 99). In the tumult of World War II, could Freud have fantasized here about the fall of Aryan-Christian empires as well?

The Mosaic Legacy "formed" the subjectivity of the Jewish people through the cycle of continued repression and return, time and again leading them to disdain "magic and mysticism" and push them toward greater "spirituality and sublimations" (Freud, 1939, p. 135). The Jewish people, then, "overcome by the consciousness of being the chosen, came to value highly all intellectual and ethical achievements . . . their sad fate, and the disappointments reality had in store for them, were able to strengthen all these tendencies" (p. 135). "It is that they defy oppression," Freud writes, "that even the most cruel persecutions have not succeeded in exterminating them" (p. 144). In the same way that the Mosaic God was repressed only to return with greater strength and his never-ending demand for justice on the lips of the prophets, so too did the oppression of the Jewish people lead to the strengthening of their intellect and ethics—traits Freud argued aided in their survival. Much like liberation theologians, the Exodus was for Freud the proof *par excellence* of the Jews' chosenness by God as survivors of enslavement and oppression. This chosenness, that the Mosaic God is a God of the oppressed and marginalized, allowed the Jews to partake in God's "grandeur," all in exchange for greater intellectual and ethical renunciations, a "progress in spirituality," also translated as "advance in *intellectuality*" (*der fortschritt in der geistichgeit*).

This preference toward spiritual, intellectual, and ethical imperatives, Freud (1939) argued, "helped to build a dike against brutality and the inclination to violence" (pp. 181–182). While the development of muscular power was favored by the Greeks, themselves valued by the European culture of Freud's time, this was denied to the Jewish people. For Freud the Jews turned toward critical intellectuality and renounced the violence and brutality they themselves were subjected to by their neighbors, a turn "made in favour of what is culturally the more important" (p. 182). Freud evokes the super-ego to make a distinction between renouncing one's instincts due to an external imposition, and renouncing them in the name of an internal, and higher, set of values and ethics. He echoes here his reading of Michaelangelo's Moses, and his psychodynamic definition of social justice—to subject one's aggressive desires in favor of a higher cause one has committed to. This renunciation of power is pleasurable to the ego, which "feels uplifted" by living a life in accordance with justice (p. 187).

What maintained this inclination toward justice and renouncing brutality against other peoples *as the Jews themselves suffered*, was the sense of guilt. Remember that in Freud's psycho-political system it is guilt, with its superegoic injunction that we love even those whom we hate, which stays the hand of oppression and cyclical violence. It is, in essence, how he conceives of social justice. It was this feeling of guilt whenever the people fell short of God's call for justice

> which the Prophets incessantly kept alive and which soon became an integral pact of the religious system itself . . . In a new transport of moral asceticism the Jews imposed on themselves constantly increasing instinctual renunciation, and thereby reached—at least in doctrine and precepts—ethical heights that had remained inaccessible to the other peoples of antiquity. (Freud, 1939, p. 212)

Through internalizing Moses' God of the oppressed and enslaved, the Jews developed a sense of justice which depended on the renunciation of violence toward the other. In so doing, Freud argued, they reached "ethical heights" which their neighbors—whether the empires of old or the European hosts of

Freud's time—were not able to reach, as evidenced by the persistent brutality of the *fin-de-siecle* that was, and the brutality that in the fires of World War II was to be.

Freud (1939) reminds us that the great ethical heights reached by the Jewish people was itself the product of a stranger—"the man Moses, who created the Jews" (p. 168). The Jewish people owed Moses their "tenacity" in surviving millennia of colonization, marginalization, and oppression. At the same time, Freud stated, the Jews owed "much of the hostility which it has met with and is meeting still" (p. 168) to this same stranger from Africa. In making these odd arguments, Freud is simultaneously re-writing and working through a number of issues. Remember that in *Totem and Taboo*, as Brickman (2003) has pointed out, Freud depends on a racially-toned and colonial theory of primitivity that maintains that what is Black is developmentally earlier, less mature, archaic, and irrational—associations also often lodged at the Jew. By configuring Moses in *Moses and Monotheism* as an Egyptian prince who bestows upon the Jews an ethics of truth and justice, Freud is essentially reversing that scheme—what is earlier and originates in Egypt is what is more mature, advanced, and ethically higher. The Jews, in Freud's mythological retelling, *deny and murder* both those values and this "great stranger" from the African continent, in turn repressing their connection to him.

This implies that Freud's conception of his Jewish identity within his immediate historical context, was one of belonging to a people who sustained constant marginalization due to European society's imaginary and mythical equation of Jewishness and Blackness, a relationship Freud in his own myth-making saw the Jewish people repress time and again in their collective memory, yet which returned time and again without end. Freud then wrestles with his existential reality as a Jew by reconfiguring his relationship to Blackness as both cause of his oppression (e.g., the association between anti-Jewishness and anti-Blackness), as well as a source of survival and liberation.

FREUD'S PSYCHOANALYSIS OF LIBERATION

From his mythology of the origins of human society in *Totem and Taboo* to his mythology of the origins of the Jewish people in *Moses and Monotheism*, Freud develops a coherent and surprisingly consistent psychoanalytic theory of the dynamics of oppressor and oppressed. He argues that in order for humans to live together in community, all must make a sacrifice of their violent, aggressive instincts *and* their libidinal desires (e.g., for sex, wealth, or domination), and be ever watchful of those who seek to rise to the level of a "strong man"—the community must not allow a member to identify with the position of the "the Father," and seek his place. However, Freud recognized that society often reflects the desires of a wealthy few who acquire control over the distribution of wealth. In order to protect this distribution of wealth, conditions are created under which the oppressed classes come to *identify with the power of their oppressors*. The oppressed are then turned from being opponents of a given society into "being its vehicles." This identification with the oppressor, and the provision of a compensation via ideology and illusion, neutralizes the envy and hostility the oppressed might otherwise feel and enact through rebellion against the powerful. This process is related to Freud's bipolar model of internalization, the structure of the super-ego, and guilt. The super-ego and the guilt that results from its injunctions can serve oppressive ends by restricting the oppressed's capacity for critical reflection and revolt against the oppressor.

At the same time, this illusory process of identification with the oppressor is maintained by splitting and projective identification of hatred toward another group of people which serves as an excluded third—women, Jewish people, and Black peoples serve this function of an external other against which the European ruling class and working class can perform an illusory White/European ego. Freud both frames and renders invisible this triadic function of oppression—oppression as a complex matrix of identifications and denigration in which one oppressed class (working-class Whites) and oppressor class (ruling White elites) enter into unholy communion over the body of a third other. What remains unsymbolized for much of Freud's work, with the exception of *Moses and Monotheism*, is an account of the psychology of the excluded third. In *Totem and Taboo*, his account of tyrannical fathers and rebellious sons renders women silent, invisible objects. In *Group Psychology*, *The Future of an Illusion*, and even *Civilization and its Discontents*, the Jew is similarly a passive object of projection with no interiority of her or his own. Freud's own analysis, then reveals a back and forth identification with the White European ruling class as oppressors, and the White working-class as sub-oppressor, through which he distances himself from his positionality as "Black" Jew. In *Moses and Monotheism*, he inhabits a most curious position, that of a secular Jew relating to the Egyptian Moses and Blackness as this *stranger* that is both a source of resilience, creativity, and ethics as well as a source of oppression, marking an ambivalent and fraught attempt to rework the relationship between Jewishness and Blackness.

At the same time, Freud had a vision of social justice in which we renounce our aggressive instincts and desires to make space for the other, a space created out of a libidinal and affectionate tie. As Brickman (2003) writes about Freud's bipolar model of super-ego structure, "guilt may tighten the noose of the civilizing superego, but it also produces the ever greater 'ethical heights' that contribute to moral progress" (p. 151). Drawing on Hegel's master-slave dialectic, Brickman also interprets Freud as claiming that the oppressed "must dare to rebel, to aspire to the violence of the father and only then to renounce it" (p. 99). This suggests a complex psychoanalysis of aggression in Freud's scheme—the oppressed must in a sense experience and use their aggression to rise up against the oppressor, *and* renounce their identification with the position of the oppressor as such. This renunciation of enacted aggression against the other restores the humanity of both oppressor and oppressed, through a "compromise of rebellious desire and its renunciation" (p. 99). Neither domination nor submission, but the desire to enact social change tempered by one's libidinal tie to an other—even one's oppressor—who is seen as a human being, is what drives progress for Freud. These themes are a set of relationships that Freud's descendants, including Frantz Fanon and Paulo Freire, struggled with in their articulation of a liberation psychology. It is to their work that we will turn to in the following chapters.

Freud's vision of social justice is fundamentally one of how dominant and subordinate groups in society negotiate and struggle with their respective desires, and how this process of struggle and negotiation can lead to social change. But this communal process of rebellion, renunciation of aggression, and recognition mirrors an internal process central to psychoanalytic inquiry. Psychoanalysis reveals that the "I," the ego, is not the dominant master of its own home, but "has to struggle against various internal forces threatening to topple it" (Frosh, 2005, p. 206). "This is a process of *decentring*," Frosh writes, "because it removes the ego from the centre of personal psychology and replaces it with the unconscious (and, in Freud's 'structural' theory, the Id or 'It'), which reveals with great intensity the alien core inside each one of us" (p. 206).

Psychoanalysis' concern with shedding light on, struggling with, and making room for the marginalized otherness within and outside of us reflects a "preferential option for the repressed" that mirrors liberation theology and psychology's own "preferential option for the oppressed" (Gaztambide, 2015). At the same time, the alien "other" that is feared and desired within the self is a symbol of external otherness. Frosh (2005) writes,

> "In" the unconscious, this means that otherness itself has a "Jewish" feel to it; the hidden recesses of sex and aggression are easily identified with anti-Semitic paradigms. It is not, then, that the Jew is just a convenient scapegoat upon whom these inner urges can be projected; it is rather that just as psychoanalysis is "Jewish" in important ways, so is the unconscious it has discovered and invented. *All* otherness in the West is Jewish, including that inner otherness that is unconscious desire. (p. 215)

But given that the way Jewishness was rendered other in Freud's world through an imaginary relationship to Blackness, so too could one say that the hidden recesses of sex and aggression reflect anti-Black stereotypes. By virtue of the wounds visited upon the world by colonialism, the trans-Atlantic slave trade, and continued deployments of racism and xenophobia, *all* otherness in the West is Black within racist discourses, an otherness that has been equated with unconscious desire.

THE AMBIVALENCE OF FREUD'S LEGACY

As we have seen across these first three chapters, Freud and his colleagues had open and ongoing dialogues in their writings, personal correspondence, and intimate discussions about race, class, and inequality. It is through wrestling with their realities as excluded Jews who identified with social democratic, Marxist, and socialist values that they rendered a psychoanalytic theory of the intersections of race, class, and inequality, and how oppression is internalized and then enacted against other groups of exploited and marginalized people. These same energies unleashed a tradition of progressive thought in psychoanalysis, one that was come to an end and become repressed. But as we will see in subsequent chapters that this tradition like Freud's Mosaic Legacy would "gradually grow in darkness" in Harlem, the Caribbean, Africa, and Latin America.

However, the progressive spirit of psychoanalysis was killed not just by the systemic forces of anti-Semitism and anti-Marxism on both sides of the Atlantic, as reviewed in the previous chapter—it was also killed by Freud himself. Rudnytsky (2015) reminds us of the split that occurred between Freud and Ferenczi just before the outbreak of World War II, and the subsequent character assassination of Ferenczi by Ernest Jones, who argued he had become psychotic as revealed in his behavior, indulging his "turning away from Freud and his doctrines" (cited in Rudnytsky, 2015, p. 45). Erich Fromm penned a rebuttal to Jones, and set upon an analysis of Freud's relationship to Ferenczi as "the most dramatic example of . . . intolerance and authoritarianism" (cited in p. 68).

Using ideas central to his classic text *Escape from Freedom*, Fromm (1941) explored how Freud's demand for intellectual loyalty set him up as a dominating authority who was to be treated by his infantilized disciples as a "magic helper," an omnipotent authority who must not be questioned. Almost as if drawing from Ferenczi, Fenichel, and even Freud's ideas on the psychology of domination and submission, Fromm (1941) wrote about how the person who

> is dependent on the magic helper also feels, though often unconsciously, enslaved by "him" and, to a greater or lesser degree, rebels against "him." This rebelliousness against the very person on whom one has put one's hopes for security and happiness, creates new conflicts. It has to be suppressed if one is

> not to lose "him," but the underlying antagonism constantly threatens the security sought for in the relationship. (p. 109)

Fromm (1958) showed how underneath the years of friendship and collaboration between Ferenczi and Freud lay a terrible ambivalence—Ferenczi's fear of breaking the taboo against speaking his mind with Freud, and thus losing the relationship. When he finally read Freud his "Confusion of Tongues" paper, his once old friend simply turned away from him without speaking a word, let alone saying goodbye. In the shadow of anti-Semitism and world war, both men would die without any repair.

Rudnytsky (2016) reminds us of Fromm's (1941) distinction in *Escape from Freedom* between a true revolutionary and a "rebel" who seeks "to overcome his own feeling of powerlessness by fighting authority, although the longing for submission remains present, whether consciously or unconsciously" (Fromm, 1941, p. 192). Applying this to Freud, Fromm (1959) argued that he "was a rebel" but "not a revolutionary." The rebel fights authority while desiring *to be* an authority others submit to, failing to "dissolve . . . dependence on and respect for authority per se" (p. 63). The rebel directs their energies against the authorities who do not provide them recognition, while maintaining an identification to authorities of their own choosing, "especially when he becomes one of them" (pp. 63–64). A true revolutionary, by contrast, "is someone who overcomes his ambivalence toward authority because he frees himself from attachment from authority and from the wish to dominate others" (p. 64). According to Fromm, Freud enacted his own internalized ambivalence toward bourgeois, upper-class values by taking a dominating stance toward Ferenczi and other analysts. But this was also a racialized ambivalence. In a terrible twist, Freud could dominate, control, and instill fear in other Jews within his movement.

Freud created a nuanced psychological system for understanding the dynamics of power and control, a system we can use to understand his own enactment of tyrannical power and domination. As the founder of the psychoanalytic movement, now *he* could be the tyrannical father, the strong man beneath whom the band of (Jewish) brothers and sisters could squabble in envy and hatred. Before the broader world, he could play the "game of superiority" and become White (Tate, 1996; cf. with Altman, 2009; Aron & Starr, 2012; Brickman, 2003). In this sense, both Jonte-Pace (2006) and Brickman (2003) are right. Freud *was* a proto-postcolonial theorist rendering a critique of a colonialist, racist, patriarchal society, *and* he also enacted colonial, racist, and cisheterosexist performances that betrayed his identification with the oppressor in each of these terms. In so doing, Freud failed to consistently follow his own psychoanalytic ethics of social justice—he did not renounce brutality and dominating authority in favor of an affective tie with the other. Not consistently at least. By the same token, Fromm shows us how the very psychoanalytic system Freud devised can be used to understand the psychodynamics of power, *including Freud's own identification with (White) power*. Freud's work, then, both provides us with a powerful set of tools for understanding how oppression is internalized within the psyche and enacted against others, *and serves as a warning—Remember*, "You too must love the stranger, for you were strangers in the land of Egypt" (Leviticus 19: 33–34). As Tate (1996) showed in her analysis, this was a symptom of Freud's ever shifting identification between Jewishness, Whiteness, and Blackness.

And so we have to tally with both baby and bath water, with a tradition pierced through the heart with both emancipatory possibilities and bourgeois anti-Blackness. But it was through Freud's wrestling with his historically contingent Blackness and his relationship to Jewishness that he created a system for looking at inner experience that upended European notions of identity, culture, and the self. And in so doing, he found a way of narrativizing the dynamics of oppression that would resonate with other non-White beings trying to find meaning in a world that subjected them to violence. I will argue it was these insights, and the genealogy it set in motion, that laid the foundations for liberation psychology, from Freud to Ferenczi and Fenichel to Fromm, to Fanon to Freire and finally, Martín-Baró.

Chapter Four

"The Possibility of Love"

Black Psychoanalysis from Harlem to Algeria

If even Freud maintained that love is the force that can overcome hatred across race, class, and nation, then post-colonial psychoanalyst Frantz Fanon can be considered a true tragic romantic. "Today I believe in the possibility of love" Fanon (1952) wrote, "that is why I endeavor to trace its imperfections, its perversions" (p. 28). And trace its perversions he did. Using a style and methodology that is at once academic and poetic, Fanon channeled his poetry teacher Aimé Cesaire—Fanon's disagreement with his views on negritude notwithstanding. Cesaire taught that decolonization and liberation were not automatic historically ordained processes, "It is always the result of a struggle, the result of strenuous efforts. Even the most peaceful form of decolonization is always the result of a rupture" (cited in Kebede, 2001, pp. 125–126). A rupture in space and time, a wound in history that will not heal and distorts the humanity of both colonizer and colonized. A rupture that for Fanon, requires a "murderous encounter" in order to be resolved. In the dialectical tension between love and murder we will soon find ourselves in familiar, Ferenczian territory.

This chapter will trace the routes through which psychoanalysis became a tool of anti-racist, post-colonial theorizing, beginning with the liaisons of Black intellectuals and psychoanalytic practitioners during the Harlem Renaissance, and how those relationships, along with those of existentialist and Marxist psychoanalytic thinkers, then flowed into the life and work of Frantz Fanon. In the middle of the chapter I will shift to an analysis of Fanon's work from *Black Skins, White Masks* to *The Wretched of the Earth*, and show how Freud and Ferenczi's insights are either echoed in Fanon or drawn upon directly, further informing this stage of liberation psychology's development.

Given the misunderstanding of Fanon's position on violence, and the dismissal of the role of psychoanalysis and his clinical practice in his thinking, I will spend time unpacking the intersections of each of these areas of his work. The spirit of the lessons we will draw on in this chapter is best captured in the music of hip-hop artist Immortal Technique's "The Harlem Renaissance":

> People of Harlem—they are the natural allies of the oppressed people of the world, whether the struggle is in Panama, in Africa, Cuba. We spend money with the wrong people. We looking for love with people who don't love us. What's wrong with us loving each other and making sure we are protected?

PSYCHOANALYSIS IN HARLEM

In her monograph *Freud Upside Down: African American Literature and Psychoanalytic Culture*, Ahad (2010) reveals how African American writers and intellectuals during the Harlem Renaissance and beyond drew on psychoanalysis in the struggle for racial justice, deploying it "as a way to create a productive space for the expression of black interiority" (p. 3). She notes the interesting liaisons between Otto Rank, French-Cuban essayist Anáis Nin, and poet/writer Nella Larsen. Anáis Nin was the one to introduce Otto Rank—her lover and former therapist—to Harlem. Ahad (2010) relates this entry from Nin's diary: "Rank could not forget Harlem. He was eager to return to it. He could hardly wait to come to the end of his hard day's work. He said: 'I am tempted to prescribe it to my patients. Go to Harlem!'" (p. 39). This history reveals a forgotten intertextuality between psychoanalysis, Latinx and Black subjectivity, and racial justice, one which would follow routes into Fanon's work, and later that of liberation psychology.

Ahad (2010) reviews how "African American writers did not simply appropriate the model and language of psychoanalysis to destabilize conventional, and often inferior, notions of blackness—they relied upon it" (p. 4). Zaretsky (2015), in his study of the role psychoanalysis played in progressive politics, examined its centrality to three periods of African-American and Afro-Caribbean liberation movements, from the Harlem Renaissance of the 1920s, through the Popular Front of the 1930s, and the postcolonial movements for liberation post-World War II. He points out how W. E. B. Du Bois set the stage for Freud's assimilation into African-American culture through his writings on double consciousness, first articulated in *The Souls of Black Folk* (1902). Although his original works were powerfully insightful and presaged psychoanalysis in America, later in life Du Bois wrestled with the fact that racism was not a logical process "based on wide-spread ignorance," concluding he in fact had not been "sufficiently Freudian to understand how little human action is based on reason" (Cited in Zaretsky, 2015, p. 48). Du

Bois wished he could have been *more* Freudian! His exploration of Black interiority and American racism opened the door for later considerations of psychoanalysis, and its relevance to racial justice during the Harlem Renaissance and later post-colonial movements. Rather than finding psychoanalysis to be somehow *alien* to the Black experience, Black writers and intellectuals found themselves reflected in it.

Ahad's (2010) analysis of the New York City periodical *The Messenger*—a key influencer of the Harlem Renaissance—shows the extent to which psychoanalysis was deployed as a Black counter-discourse to American racialist ideology. In its pages, the *Messenger* articulated a "coloured psychoanalysis" seeking to reconcile psychoanalytic, African-American, and socialist thinking. "For a community of people who were bound by the politics of the exterior," Ahad writes, "psychoanalysis served the desire of many African American writers and scholars who sought to promote the psychological depth of the black subject" (p. 16). Ahad is cognizant of how psychoanalysis contributed to discourses of primitivity, yet draws attention to how "black subjects used psychoanalysis as a counterdiscursive method to assert a psychologically superior subjectivity" (p. 16). We should notice the historical irony, that in many respects this parallels Freud's own project to create a counter-discourse to anti-Semitism via psychoanalysis, asserting a "psychologically superior subjectivity" in the Jews' ability to resist oppression while nurturing a preference for intellectual and "interior" pursuits. The project of integrating psychoanalysis and socialist thought is similarly interesting given how the majority of early psychoanalysts were themselves socialists, Marxists, communists, and social democrats. Equally notable is how Black writers used psychoanalysis to subvert stereotypes of Blackness and Black people as excessively sexual, aggressive, criminal, chaotic—the very same terms deployed against Jews in fin-de-siecle Europe, terms which emerged from the White-Aryan fantasy of their relationship to Africa and Blackness.

The Harlem Renaissance gave us unsung heroes of psychoanalysis who crafted novel ways of thinking psychoanalytically about race, such as Floyd Calvin and his "coloured psychoanalysis," or William Pickens and his theorizing on the "racial unconscious." Pickens in particular theorized that "whites had repressed their historical memory of amity with blacks," arguing that a super-ego "watch-dog" stood between conscious hatred and unconscious libido (love), dissociating affective ties to their fellow humans based on the color of their skin, replacing them with "abnormal behaviors, such as mob violence and lynching" (Ahad, 2010, p. 28). Biracial novelist Nella Larsen, an avid reader of Freud and Rank, engaged in psychoanalytic meditations on biracial subjectivity, holding the tension between different worlds, and finding community as a biracial subject. Through creative reinventions and applications, "postwar psychoanalysis was imagined as an 'emancipatory therapy' that could effectively articulate and respond to the psychological crisis of the African American experience" (p. 83).

Ralph Waldo Ellison and Richard Wright presented perhaps the clearest example of this vision. In Wright's "Psychiatry comes to Harlem" and Ellison's "Harlem Is Nowhere," both published in *The Messenger*, they argued that psychoanalysis "was the most effective methodology available to interpret and explain the prevalence of mental illness and social deviance within black communities" (Ahad, 2010, p. 83). Ellison and Wright, in collaboration with psychoanalytic psychiatrist Fredric Wertham, opened the Lafargue Mental Hygiene Clinic in 1946. Reflecting yet another integration of Black thought, Marxism, and psychoanalysis, the clinic was named after Marx's son-in-law, the Afro-Cuban socialist Paul Lafargue. Echoing the spirit of Freud's free clinics, treatments were provided at a low fee, "but if a patients lacks this, it is waived," wrote Wright (1946) "anyone may literally walk in off the streets and tell his troubles" (p. 51). Wright clarified that the coming of psychiatry to Harlem was not some act of charity, but rather

> it is the extension of the very concept of psychiatry into a new realm, the application of psychiatry to the masses, the turning of Freud upside down. The Clinic has found that the most consistent therapeutic aid that it can render Harlem's mentally ill is instilling in them what Wertham calls "the will to survive in a hostile world"; that the many Negroes sink under their loads because of hopelessness, social fear, worry, frustration, and just plain hunger. (p. 51)

Wertham, Wright, and Ellison's collaboration on a Black, Marxist, and psychoanalytic project was also informed by Wertham's background as a psychoanalytically oriented psychiatrist. Given how his work is often associated with moralistic fearmongering about comic books (Beaty, 2005), some words about his involvement with Wright and Ellison are in order.

Born to a middle-class Jewish family from Nuremberg, Germany in 1895, Wertham had a personal correspondence with Freud during medical school and later visited him in Vienna in 1922. Freud was impressed with the young physician's enthusiasm for psychoanalysis, and encouraged him in his choice of psychiatry as a career. Wertham later moved to America, where he—like Fromm—became increasingly critical of the conservative turn in psychoanalysis (Beaty, 2005, pp. 24–25). "We psychoanalysts who wish to guard the true heritage of Freud and develop in a truly progressive manner," Wertham wrote, "do not visualize the future scientific development of psychoanalysis in terms of a formalistic allegiance to dogmatic doctrine as it stands" (cited in Beaty, 2005, p. 25). Upon his move to New York City in 1932 his writing took a significant turn to the left, in part due to his forensic work in the court system. He wrote about the lack of communal and safety net support for single mothers penalized by a patriarchal and misogynist society, and drew attention to how psychiatry became invested in rendering class and racial inequality invisible (Beaty, 2005, p. 44).

Wertham engaged in recurrent psychoanalytic commentary on segregation and anti-Black and anti-Puerto Rican racism, writing an insightful historical, psychodynamic, and socio-economic analysis of Puerto Rico's colonial situation, as well as participating in the landmark *Brown v. Board of Education* Supreme Court decision in 1954 (Beaty, 2005, p. 91; see Wertham, 1955). Although his long-term goal was to write an opus on Marx and Freud, he wrote an incisive analysis of fascism and colonialism as symptoms of capitalism (Wertham, 1966). Hence, in citing Wertham's assertion that psychoanalytic therapy instills "the will to survive in a hostile world" (p. 51), Richard Wright's "Psychiatry Comes to Harlem" renders a striking similarity to Freud's (1919) call in "Lines of Advance" for outpatient clinics to help the poor become "capable of resistance" (p. 167), applying "psychiatry to the masses" to create a "psychotherapy for the people."

Born in 1908 at Rucker's Plantation by Natchez, Mississippi, Wright and his family experienced what it was like growing up in the Jim Crow South. Wright's parents were born free, whereas his grandparents had been born slaves until after the end of the American Civil War. For a period of time, there was the hope that African-Americans could be socially, economically, and politically integrated into American society, as Blacks received hard-fought enfranchisement through universal (though male) suffrage, and winning election into state and federal legislatures. With reconstruction, however, came a visceral backlash, as "black codes" were enacted to force African-Americans into low wage or debt slave labor, and the Ku Klux Klan arose to reinstate daily and public White Supremacy. The economic and social oppression of Black people led Wright as an adult to join the Great Migration to the North, seeking greater economic opportunities. Wright would run in Black Socialist circles in Chicago and later New York City, as well as develop an appetite for psychoanalytic thinking. Tuhkanen (2009) notes the influence of psychoanalytic writers on Wright beyond his association with Wertham, as reflected in the texts he kept in his library among them books by Karl Abraham, Helene Deutsch, Otto Fenichel, Sandor Ferenczi, Anna Freud, Sigmund Freud, Ernest Jones, Melanie Klein, Theodor Reik, and Geza Roheim—attest to his familiarity with psychoanalysis. According to one biographer, Wright combined Marx with Freud in order to discuss the social and historical basis of mental illness to combat biological and deterministic explanations of African-Americans supposed proneness to hysteria. For Wright, this bias reflected White people's "blind inability" to understand the psychology of the Negro (Zaretsky, 2015). His contemporary Horace Cayton explored how structural racism breeds fear as a predominant and guiding affect for African-Americans navigating their lives in the United States. Racial inequality similarly generates a mirror fear in the form of an "oppressor's psychosis" among White people, in which they fear retribution from oppressed people of color for the violence they have subjected them to. Cayton, who himself was an analysand of Helen McLean, arranged for Wright to deliver a lecture at the Chicago Institute on the use of psychoanalysis to shed light on the dynamics of fear and hate among African-Americans (Zaretsky, 2015, p. 58).

Born in 1914 to a homemaker and a small business owner in Oklahoma City, Ralph Waldo Ellison suffered the loss of his father at an early age to a freak accident. Like Wright, Ellison's mother moved north with her children seeking better living conditions and a future for their family. As a young adult Ellison enrolled in the Tuskegee Institute, which proved an ambivalent experience for him as was both exposed to literature that sharpened his writing style and voice as well as a class-conscious elitism that seemed to go against racial solidarity. It was in New York City where he would meet his best friend and kindred spirit Richard Wright in 1937, who introduced him to Marxist and communist activist circles. But it was a year earlier that Ellison kindled an interest in psychoanalysis.

Ellison's immersion in psychoanalytic thought was facilitated by his relationship with psychoanalyst Harry Stack Sullivan, for whom he worked as a clerk in his private practice in 1936. Sullivan, an American-born son of Irish immigrants who self-identified as gay, had heard Ferenczi speak at a meeting of the American Psychoanalytic Association in 1926, and participated as a discussant of one of his papers a year later in Washington, D.C. Sullivan had become infatuated with Ferenczi's thinking, urging his dear colleague and friend Clara Thompson to go to Budapest to study with him. Interested in Ferenczi herself, she undertook the trip in the summer of 1928, entering into analysis with him for two months—a ritual she would repeat with Ferenczi over the next two years (Hoffman, 2003). When Thompson would return to New York after each summer, she shared what she learned with Sullivan, as Hoffman (2003) notes, "in an unusual way"—she psychoanalyzed him using Ferenczi's style and technique. Like Ferenczi, Sullivan and Thompson believed psychoanalysis revealed "the real conditions in the various levels of society . . . just as they are mirrored in the individual" and that it could help address the impact of poverty and inequality in both psyche and society (Hoffman, 2003). Thompson would integrate Ferenczi, Sullivan, and Erich Fromm's thinking in her own interpersonal-cultural model of psychoanalysis, as well as develop a more emancipatory view of gender and women's experience. She, together with Sullivan and Fromm, would found the William Alanson White Institute in New York City in 1942.

The influence of Ferenczi's thinking and clinical style on Sullivan can be gleaned from his relationship with Ellison. Rampersad (2007), an Ellison biographer, relates how Sullivan asked Ellison to read excerpts from a book he was writing, the White psychoanalyst consulting with the Harlem Renaissance novelist "to vouch for the clarity of his prose" (p. 84). Ellison and Sullivan enjoyed having lunch together and talking about literature, culture, psychoanalysis, and art. Ellison later reflected, "I was encouraged to talk about myself . . . and under his quiet questioning I learned to relax and talk quite freely" (cited in Rampersad, 2007, p. 84). As a White man in a racist society, Sullivan's ability to mentalize and hold a safe space for Ellison allowed him to build trust and connect, and through that connection, mutually enrich one another. Ellison's employment with Sullivan also exposed him to the integration of sociology and psychoanalysis—Sullivan had interests in the social and cultural implications of psychoanalysis—leaving Ellison "curious as to how one could put Freud and Marx together" (cited in Ahad, 2010, p. 102).

After these liaisons both men would go on to engage in psychoanalytically informed work on race and racism. Sullivan (1940; 1941) would conduct a series of psychoanalytically informed studies on the impact of racial segregation on the emotional and educational well-being of Black youth in the south. As mentioned above Ellison went on to collaborate with Wright and Wertham in the development of the La Fargue Clinic and a Black Marxist and psychoanalytic perspective. Ellison had a keen understanding of "the blind spot in our knowledge of society where Marx cries out for Freud and Freud for Marx" (cited in Doane, 2004, p. 162), balancing a dialectic between understanding African-Americans' psychological depth and sociological context. By reading Freud's theory of hysteria in the context of Jim Crow, Ellison in his essay "Harlem Is Nowhere" suggested that perceived psychiatric disorder among African Americans "mask deeper intellectual energies that are repressed due to southern law" (Ahad, 2010, p. 98). Blacks who apperceive the irrational inequality which places them in a "lesser than" position were deemed at-risk for the classical symptoms of hysteria—repressing and dissociating the feelings that result from oppressive circumstances becomes necessary for survival. By lifting the repression that restricted the critical and intellectual energies of African Americans, Ellison identified "psychoanalysis as a form of therapy that . . . liberates the individual from the shackles of a degraded social position" (Ahad, 2010, p. 99). This idea, that oppression restricts the critical use of the intellect, including a critical consciousness of one's position within society, is conversant with Freud's own theorizing in *The Future of an Illusion* (1927).

These liaisons between intellectuals of color and White psychoanalysts form a missing link in psychoanalysis' cultural history, as well as an oft-ignored chapter in the history of liberation psychology. This link would be crystallized in a "fan letter" (Ahad, 2010) from one of Richard Wright's most famous Afro-Caribbean fans, often recognized as Freud's "most disputatious heir" (Said, 2003).

FREUD IN THE CARIBBEAN: FRANTZ FANON'S PSYCHOANALYTIC HERITAGE

Richard Wright and other members of the Harlem Renaissance engaged deeply with psychoanalytic ideas in their analysis of race, racism, and racial identity, ironically keeping "Freud moving" by turning him "right side up." This dialogue between African-American Blackness and the dynamics of interiority drew the attention of an eager young psychiatrist and psychoanalyst from the Caribbean, who wrote Wright an earnest, enthusiastic letter in 1953. This young psychiatrist, Frantz Fanon, gushed over Wright's novels *Native Son*, *Black Boy*, and *Twelve Million Black Voices*, noting the influence they had on his postcolonial theorizing. Ahad (2010) noted the dialogue and "symbiosis" this created between Black intellectual thought and psychoanalysis. Zaretsky (2015) refers to this as the third form Freudian thought took within Blackness and Black psychopolitical discourse, which he dubbed "the Freud of the Black Atlantic" (p. 63).

Fanon was born in 1925 to a middle-class Martinican family in the French West Indies. Raised in a colonial context, the young Fanon taught himself French history, and later became a student of Aimé Césaire, who taught him poetry in high school and introduced him to the negritude movement (Nicholls, 2015). He left the colony in 1943 at 18 to fight with the French army during World War II, where he first experience institutionalized racism despite fighting for the French motherland. After the war, he enrolled in the school of medicine at the University of Lyon. Fanon experienced the charged political climate at the university, witnessing worker strikes taking place during that time, while also bearing witness to day-to-day racism. These experiences left an impact on the young Fanon, who would go on to chronicle the psycho-existential crisis he suffered in *Black Skins, White Masks*, a project that proved both intellectual and therapeutic for Fanon (Bulhan, 1985). In his attempt to make sense of the persistent attacks and exclusion he suffered as a Black man, as a French citizen relegated to "second class" status by virtue of racism and colonialism, Fanon initially drew on the influence of Cesaire's negritude movement. When Cesaire later advocated for the total integration of Martinique with France, rather than committing to the independence movement, Fanon turned to existential-psychoanalytic thinker Jean-Paul Sartre, who argued that negritude seemed to subject itself to the authority of White domination (Bulhan, 1985).

Fanon and Sartre would later start a friendship, which was recorded by Sartre's intellectual collaborator and partner, Simone de Beauvoir. The three once met for lunch, starting a conversation that lasted until two in the morning (Bulhan, 1985, p. 31). Sartre and de Beauvoir's brand of socially critical and existential psychoanalysis would prove fruitful to Fanon's thinking on colonization and identity. Negritude's position of discovering an idyllic, positive, and idealized Black identity in the past then seemed like posturing for him—a positive image to contrast with a negative one, rather than a wrestling with the fissures of identity as such.

Fanon graduated from Lyons as a psychiatrist in 1951. His training in psychoanalytic theory and practice would place him in a lineage of mentors going back to the first generation of psychoanalysts. During his psychiatric residency in Saint Alban, France, he was exposed to the Catalan-born Marxist psychiatrist Francois de Tosquelles, who pioneered the idea of "socio-analysis," emphasizing the role of cultural and communal life on psychopathology (Zaretsky, 2015, p. 69). Originally from Catalonia, Spain, de Tosquelles was exposed to Marx at an early age, and would become an ardent supporter of Catalan nationalism and independence. After graduating as a medical doctor in 1927, de Tosquelles completed his psychiatric residency with Emilio Mira y Lopez in Reus at the Institute Pere Mata (Macey, 2012, p. 143). Mira y Lopez, born in Cuba in 1896 though raised in Catalonia after the revolution, began his career as a psychometric researcher, later adopting psychoanalysis and practicing it therapeutically based on his reading of Freud (Diaz-R. Labajo, 2016; Garcia, 2014). Even without "formal" psychoanalytic training, Mira y Lopez was considered by his peers a psychoanalyst, conducting a series of studies interpreting Freud's writings within a Spanish and Latin American context (Garcia, 2014; Sanchez Lazaro, 1986), as well as quantitative studies of the impact of social and economic inequality on mental health (Mira y Lopez, 1937). A leftist and anarchist, he encouraged de Tosquelle to take courses in Freud and Marx during his training (Basauri, 1997, p. 234). It was through his residency at the Institute Pere Mata that Tosquelle came into contact with Jewish refugees from Germany and Hungary who were influenced by Freud and Ferenczi (Zeilig, 2016, p. 43).

Among those refugees then operating at the Institute was one of Mira y Lopez's colleagues, a Hungarian psychoanalyst named Sandor Eiminder. Eiminder was a pediatrician who had worked with August Aichorn—an educator turned psychoanalyst—and Freud's circle in Vienna. Prior to that, however, Eiminder was a student of Sandor Ferenczi interested in developing innovative treatments for patients with borderline and psychotic experiences (Berti et al., 2012, footnote 23; Basauri, 1997, p. 235; Delion, 2014, p. 22). Tosquelles would enter into psychoanalysis with Eiminder from 1931 to 1935, during which time he also started leading an evening seminar on Marx and Freud, as well as take part in a study group reading Jacques Lacan's thesis (Macey, 2012, p. 144). The presence of Hungarian psychoanalysts taking refuge in Reus, as well as being in analysis with Eiminder, exposed de Tosquelles to Ferenczi's work (Garcia Siso, 1993, p. 199). In his clinical writing, Tosquelles would show an interest in Ferenczi's trauma-informed approach and his concept of introjection (De Macedo, 2019, footnote 24).

Mira y Lopez would later join the Spanish Republican army as a medical doctor during the Spanish Civil War, while de Tosquelle would become part of the Partido Obrero de Unificación Marxista (Workers Party for Marxist Unification), throwing themselves in what would become "Europe's first armed struggle (and revolution) against fascism" (Zeilig, 2016, p. 44). Both men would become refugees—Mira y Lopez fled to Cuba and later Argentina, de Tosquelles to France—after Franco's victory (Garcia, 2014; Zeilig, 2016). After the Civil War, Tosquelles would flee on foot through the Pyrenees, hoping to join his wife and children on the other side of the border, carrying nothing but light luggage and "his prized copy of Lacan's thesis" (Macey, 2012, p. 145). After World War II, de Tosquelles would establish himself as the chief psychiatrist at Saint Alban, which had served as a haven for both resistance fighters and people rendered outcast due to their race or political background. It was here that Tosquelles began experimenting with his socio-psychoanalytic methods, maintaining that making the psychiatric unit a liberatory space in turn helped liberate the world. It would be here that he would train Fanon and build a relationship with him.

The psychiatrist Nicole Guillet recalls that after introducing the two men, they were at times prone to "loud and at times angry exchange of views" (Macey, 2012, p. 147). This passionate encounter between de Tosquelles and Fanon belied the deep kinship the two would develop over their shared experience of marginality. In Ferenczian fashion, de Tosquelle listened empathically as Fanon shared his experiences of racism, telling of how one night while walking in Lyon with his fiancée, who happened to be White, he was arrested by the police on suspicion of trafficking White women (Zeilig, 2016, p. 46). De Tosquelle could never know what it was like to be a Black man in a racist society. He could only extend his empathy to Fanon based on his own experience of marginality as a Catalan man. As Harper (2012) put it, "The theme of refugee, exile and outsider transfers itself, via the lived ritual enactment of analysis, from Freud to Fanon in the analysis of Tosquelles by Eiminder and mentorship of Fanon" (p. 184). The senior psychiatrist was impressed with his pupil's knowledge, scholarship, and commitment to reforming society and psychological practices:

> We were in the capital of Lozere, Mende, one evening, with people concerned by culture, and by extension, with the issue of madness. We talked about the importance of space, and certain spaces. What is the space of madness? And Fanon was moved to speak and develop the theme with the aid, take note, of certain cultural texts: specifically the space of tragedy. This was not a topic touched upon by the literature . . . [Fanon asked] What were the professional limits of action for psychiatrists? Where do we practice such action in regard to mental hygiene, even therapy? . . . Fanon' life was consumed with this. (Tosquelles, 2007, p. 225, my translation)

After completing his residency with de Tosquelles in France, Fanon finished his studies back in the Caribbean in 1953, and after a brief placement in Paris finally accepted a position as chief of staff for the psychiatric unit of the Blida-Joinville Hospital in Algeria (North Africa). The following year the Algerian revolution erupted under the leadership of the *Front de Libération Nationale* (FLN). As a faculty member at a French hospital, Fanon was responsible for treating both civilians victimized by the conflict, and soldiers and officers of the French army.

Fanon drew on a full array of interventions as a practicing psychiatrist, combining psychopharmacology with individual and group therapy. Gibson and Beneduce (2017) researched the clinical theory Fanon drew on as a therapist, offering translations of his clinical work with the aid of Lisa Damon. They cite a clinical paper by Fanon and Geronimi in which they advocated avoiding "as far as possible, assaulting the patient's consciousness" (cited in Gibson & Beneduce, 2017, p. 211). Echoing de Tosquelle and Ferenczi, the hospital would be a safe place of healing in which the patient's narrativization of their trauma would prove possible, emphasizing the telling of one's story in group therapy. In telling their story in a group setting, patients "demonstrate, comment on, and gain awareness of their own responses to conflict, provoking the listeners to take a position, offer criticism and express reservations" while at the same time inviting the patient to explore the thoughts and feelings behind their behavior, "thereby prioritizing the use of reason over phantasmatic and imaginary attitudes" (cited in Gibson & Beneduce, 2017, p. 211). In essence, Fanon was helping patients exchange different perspectives with one another as a way of helping them mentalize about their experience. I will expand further on mentalization and its psychological and political implications in Chapter 6.

Alice Cherki (2006), a psychoanalyst and psychiatrist who worked alongside Fanon in Blida and later in Tunis, noted how he re-engaged psychoanalytic thinking in what she called "his return to Freud," reading Melanie Klein as well as Sandor Ferenczi (Gibson & Beneduce, 2017, p. 211). Fanon discovered Ferenczi's work in a bookstore in Tunis, and became fascinated with the latter's ideas around trauma, war, and violence (Cherki, 2006, p. 118). Cherki recalled that Fanon would be "on the look out for people who could translate Ferenczi's other works" (cited in Gibson & Beneduce, 2017, p. 214). She (2006) relates her reading of an unpublished case study written by Fanon, which revealed "his command of psychoanalytic theory and his understanding of the workings of the unconscious as well as his acute intuition" (p. 120). In this case report, Fanon described an intensive five session a week treatment of a 27-year-old patient, in which he paid exquisite attention to the patient's defenses, slips of the tongue, and shifts in affect. However, he initially experienced intense discomfort with the transference, and with his role as a second subjectivity in the room. Fanon initially side-stepped the patient's yearnings, "I would have liked you to be my father" by redirecting him to focus on childhood memories, or by proclaiming, "I cannot be your father, I am your doctor," maintaining an impasse in the therapeutic relationship. Likely with inspiration from Ferenczi, with time Fanon allowed himself to be more vulnerable in the transference and engage his patient's feelings—Cherki (2006) tells us that, "The young man in question made incredible progress. As did Fanon" (p. 121).

Fanon's shift to an interactive, relational approach helped him to grow more comfortable with the counter-transference. Gibson and Beneduce (2017) identify this shift in his clinical writing as well, with Fanon's turn to "the importance of cultivating the body as a means of avoiding anxiety" (Fanon & Geronimi, 1959, p. 723, cited in Gibson & Beneduce, 2017, p. 212). Fanon identified building of self-awareness by putting thoughts and feelings into words, having an empathic other explore one's internal state, and increasing the capacity for action (all components of mentalization) as core goals of psychotherapy. How this was accomplished was grounded in a psychodynamic, relational encounter. In Corcoran's translation Ferenczi's influence is even more explicit, "In the psychoanalytic treatment, we practice *appeasement*, we foster fantasy reconstruction and, as a rule, adopt an active attitude in Ferenczi's sense" (Fanon & Geronimi, 1959, pp. 506–507; cf. Gibson & Beneduce, 2017, p. 213). Note again, for Fanon as for Ferenczi "appeasement" or "indulgence" was not a mere "giving in" to the patient, but opening the space toward a distinct freedom which is vulnerable, open, and receptive to them.

Gibson and Beneduce (2017) review Ferenczi's concerns with the body as a site of trauma, as well as his ethics toward the Other, which "resonated with what Fanon understood as a first principle of Tosquellean sociotherapy; that is, to break down the hierarchies inherent in doctor-patient relationships" (p. 214). One could just as easily see this as the first principle of Ferenczian psychotherapy! Echoing a similar thought process, Alice Cherkin, in a foreword to Gibson and Beneduce's text, noted how for Fanon the hospital is meant to be a space where the patient may "finally feel understood" rather than re-traumatized (Fanon & Asselah, 1957, p. 22, cited in Gibson & Beneduce, 2017, p. xi). Fanon's adoption of a Ferenczian sensibility "left space for the possibility that the caregiver-patient relationship could be an encounter of two freedoms" (Cherki, in Gibson & Beneduce, 2017, p. xi). But Fanon's encounter with Ferenczi was more than clinical—it also had clear implications for the transformation of societal and political systems. In a manner that would resonate with Fanon's post-colonial psychoanalysis for liberation, Cherkin recalled how "To this day, former nurses who worked with 'Dr. Fanon' at Blida-Joinville Hospital in Algeria, still remark on their change of status: they stopped being repressive guards, and became instead active agents in their relationship with the alienated person" (in Gibson & Beneduce, 2017, p. xii).

After treating military personnel who carried out torture against Algerian citizens and freedom fighters, Fanon realized he could no longer be complicit with the French. In 1956 Fanon resigned his position at Blida. In his resignation letter to the chief resident, Fanon (1964) recognized that, "If psychiatry is the medical technique that aims to enable man no longer to be a stranger to his environment, I owe it to myself to affirm that the Arab, permanently an alien in his own country, lives in a state of absolute depersonalization" (p. 53). Similarly, he argued that the purpose of society and its institutions is to help people meet their emotional and material needs. Echoing Freud's injunction "that a civilization which leaves so large a number of its participants unsatisfied and drives them into revolt neither has nor deserves the prospect of a lasting existence" (1927, p. 12), Fanon proclaimed that, "A society that drives its members to desperate solutions is a non-viable society, a society to be replaced" (1964, p. 53). No longer able to be a bystander, Fanon joined the Algerian revolution.

Ahad (2010) and Zaretsky (2015) traced a genealogy of Black, existential, and psychoanalytic thought influencing Fanon, from Sullivan and Wertham to Richard Wright to Stuart Hall to James Baldwin, and from Jean-Paul Sartre, and Simone de Beauvoir, to Albert Memmi and Octave Mannoni—and I also add Freud, Ferenczi, Mari y Lopez, Eiminder, and de Tosquelle. Fanon wrote in direct response to his intellectual antecedents and ancestors. "Diverse though they were," Zaretsky (2015) writes,

> the long-term result of their labors was one of the great paradigms of the postwar world: the antagonistic self/other relations of domination exemplified by the anti-Semite and the Jew (Sartre), colonier/colonized (Fanon, Memmi, Mannoni), sexism (Beauvoir), knowing subject/object of knowledge (Foucault), racism (Stuart Hall), and orientalism (Edward Said). (p. 64)

Each of these thinkers built on a psychoanalytic tradition of critical reflection on psyche and society that began with Freud and the first generation of psychoanalysts, each one a tributary flowing into the river of liberation psychology. Fanon drew on this tradition in order to examine the "inferiority complex" suffered by colonized peoples, and how this "complex" results in "explosions" of both hatred and liberation.

Black Skin, White Masks: A Psychoanalysis of Colonization

In his first book, *Black Skin, White Masks* (1952), Fanon believed that only a psychoanalytic perspective (p. 3) can shed light on the distortions of self, affect and other that maintain racist, colonialist systems. Psychoanalysis for Fanon is concerned with language as a phenomenon providing a link to *the other*—the other person, the sociological other, the other of the unconscious—the act of what is said and left unsaid as an existence *for* the other (p. 8). The Black person and the colonized are forced into a relation of domination to the White man, the colonizer, the titular subject of Western civilization. This relation breeds a desire within the Black man exist for Whiteness and to become White—taking on the colonizer's language, mannerisms, while also lusting to sleep with a White woman as an act of revenge. Just as the Black man desires to be White in order to be human, the White man enslaves to achieve humanity. Akin to Dubois' double consciousness, Fanon diagnoses two dimensions to Black subjectivity—a self that conducts itself with other colonized people, and a self that lives for the White man, a split produced by social and pseudo-scientific discourses that defines Black people in a regressed stage in human evolution (p. 8). Fanon identifies the *scala naturae* of the Caribbean, with Whiteness and Europe at the top, with humanity defined by one's relative closeness to Whiteness—whether by adopting the colonizer's language, or bearing lighter skin. This hierarchy is as much bodily as it is geographic and national, a literal body politic defined by the relationship of center-periphery, civilizing nations and subjugated colonies.

This hierarchy and its associated body-maps are swallowed whole by the oppressed, who play this violence off against one another in a race to the top—or more properly, the bottom. Fanon (1952) describes this dynamic within his Caribbean context, noting how Black people from Antilles are irritated when there are suspected of being Senegalese, as if Afro-Caribbean people were somehow more civilized than Africans. He also shared a conversation with a fellow Martinican who expressed with resentment how Blacks from Guadeloupe were trying to "pass" as Martinicans. His friend scoffed at how their "passing" would be discovered due to how more savage Guadeloupans were than Martinicans, "which, again, means they are farther away from the white man" (p. 15). The narrative of "White is right" bleeds over into family and relationships with the credo "Whiten the race, save the race," familiar among Latinx Caribbean and Latin American cultures as "*mejorar la raza*"—improve the race. Fanon clearly identifies how colonized and oppressed people internalize this identification with the values of the oppressor. Ever present in his work is how the oppressed also internalize an idealized identification with the *position* of the oppressor.

"Affect is exacerbated in the Negro," Fanon (1952) writes, "he is full of rage because he feels small" (p. 35), isolated within the contours of his mind, unable to break free of the yoke that burdens them. The Negro feels small because of the profound humiliation they experience at the hand of Whiteness, locked into an eternal cycle of shame and self-contempt. This cycle is accompanied by gaslighting that invalidates one's experience of racism—if you are loved, you are told that it is *despite* your color, and if hated, told that it is *not* because of your color (p. 72).

In ways that foreshadowed his prescription for the toxic effect of shame and rage in *Wretched of the Earth* (1963), Fanon (1952) tells the story of a Black medical student who had an "*agonizing* conviction" that he would not be accepted by his White patients and colleagues. In despair, he would be driven to drink to quell his pain, until one day, he decided to enlist in the army as a medical officer. The doctor turned officer refused to be assigned to one of the colonies or serve in a "colonial unit" alongside other Black soldiers, as he desired to have white men serve under him in his unit. Fanon writes that as an officer this Black man commanded fear and respect to fulfill his wish, "to make white men adopt a Negro attitude toward him. In this way he was obtaining revenge for the *imago* that had always obsessed him: the frightened, trembling Negro, abased before the white overlord" (p. 43).

The agony this man suffered made him desire a *reversal* of his social world, one in which it would be *he* who was in command of White men, *he* would be the one to denigrate and control, *he* would amass power and capital. Fanon referred to this desire, a symptom of internalized oppression, as a "poison" that contaminates the psyche of the marginalized and must be expunged. Depending on where we read Fanon, it would seem that such a poison could only be cancelled with another poison.

This poison distorts the bonds of love (Benjamin, 1988), turning them into chains of domination in which Black people are alienated from Blackness, the colonized from their own cultural identity, and exploited in their relation to capital. In the gaping lack left behind by the wound of colonialism, there is a yearning to fill it with the desire and recognition of Whiteness. Fanon devotes much ink to the Black man's desire for recognition in the arms of the White woman. Revealing the influence of Aime Cesaire's poetics, Fanon writes about this desire with the cadence and pain of poetry:

> Out of the blackest part of my soul, across the zebra striping of my mind, surges this desire to be suddenly *white* . . .
> . . . who but a white woman can do this for me? By loving me she proves that I am worthy of white love. I am loved like a white man.
> I am a white man . . .
> I marry white culture, white beauty, white whiteness. When my restless hands caress those white breasts, they grasp white civilization and dignity and make them mine.
> (1952, p. 45)

In the realm of oppression and interracial love, Fanon lifts up the case of Jean Veneuse, whom he sees as "the crusader of the inner life" (p. 57) in his yearnings for White women and Whiteness, while he treats Mayotte Capecia—with her yearning for the love of White men—as an object of lust, lost in passion. Fanon's idealization of Black male subjectivity and his quest for recognition stands in contrast to his dismissal and denigration of Black female subjectivity. Of the woman of color he writes, in effect, "I know nothing about her" (p. 138). We will return to this contradiction in Fanon later on.

For now, it is important to recognize that it too stands in contrast to another trend in his work. Fanon argues that Jean Veneuse's idealization of Whiteness is understandable, given the hierarchy created to elevate it. In this sense, for Fanon, Jean Veneuse is trying to rise to the white man's level. Fanon posits, however, that another solution to the complex of race is possible, one which would necessitate "a restructuring of the world" (p. 60). The colonized cannot aspire to be like the Anglo-Patriarchal master and sit at his table. The table itself must be dismantled—not simply flipped upside down.

Fanon engages Sartre's existential-psychoanalytic reflections on anti-Semitism, who noted that Jews become "poisoned" by the stereotypes society projects upon them. For the colonized Negro as for the colonized Jew, Fanon argues that shame and self-contempt lock them in an "infernal cycle" in which they experience rejection and marginalization from both the White-Aryan world, and from their peers. Citing Sartre's argument that anti-Semitism in a sense makes or creates the Jew it so hates, Fanon argues that it is the racist that creates the Black and the Jew into the lesser than (p. 69). In dialogue with the Jewish experience, Fanon recalls his philosophy professor, a man of the Antilles, who said: "Whenever you hear anyone abuse the Jews, pay attention, because he is talking about you." Reflecting on his mentor's words Fanon realized that "an anti-Semite is inevitably anti-Negro" (p. 92). Echoing Fenichel, the Black man and the Jewish man for Fanon share a basic commonality as scapegoats who stand in for what is evil, "The black man more so, for the good reason that he is black" (p. 139). Fanon relates a story where in New York, Simone de Beauvoir went for a walk with Richard Wright, only to be harassed in the street for being a White woman accompanied by a Black man. Fanon summons Sartre anew: whether the hated object is the Jew or the person of color, the scapegoat is essential to the functioning of a capitalist, anti-Black system.

It is here that we come across another symptom of this system that poison's Fanon and his text. Referring to the White man's fault for committing violence, his guilt, refusal of guilt, and paranoia toward the other, Fanon writes that when one recognizes that what has been said about the Jew applies perfectly to the Black man, "one is back in homosexual territory" (p. 141). Similarly, he writes, "the Negrophobic man is a repressed homosexual" (p. 131). Subtly, Fanon comes to identify the position of the oppressor with a kind of repressed homosexuality, something he clearly sees as pathological. This turn in his writing seeks to denigrate the White man as degenerate through an association with homosexuality as a denigrated identity. Somewhere it *is* the Jew, somewhere else it *is* the Black man—here it is the homosexual. I will comment on this turn in Fanon's thought further below.

THE CURE OF PSYCHOANALYSIS: AGGRESSION, ACTIVISM, AND CATHARSIS

Fanon (1952) saw activism as a psychoanalyst or psychoanalytic practitioner to infer action at both the individual and collective level. To help his Black patient is to make him "*conscious* of his unconscious and abandon his attempts at a hallucinatory whitening" (p. 74). When confronted with the call of acculturation, "*turn white or disappear*," the goal is to help the oppressed, colonized person to "take cognizance," or we might say in contemporary terms, *concientizar* or *mentalize* the possibility of existence. When the unconscious desire to "change color" by assimilating to the logic of the oppressor is made conscious, Fanon's objective shifts to "put him in a position to *choose* action (or passivity) with respect to the real source of the conflict" (p. 75), the system of inequality itself.

But this act of individual liberation is inert without the power of a collective affective experience (Fanon, 1952, p. 112). What this looks like between *Black Skin, White Masks* and *The Wretched of the Earth* changes dramatically, as we will see. But in 1952 Fanon, like Freud before him (see Chapter 3), discusses how every society or collective needs an outlet to release the aggression accumulated due to violence, inequality, and oppression. The identification with the oppressor serves as precisely that outlet for aggression. He gives the example of Black schoolchildren in the Antilles of his time, who identified with the white man as an explorer who civilizes the savages,

> There is identification—that is, the young Negro subjectively adopts a white man's attitude. He invests the hero, who is white, with all his own aggression—at that age closely linked to sacrificial dedication, a sacrificial dedication permeated with sadism. (p. 114)

This identification with the oppressor becomes a vehicle for the oppressed's own aggression. By attempting to idealize the Black identity that had formerly been denigrated, this pathway results in an attempt to reverse the polarities of good/White, bad/Black. Otherwise, the oppressed internalize their aggression until it destroys them from the inside, making them disappear. He sees both of these choices as the result of a "neurotic situation, in which I am compelled to choose an unhealthy, conflictual solution, fed on fantasies, hostile, inhuman" (p. 153).

In 1952, Fanon argued there was only one solution to the impasse between sadist activity and subjugated passivity: "to reject the two terms that are equally unacceptable, and, through one human being, to reach out for the universal" (p. 153). This involves a risk on the part of the oppressed, a risk taken with the end goal of breaking the vicious cycle of oppressor and oppressed—"to restore to the other [the oppressor], through mediation and recognition, his human reality" (p. 169). An act of challenge and recognition by the oppressed restores the humanity the oppressor has surrendered through brutality. In this same spirit, Fanon concludes his book with a final stream of poetry—"I find myself suddenly in the world and I recognize that I have one right alone: That of demanding human behavior from the other" (p. 179).

In a series of beautiful stanzas, Fanon laments the "disaster" befalling people of color being a symptom of their enslavement, while the "disaster" of White people lies in their having killed their fellow man. He proclaims,

> Superiority? Inferiority?
> Why not the quite simple attempt to touch the other, to feel the other, to explain the other to myself?
> Was my freedom not given to me then in order to build the world of the *You*?
> At the conclusion of this study, I want the world to recognize, with me, the open door of every consciousness.
> My final prayer: O my body, make of me always a man who questions! (pp. 180–181)

With this, Fanon ends with a call for recognition that is equal parts plea and demand. It is a call to open the consciousness of White and Black people, oppressor and oppressed, toward a restored humanity for both. By 1963, however, there would be no more plea. Only a great reversal.

The Cry of the Wretched of the Earth

Before the posthumous publishing of *The Wretched of the Earth* (literally, the *Damned of the Earth* in French), Fanon (1963) was involved as a doctor and a fighter in the Algerian revolution. In the first pages of his most renown text, there is no more talk of recognition or mediation—only of decolonization as the creation of a "new man" (p. 2). The emancipatory process for him turns colonized "things" into human beings through a process of reversal. Fanon defines the logic of decolonization using an age-old and apocalyptic phrase—"The last shall be first." He argued that this great reversal can take place "only after a murderous and decisive confrontation" (p. 3). This language calls us back to Ferenczi's painful recognition that in the encounter between others, an act of murder is an inevitability. For Fanon, the colonized rising up to respond to the colonizer's act of murder is similarly a natural, inevitable, *human* response to violence and subjugation. In what is an uncanny resonance with Freud's *Totem and Taboo*, Fanon states that for the colonized, "it is obvious to them that their cramped world, riddled with taboos, can only be challenged by out and out violence" (p. 3). Coupled with this rage, the colonized regards the colonizer with envy, lust, and a desire to posses all that is the colonizer's, to become like the colonizer, all the while retrieving what the colonizer has stolen (1963, p. 5). Again, for Fanon the measure of progress remains the same—the last shall be first (p. 10).

Liberating the Affect of the Oppressed

Oppression for Fanon (1963) breeds rage, anger, and frustration that emerges from experiences of humiliation, carried in the body. He articulates how many dreams of colonized subjects "are muscular dreams, dreams of action, dreams of aggressive vitality. I dream I am jumping, swimming, running, and climbing" (p. 15). Dreams then become dreams of freedom and liberation of the strangulated affects the oppressed must dissociate within herself to survive. Fanon also sees the discharge and regulation of aggression in cultural formations such as dance. Through dancing, the colonized relaxes the tension in her body by discharging, sublimating, and channeling their aggression (p. 19). The dance becomes a kind of speech-act, a somatic form of free association in which everything is permitted to come to and through the body, "the supercharged libido and the stifled aggressiveness spew out volcanically. Symbolic killings, figurative cavalcades, and imagined multiple murders, everything has to come out. The ill humors seep out, tumultuous as lava flows" (p. 20).

These non-violent ways of coping with, expressing, and discharging violence become a source of fear for the colonizer, who may seek to abolish the dance and folklore of the colonized. The colonizer fears the rage implicit in these manifestations, and becomes preoccupied with preventing the colonized's rage "from boiling over." With no external discharge or mode of expression, this aggression becomes "sedimented in his muscles" (Fanon, 1963, p. 15). When not regulated, this "muscular tension" often becomes discharged initially not against the colonizer, but against other colonized peoples and individuals. While the colonizer or the police officer may subject the colonized to routine violence and humiliation, "it is not uncommon to see the colonized subject draw his knife at the slightest hostile or aggressive look from another colonized subject" (p. 17). The fellow oppressed becomes an object for the self to discharge the anger restricted within the body, an "aggressiveness which has been deposited in his bones against his own people" (p. 15). Through this discharge, power may be both experienced (feeling of release) and accumulated (taking from the other). The alternative to this discharge of affect for Fanon is to withdraw into a fatalistic mindset. Fatalism absolves the oppressor from responsibility, as the violence, inequality, and brutality they have committed is abstracted from its socio-political context, turned into acts of God. Indeed, they are *decreed* by God. The oppressed in the thrall of fatalism bows to the colonizers will as the hand of fate itself, "and mentally readjusts to acquire the serenity of stone" (p. 18).

Fanon (1963), at this stage of his activism and revolutionary career, sees non-violence as a product of the bourgeoisie trying to reach an agreement for the "common good," and is in essence a compromise with the oppressor. For true liberation, according to Fanon, there can be no such compromise, only independence and violence as a decolonizing act brings reparation and recognition (p. 40). The violence of the oppressor demands a necessary counter-violence by the oppressed which balances the scales of justice (p. 46). If the work of the colonizer is to make the colonized's dreams of freedom impossible, then the work of the colonized is to eradicate the colonizer. The rendering of the colonizer as an absolute evil to be annihilated is a natural and expectable response to the eradication and denigration of people of color, and the indigenous people of Africa, Asia, and the Americas.

Fanon (1963) is fully aware at this point in his text of how calculated, how *Manichaean* (to use his term) this thinking is. But this is no mere endorsement of revolutionary violence—this is Fanon's *analysis* of violence as a *symptom* of a colonial situation. He has framed for us one of the problems of both oppression and acts of resistance against oppression—they form part of a cycle of violence that both natural and expectable. The only way out is destruction of the other. And yet, there is another current in *The Wretched of the Earth*, one that is reparative and almost mournful. Fanon defines the "colossal task" of the oppressed as one of "reintroducing man into the world, man in his totality," which he feels can only be achieved with the "crucial help of the European masses" who have often allied with their wealthy masters against the colonized. He argues that the European working-class must "wake up," start thinking, and ally themselves with colonized peoples as a natural ally (p. 62). Furthermore, he criticizes the colonized's attempts—in resisting the colonizer—to idealize and emulate him. Only by both the European working-class *and* the Black revolutionary divesting themselves of the master's poison can true international, class, and racial solidarity take place.

Fanon's Desire for a Third

At the end of his text, Fanon (1963) calls on the colonized to cease attempting to copy European models of identity, to leave "this Europe which never stops talking of man yet massacres him at every one of its street corners, at every corner of the world" (p. 235). In its violence toward the non-White peoples of the world, Europe "has denied itself not only humility and modesty but also solicitude and tenderness" (p. 235). The desire to imitate the oppressor—their power, their culture, their achievements—leads the oppressed astray. Alongside the rage and indignation spilling over the pages of *The Wretched of the Earth*, Fanon slows down and reflects on the need for a new creation, which emanates a vulnerability and desire for rapprochement previously hidden behind calls for the loosening of one's rage. A new model of being that is not buried in an overly idealized, imaginary, and fossilized past, but which reaches out toward a revolutionary futurity which restores the humanity of both oppressor and oppressed. He calls on the oppressed people of the Third World to

> start over a new history of man which takes account of not only the occasional prodigious theses maintained by Europe but also its crimes, the most heinous of which have been committed at the very heart of man, the pathological dismembering of his functions and the erosion of his unity, and in the context of the community, the fracture, the stratification and the bloody tensions fed by class, and finally, on the immense scale of humanity, the racial hatred, slavery, exploitation and, above all, the bloodless genocide whereby one and a half billion men have been written off. (p. 238)

We find ourselves back at the project he began at the end of *Black Skin, White Masks*. Fanon was not simply caught in the throes of reversal, violence, and rage—he contextualizes them as a natural, human response to oppression, and furthermore, correctly diagnosed each of these as a result of the natural dysfunction of an economic and racial system of inequality—one which keeps the working-class at odds with one another, and in turn prevents white people and people of color from banding together against the (White) ruling class. At the same time, he also held out the possibility for a new form of subjectivity outside the bounds of a murderous encounter of kill or be killed.

Fanon (1963) was equally cognizant of the ways that the oppressed can, by falling prey to sectarian politics, seek then to oppress and enact violence against other vulnerable peoples and nations (p. 104). He argued that any revolutionary movement, or post-colonial government, needs not only an economic program, but also a program that impacts the health of social relations, built on "a concept about the future of mankind. Which means that no sermon, no complicity with the former occupier can replace a program" (p. 143). Fanon pointed to the danger of an under-developed political consciousness (something Freire wrestles with, as described in the next chapter) in which "violent calls for social justice are combined, paradoxically enough, with an often primitive tribalism" (p. 143). By this he refers to the splintering that often takes place in leftist, revolutionary, even post-colonial movements for liberation. The colonized, still adherent to a model of politics, economics, and subjectivity based on territorial and identity "chauvinism," demands the domination of another—the Senegalese ridding themselves of the Sudanese, the Congolese wishing to expel the Senegalese, and so on (p. 104). Worse still, the post-revolutionary forces erect their own bourgeoisie—a Black bourgeoisie—that can now amass capital and engage in economic exchange with Europe, while the masses of people continue to starve. This Black bourgeoisie "has learned by heart what it has read in the manuals of the West and subtly transforms itself not into a replica of Europe but rather its caricature" (p. 119). We are not far from Freud's band of brothers breaking down into memetic violence due to identification with—and desire to be—the dominating father. We are also right at the center of a history and a system in which capital and identity chauvinism pits Black people against Native people, White against people of color, people of color against one another, men against women, straight against non-straight, and so on.

Here emerges Fanon's (1963) condemnation—a leadership class that can only offer a chauvinistic, tribal, and hubristic nationalism "to feed the people fails in its mission and inevitably gets tangled up in a series of trials and tribulations" (pp. 143–144). If post-colonial nationalism is not explained and deepened through relation with the people, "if it does not very quickly turn into a social and political consciousness, *into humanism*, then it leads to a dead end" (p. 144, my emphasis). It is not a Black middle-class wearing white masks that is needed, but an economic, social, and pedagogical program which can "elevate the people, expand their minds, equip them, differentiate them, and humanize them" (p. 137). Anything less risks enacting an identification with the colonizer, which continues to maintain a system of racial, colonial, and economic exploitation. This likely explains how Fanon ends *The Wretched of the Earth*—by making an appeal to the European White working class. They too, Fanon observed, failed to answer the call for liberation, due to their own identification with Whiteness representing the rich and powerful (p. 237). For the sake of all humanity, Fanon concludes "we must make a new start, develop a new way of thinking, and endeavor to create a new man" (p. 239).

From Harlem to the Caribbean to Europe to Africa a voice calls out across time and space, one which echoed Fanon's ethics—"We spend money with the wrong people," the wealthy rulers and their system, looking for their love even though they *clearly* don't love us.

"What's wrong with us loving each other," from Harlem to Cuba to Puerto Rico to Africa to the Middle East to Europe and the Americas, "and making sure we are protected" from economic inequality, from exploitation and racial marginalization, from exclusion, from brutality and violence?

FANON, FREUD, AND THE PROJECT OF EMANCIPATORY SUBALTERN MALE SUBJECTIVITY

Despite Fanon's revolutionary work serving as a foundation to post-colonial psychoanalysis and liberation psychology, it is important to recognize certain limitations in his thinking. Not unlike Freud, they reside in part in his handling of gender and sexuality, specifically the subjectivity of women of color and the humanity of LGBTQ people (and by extension, that of queer people of color)—both are sacrificed on the altar of (Black) cis-heterosexual male emancipation. Such a trend among subaltern men is not unique to Freud or Fanon. Martin Luther King, for example, was of course a civil rights leader and activist on behalf of racial justice and equality for Black Americans and other people of color. But he was also known to have a homophobic trend in his thinking, such as when a young man wrote to Dr. King about what to do about his homosexual feelings. King advised that he see a "good psychiatrist" to solve his problem. Racial justice had a limit—one set by cis-heterosexual male agency.

Ahad (2010) notes the intersection in Fanon of psychoanalytic ideas, sexual normativity, and Black cismasculinity. While Fanon provided the most incisive analysis of Black male subjectivity (one that can be related, by the way, to the experience of other Caribbean subjectivities including Latinx males), his interpretation of Black female subjectivity "is at best dismissive, and at worst disparaging" (Ahad, 2010, p. 112). Ahad cites Gwen Bergner to discuss how Fanon glosses over how colonialism maintains racial inequality precisely through sexual and gender difference, re-enacting the very colonialist discourse he is trying to deconstruct (pp. 112–113). For Fanon, Black male subjectivity is a victim of racism, whereas women of color are in collusion with the colonial project, taking up the role of "race traitors." In effect, Ahad notes how in Freud's and Fanon's paradigms women are reduced to passive objects of desire with no separate agency, "primarily understood through their sexual relationship to men, whether as wife (in the case of Freud) or race traitor (in the case of Fanon)" (p. 116).

Bergner (1995) also recognized that despite Fanon's work serving as "a foundational text for reconfiguring psychoanalysis to account for race, Fanon, like Freud, takes the male as the norm" (p. 76). Although the colonial struggle for recognition is played out between White and Black Men, "this process is played out through the bodies of women" (p. 80). Black female agentic subjectivity, outside of the White or Black male gaze, implies an incompatibility with Fanon's revolutionary masculinity. Nagel (2000) notes a similar incompatibility posited in Fanon's work between Blackness and homosexuality, citing his argument "that homosexuality was 'an attribute of the white race' and did not exist in the Caribbean because blacks there don't experience the Oedipal tensions that putatively give rise to same-sex desire" (pp. 123–124).

Fanon's centering of Black cisheteromale subjectivity necessarily narrowed the emancipatory scope of his work (the liberationist credo "we are not free if we are not all free" is worth reiterating). But to delineate the contours of Fanon's subjectivity is not to dismiss him wholesale any more than it is to dismiss Freud. Rather it is to situate him within a certain positionality, and at the same time to recognize one of the symptoms of what he so eloquently diagnosed across both his titular works—the oppressed's identification with the position of the oppressor. This identification—explored as we have seen in Freud as it is in Fanon—leads the oppressed to engage in acts of violence toward *other* oppressed people and communities. In relation to Black women and LGBTQ people, he can take the position of the Master, the powerful one who inhabits the "standard" against which others are judged for their deviancy. In the tripartite structure of White man, woman/LGBTQ people, and Black man, Fanon can disown his own feelings of denigration and humiliation by projecting them upon other victims of White heteropatriarchy. At the same time, this position of the powerful, the "do'er" who engages in power and violence, also allows for a reversal of terms between oppressed and their oppressor. It is the latter that will now suffer vanquishing at the hands of the former.

Fanon and the Question of Violence

Kebede (2001) writes on Fanon's psychoanalysis of violence as both a revolutionary and therapeutic act. He argues that Fanon "sees violence as a necessary therapy for a cultural disease brought about by colonial subjugation" (p. 529). It is not enough for the colonizer to leave or end their occupation. The colonized must engage in "violent performances" in order to restore their dignity. Following Hegel, Kebede notes that violence would typically signal a necessary moment in the dance of recognition. However, for Fanon, the colonial situation renders the possibility of mutual recognition always already fraught due to the oppressed not being equals to begin with. Hence, this "obstructed dialectics" leads Fanon to conclude that the colonial struggle is not a struggle for recognition—"Fanon's Negro aspires to be like the master, he aspires toward freedom" (p. 548). Mutual recognition is impossible. Violence is the only answer, as it is the only device that can subject the oppressor to *fear*, as it "inculcates in them the respect of that which prefers death to continued servitude" (p. 549). Violence serves as both act of self-recognition and epistemology for Fanon, becoming the way through which the colonized can come to know the social world and act upon it. This violence is cathartic, as it "purges the colonized of the aggressiveness that is eating them" (Kebede, 2001, p. 551) by directing it toward the "real culprit." Violence for Fanon is then, Kebede ascertains, "a cure, a therapy" (p. 551). Through the curative fires of violence, the oppressed recreates themselves.

Although empathic toward Fanon's argument, Kebede (2001) recognizes that this same kind of male subaltern "bravado" has led to authoritarian violence in both colonial and post-colonial contexts. As stated above, such a model of violence is just as likely to "spill over" and hurt other oppressed peoples within one's perceived community, as well as other members of the community seen as "other" (i.e., non-cisheterosexual, female, etc). If, as Fanon has argued, this violence is a natural outcome of oppression, then it is unclear how it can be curative as such. Rather than curing the "disease" of oppression, it prevents "the administration of the real remedy" (p. 557), which would be "to decontaminate one's soul from such a perversion" (p. 558). Ushering an argument that echoes Freud, Kebede writes,

> But then, this therapy of violence needs to explain how capitulation to an impulse amounts to a victory over that impulse. All ethical thinking teaches that resistance to impulses is the manner the will and the good triumph. Even those theories that resent resistance admit that the best way to deal with uncontrolled impulses is to sublimate them, that is, to channel them into superior and creative works. Fanon rightly took note of the accumulated anger of the colonized people but never shows how this immense anger could be transformed into a creative work. (p. 558)

Here is where I both agree with Kebede regarding the solution to this impasse, and *disagree* with his assessment of Fanon. I will unpack that statement further below. For now, it is important to note how Kebede favorably cites Gandhi's idea that "to conserve my anger, to control it, and just as heat conserved is transmuted into energy, so also our anger, conserved and controlled, can result in a power that becomes irresistible throughout the world" (cited in Kebede, 2001, p. 558). Similarly, Kebede appeals to how violence, even the violence of the oppressed, distorts our humanity. Violence is "the value of the colonizer . . . acting like beasts, there is no reason to aspire after their values. Instead, one must refuse to become beasts like them" (p. 559).

Rather in line with Freud's theorizing on ethics and social justice, Kebede (2001) argued there need to be processes by which the oppressed are able to restore the humanity violated by oppression, while renewing a reluctance—Freud might say renunciation—of cyclical violence. "Unless the colonized extirpate the violence that was instilled into them by colonial rule," Kebede writes, "they will never activate their own suppressed creativity. Far from violence being a cure, it is the very disease that must be wiped off the soul of the colonized" (pp. 561–562). Oppression is internalized within the oppressed in the form of a *disease*, one which contaminates the oppressed, and leads them to spread it in a form of what Paulo Freire would call *horizontal* violence. This epidemic spreading within and between oppressed people poisons the struggle for social justice. Not mere coincidence, yet more than synchronicity, Black and Afro-Caribbean authors formulated an antidote not unlike Freud's own—to refuse to pass on this disease, and instead recognize the humanity of the other as an ethical act.

Fanon's Plea for Justice

Earlier I described my agreement with Kebede's answer to Fanon, while at the same time, noting my objection to his assessment of Fanon. Similarly, one can note the tendency to sidestep or dismiss Fanon as a source of psychoanalytic theorizing for his position on race and violence. While one can take issue with his underlying assumption that mutual recognition—a mutual humanization—between oppressor and oppressed is impossible, I argue there is another dynamic at play within Fanon's work.

As noted in my analysis of *Black Skin, White Masks* (1952), Fanon evidenced a flourish for the rhetorical and poetic, switching back and forth between a psychoanalytic critique of racial and colonial relations, and an existential expression of his own subjectivity as an Afro-Caribbean, colonized subject, using poetry as a vehicle (if only such conventions were still allowed in academic writing!). There is an oscillation between content and process in Fanon. So too in *The Wretched of the Earth* (1963). Although he begins with the "murderous encounter" between oppressor and oppressed as the natural response to colonization, he ends his text with the same kind of poetic invocation which so textures *Black Skin, White Masks*. He points out how for the "Third World" to emulate Europe will only lead to destruction, for "only toward man has it shown itself to be niggardly and murderously carnivorous" (1963, p. 236). Fanon states that while the "European model" of subjectivity presents itself as an ideal before people of color, they must not subject themselves to imitating it. "When I look for man in European lifestyles and technology," Fanon writes, "I see a constant denial of man, an avalanche of murders" (p. 236). Imitating the colonizer, the oppressor, Whiteness, European culture, can only lead to further chaos, violence, and destructiveness.

Fanon also recognized the role that European White workers have to play in this conflict. Although themselves marginalized by the inequality that rampant capitalism endows upon its denizens, White workers did not answer the call for change and liberation, Fanon argues, but instead saw in their masters their ideals. Interestingly, as discussed in a previous chapter, this mirrors Freud's own theorizing and positionality as a Jew vis-à-vis the White-Aryan working class, who saw in the wealthy and powerful their "ego ideal," and turned against Jews as an other to distract them from operating to change society (see Chapters 1 and 3). Fanon believed that the oppressed must take up the task of starting over "a new history of man" (p. 238) that supersedes the models of identity held up by the oppressor—an emancipatory act that liberates both colonizer and colonized, and breaks out of the cycle of murder, violence, and brutality.

How can this be? How can Fanon seemingly "advocate" for a murderous encounter, while also calling for models of subjectivity that subvert murderous carnivorousness? I argue that the *process* of Fanon's writing frames his *content*. Grasping this involves taking something akin to Zizek's (2006) pallarax view. In brief, the parallax refers to the apparent motion of a object when one shift between different perspectives on said object. Zizek capitalizes on this concept to rework Hegelian dialectics. Rather than seeking a unitary integration that collapses the tension between two positions, a proper synthesis from Zizek's view lies in the recognition of an unassimilable "gap" between them. True synthesis is then only capable by taking a parallax view, the "sense of motion" perceived in the object when shifting back and forth *between* two positions.

Shifting lenses between Fanon the revolutionary who seeks transformation through violence, and Fanon the coalition builder who seeks transformation through solidarity and reconciliation, reveals a parallax view in which violence and reconciliation are both *incommensurate* and *codependent* on one another. Not in the sense of a cheap appeal to paradox, but rather a view in which Fanon both threatens and appeals, condemns and reaches out. In this sense, Fanon emerges as an example of Levinas' *autrui*—the Other who appeals for justice. The encounter with the Other for Levinas indicates an encounter with death, a death that "indicates that we are in relation with something that is absolutely other" (Levinas, 1989, p. 43). This brings us to awareness of an intersubjective relationship with the other that is asymmetrical. We are confronted by an Other defined by alterity, the "not-me," who is "the weak, the poor, the 'the widow and the orphan', whereas I am the rich or the powerful" (p. 48). This Other confronts us with a cry for justice—a cry that results from a rupture upon history, a violation of the humanity of the stranger, the poor, and the widow. This cry disturbs us, fills us with fear and trembling. Perhaps even disgust. But the cry calls us to responsibility for this other, and an understanding of this cry. Our responsibility for the other means becoming "one's brother's keeper; to be one's brother's keeper is to be his hostage" (p. 181). Responding to this cry means not trying to smother it, dismiss it, or cover it over, for to respond to this cry in an act of repair is to bring upon the transformation of the world. This is an appeal to make a repair to Fanon's cry—the cry of the wretched of the earth.

At the same time, it is important to recognize the strategic and diagnostic role of Fanon's discussion of violence. Cherki (2006) recognizes that

> Fanon may not explicitly refer to the writings of Freud—*Totem and Taboo*, *Moses and Monotheism*, *Why War?*—but he does concur, in his own way, that the one who possesses power, women, and wealth does not step down of his own accord. He has to be put to death if the society of equals that Freud would have qualified as democratic is to occur. (p. 183)

She adds that while Fanon spoke of a liberating violence that is the natural response to the violence of oppression, he *did not* believe in a "purifying" violence. What was crucial for Fanon was "confronting the violence that impedes being, appropriating it in an act of desubjugation, and turning it against the oppressor, especially when the historical conditions were such that the space of language had been obliterated" (p. 183). Anger, aggression, even violence are attempts to restore humanity in a context in which dialogue and intersubjectivity are destroyed. As Freire will show us in the next chapter, this natural resistance of the oppressed toward their oppressors can lead to fanaticism, seeking to topple the gods in order to lift up their own idols, but it can also lead to dialogue, transformation, and a "call to the other." In this sense, one may disagree with Fanon's argument for the necessity of physical violence per se, but one cannot deny that affect, even the anger, of the oppressed necessitates a form of expression, one that can be met by a humanizing response. In this way oppressor and oppressed must survive the murderous encounter, in order to find the human on the other side.

PSYCHOANALYSIS AND BLACKNESS: A REJOINDER

From the streets of Harlem to the seas of the Caribbean, psychoanalysis was employed by African-American and Afro-Caribbean voices seeking to explore the depths of Black interiority, challenge the non-logic of anti-Blackness, and develop strategies and methodologies for reconciliation with, and resistance and rebellion against, Whiteness. Psychoanalysis became a methodology through which oppressed, colonized voices could bring the intersubjective and political relationship between Blackness and Whiteness into sharp relief, and track its distortions, projections, and interpellations. But it is important to note that for these Black psychoanalytic thinkers, an analysis of the unconscious depths of race stood in a dialectical relationship to an analysis of socio-economic inequality, and how the ruling classes proliferated and exploited a racial caste system in order to maintain inequality as such. This was influenced as much by the intellectual history of psychoanalysis, as by the accidental and synchronous relationships between socio-cultural and socialist psychoanalysts like Fredric Wertham and Harry Stack Sullivan, and Harlem Renaissance activists and essayists like Ralph Waldo Ellison and Richard Wright, which led to the development of Harlem's first psychoanalytic free clinic. These same Black psychoanalytic voices were to influence Freud's "most disputatious heir" Frantz Fanon, who under the tutelage of Marxist psychoanalysts like Tosquelles, engaged in ongoing correspondence with Richard Wright, while also drawing on psychoanalytic theory in the form of Ferenczi, Lacan, and Freud. It is of utmost import to recognize that for this tradition a Marxist/Socialist critique of capital went hand in hand with a psychoanalytically informed anti-Racist critique. We would do well to heed both of these currents today. These missing links in the history of psychoanalysis and liberation psychology find further elaboration in the intersection between American and Latin American voices seeking to continue psychoanalysis' tradition of social justice.

Fanon's life was tragically cut short at age 36 by leukemia. He had engaged in psychoanalytic therapy at the Blida-Joinville Hospital by day, and fought as an Algerian revolutionary by night. Living at the intersection of healing and revolution, Fanon shared with Cherki (2006) his intentions for after the war—"when all of this is over . . . I'd like to have time to go into analysis" (cited in p. 118). With his passing at such a young age, he was not to have this opportunity. As far I am concerned, he already was a psychoanalyst. Perhaps the most ingenious, creative, and heroic one of us all. We can only hope to be *his* disputatious heirs.

Chapter Five

"A Loving Encounter of People"

Freud, Marx, Freire, and the Afro-Latinx Origins of Conscientizacao

As the birthplace of Martín-Baró's (1994) liberation psychology, Latin America stands at the crossroads of time and space, the result of a five-hundred-year-old wound that brought together European colonizers, captured Black people sold into slavery, and the indigenous people who inhabited this land long before. Through the wounding wrought about by colonialism, slavery, and genocide, a complex multiracial and multicultural tapestry was woven, one that would also be influenced by the neighboring Caribbean and later waves of refugees from Europe after World War II. These refugees would include psychoanalysts of Jewish heritage (as well as other backgrounds) fleeing political persecution, war, and violence. It was this intersection of past, present, and future traumas that would inspire Martín-Baró's liberation psychology, as well as reflect the continuing recognition and denial of psychoanalysis' progressive origins. In this chapter, I will paint a sketch of psychoanalysis in Latin America, and how it influenced one of liberation psychology's progenitors—the Brazilian educator Paulo Freire. I will show that Freire became a lightning rod for psychoanalysis and liberation psychology, drawing together numerous influences while reconfiguring them within his own context and experience.

SICOANÁLISIS EN LATINXAMERICA

Hollander (1997) gives us a unique window into the heart and soul of progressive psychoanalysis in Latin America, and how the social justice spirit of early psychoanalysis survived in its new home. Inspired by the development of liberation theology during the 1960s in the Latin American Catholic Church, she called these psychoanalytic movements "liberation psychology" (p. 13). Much like liberation theologians saw no contradiction between the Christian Gospel and social responsibility inspired by their readings of Marx, Hollander describes how these Latin American psychoanalysts saw "no contradiction between Freud and Marx," seeking "a convergence between a psychoanalytic theory of unconscious roots of mental anguish and a Marxist theory of the economic origins of social violence and exploitative class relations as the basis for a praxis bent on combating both" (p. 17). Hollander argues that these analysts practiced a "preferential option for the poor," an insight reinforced by her discovery of Martín-Baró's work, who independently made his own integration of liberation theology and psychology. Psychoanalysis itself has a unique history in Latin America as a whole. It is documented that the first use of psychoanalysis as a theory and form of treatment took place in Brazil in 1899, in the work of the eminent Afro-Brazilian psychiatrist Juliano Moreira, who first taught Freud's ideas in medical faculties before the latter published the *Interpretation of Dreams* (Valladares de Oliveira, 2012), representing the earliest adoption of psychoanalysis in the world outside of Vienna (Plotkin & Honorato, 2017; Plotkin, 2018).

Moreira was born from an interracial relationship in the predominantly African-descended state of Bahia in 1873, and grew up witnessing the end of formal slavery in Brazil in 1888. Moreira was renown for reforming Brazilian psychiatry and rendering more humane treatment for the mentally ill, and for fighting assiduously against racism and arguments of Black inferiority in racial pseudoscience (Fikes Jr. & Cargille, 1986). Moreira critiqued racially biased applications of intelligence tests such as the Binet-Simon, noting that racial IQ differences "depend more on the level of instruction and education of each individual being examined than on his ethnic group" (cited in Skidmore, 1993, p. 189). Moreira argued that environmental and socio-economic factors, such as whether one was raised in the countryside with less access to resources versus a large city, had a stronger and more measurable impact. Similarly, in a 1905 article titled "Assistance to the Alienated," he maintained that those elements which predisposed Brazilians to physical, moral, and social malady "have been unfairly attributed solely to fact of mesticagem [racial mixing]" (cited in Gates & Appiah, 2005, p. 67). After his passing in 1932, his wife would write a chapter summarizing his work for Brazilian sociologist Gilberto Freyre (Skidmore, 1993).

Moreira and his students practiced a form of psychoanalytically informed treatment, although there were no "formal" training analysts until much later in the 1930s. Much like with Mira y Lopez, this did not stop his students and colleagues from referring to Moreira as a *psicoanalista*, or stop him from supervising the first psychoanalytically oriented doctoral dissertation in 1914

(Theiss-Abendroth, 2013). We will return to considering Moreira's legacy in Brazil, and the influence of its trajectory on Paulo Freire's work below.

The first training analysts in Latin America would include Adelheid Koch in Brazil in 1936 (Russo, 2014; Valladares de Oliveira, 2012), and Angel Garma and Celes Carcamo in Argentina in the 1940s (Dagfal, 2012). Koch, a Jewish doctor, trained with Otto Fenichel at the Berlin free clinic until she and other Jewish analysts fled Europe due to Nazi occupation, whereas Garma was a Spanish psychiatrist fleeing Franco's fascist regime during the Spanish Civil War. In South just as in North America, European psychoanalysts turned refugees sought home in a new world. Much like in North America, a turn toward conventional norms and power signaled a shift away from the progressive values so critical to its development. Despite the work done by Juliano Moreira and his followers in the early 1900s to disseminate psychoanalysis, the institutionalization of psychoanalysis in the 1940s in Brazil would work to erase this history, becoming increasingly clinically and politically conservative, much like the institutionalization of psychoanalysis in Argentina. But unlike in the United States, there were still those who continued elaborating on the relationship between psychoanalysis and social justice. One example of such a psychoanalytic voice was Marie "Mimi" Langer. I will depend on Hollander's (1997; 2010) contributions for my discussion of Langer, as she has written the most complete account of her life and work.

THE CURIOUS CASE OF MARIE LANGER

Marie Langer was born in Vienna in 1910 to Jewish parents during the time of "Red Vienna," when the Social Democrats where in control of the both the mayorship and the city council. An era of increasingly progressive healthcare, welfare, and domestic policy followed the end of Karl Luger's "reign." In her childhood and adolescence, Langer was introduced to the leading artists and thinkers of her time at her all-girls school, as well as social scientists seeking to integrate psychoanalysis and Marxism to address both the material and psychological factors of oppression (Hollander, 2010, pp. 62–63). Langer would go on to medical school at age 19, during the time in which Austro-fascism rose to power, winning regional and municipal elections. With their newfound political influence, the Austro-fascists erected laws banning Jews from working in public hospitals and limiting their access to education and employment. When Langer graduated in 1935, she found herself unable to train as a psychiatrist due to structural anti-Semitism, and so decided to train as an analyst at the Vienna Psychoanalytic Institute. She was accepted as a candidate following an interview with Anna Freud, and went on to study under the supervision of Helene Deutsch and Jeanne Lampl de

Groot. Cognizant of the increasing presence of anti-Semitic, populist fascism in her home town, Langer split her time between training at the institute and engaging in activism with local anti-fascist organizations (Hollander, 2010, p. 64).

As psychoanalysis was seen as a "subversive" discourse by the now dominant fascists, the Vienna Psychoanalytic Institute enacted a policy that would scar the history of psychoanalysis—they declared "neutrality" with respect to politics, and prohibited analysts from participating in activist organizations. Unable to abide this policy, Langer and her soon-to-be husband Max joined a medical brigade bound for Spain to provide relief in the midst of the Spanish Civil War. As the fascist forces in Spain gained the upper hand, however, Langer and her husband were forced to flee. Later in Reichenberg, following a tragic miscarriage, Langer reflected on the prospects of bringing a child, especially a Jewish child, into this world:

> I'll never forget what it was like lying in the hospital bed at night, alone, my gown soaked with blood . . . Through the open window of my room I could hear the terrifying sounds of a passing Nazi demonstration and hundreds of voices yelling, "Kill the Jews." (cited in Hollander 2010, p. 65)

In 1939, Langer would flee Nazi Germany with her family to Uruguay, where she encountered a German immigrant from the Spanish Republic solidarity movement who invited her to deliver a talk on Marx and Freud. This reignited Langer's interest in psychoanalysis, and upon moving to Buenos Aires, Argentina, she decided to study all of Freud's works. Later in 1942, she would, along with Enrique Pichón-Rivière and Arnaldo Rascovsky, become a co-founder of the Argentine Psychoanalytic Association (APA) (Dagfal, 2012; Hollander, 2010). She developed a training program that attracted free thinkers interested in psychoanalysis, culture, and art, counting Salvador Dali and Federico Garcia Lorca among the participants (Hollander, 2010, p. 67). Later, with the arrival of Angel Garma and Celes Carcamo, both trained analysts, they developed an official chapter of the International Psychoanalytic Association (IPA), where they conducted formal psychoanalytic training. Buenos Aires became a hotbed for psychoanalysis, training psychoanalysts throughout Latin America, while also becoming a force to be reckoned with in the international psychoanalytic scene. This brought with it renewed conflict between a rising conservatism in psychoanalysis, as well as new, radical energies.

By the 1950s, psychoanalysis in Argentina had become a powerful tool for theorizing about culture and society, as well as political activism. The psychoanalytic and political works of Herbert Marcuse, Wilhelm Reich, Otto Fenichel, and Erich Fromm were widely consumed and debated. However, as psychoanalysis became institutionalized in Argentina, it became increasingly withdrawn from questions of politics and social justice. This spurred a younger generation of psychoanalysts to develop what Hollander called "a politics of engagement, urging their profession to come down from its ivory tower to address the dramatic social crises facing the country" (2010, p. 74). Many in this new generation would be trained by Marie Langer.

Juan Carlos Volnovich was an example of just such a trainee. Hollander shares with us his telling of his interview with Marie Langer prior beginning psychoanalytic training:

> She [Langer] asked me whether I'd already had interviews with other training analysts, and I said, "Yes, two." And she replied, "*Pobrecito*, how unpleasant to have to tell your life story so many times!" I felt, "Thank goodness, she understands me," and during that interview the only thing I talked about was [the Cuban Revolution]! I don't know why. When I left I wanted to die. I didn't know Mimi was a leftist then, and I thought, "You're nuts, how could you talk about Cuba to get into the APA?" I was convinced it was all over for me. (Hollander, 2010, p. 76)

Langer recognized that candidates like Juan were precisely the kind of people that psychoanalysis needed. Juan was not only admitted to the institute, but later had Langer as a supervisor. Inspired by her students and the rising call for psychoanalysis to recognize the needs of the poor and dispossessed, Langer represented Argentina and Latin American psychoanalysis at the 1971 congress of the IPA in Vienna. In this, the first meeting of the IPA in Vienna since Freud's flight to England during the Nazi occupation, she presented her controversial paper, "Psychoanalysis and/or Social Revolution." It was in Vienna that psychoanalysis was born, and where psychoanalysis would first betray its progressive roots. It was also here that in her youth, Langer was forced to choose between her profession and her values. "It was precisely in Vienna," Langer would tell Hollander, "that I would speak not only of psychoanalysis but of Marxism and revolution to boot!" "This time," she declared, "we will renounce neither Marx nor Freud" (cited in Hollander, 2010, pp. 78–79).

Langer, together with like-minded analysts, resisted the conservative elements within the IPA. Other progressive analysts like Eduardo "Tato" Pavlovsky similarly argued that as Latin American psychoanalytic thinkers, "our project in the grand scheme of things was to contribute to the popular will to change our society" (cited in Hollander, 2010, p. 80). Volnovich in turn wrote an article criticizing the APA's criteria of mental health emphasizing "good work relations, good sexual relations, and good relations with friends," adding another criterion he considered just as crucial—"a sensibility toward social injustice" (cited in Hollander, 2010, p. 80). This led to a rupture within the APA, but as Pavlovksky explained, a necessary one, as it led to the possibility of creating "a new subjectivity, a new way of thinking, a new consciousness about the possibilities of a noninstitutional psychoanalysis, a socially committed psychoanalysis" (p. 81). As we will see, this theme in progressive Latin American psychoanalysis of creating a new subjectivity that leads to social change, would dovetail with similar trends in Black psychoanalytic thinkers (Fanon, Wright, Ellison), and flow into one of the bedrocks of liberation psychology—Paulo Freire's *Pedagogy of the Oppressed.*

Langer would go on to collaborate with the Organization of Mental Health Workers. Within their Research and Training Centers, she taught Marx and Freud, making connections between theories of ideology, the super-ego, and the defenses that maintain socio-political alienation. Langer argued that while Marx called for political and economic revolution, Freud argued for a "psychic revindication, a process based on the recovery of that which has been forced out of consciousness" (Hollander, 2010, p. 84). Following Freud and later Melanie Klein's work, Langer articulated a psychodynamic ethic toward the other, stating that,

> it is the recognition, rather than the disavowal, of the capacity for envy, greed, and destructiveness that produces the reparative impulse in human beings . . . only when the conflict and ambivalence that characterize the psyche and all human relations are recognized and worked with, rather than denied, could people act out of concern for others and build a just social order. (cited in Hollander, 2010, p. 85)

This bears a striking resemblance to Freud's musings on social justice—we must understand and work through the underlying hostility, envy, and competitiveness we feel under systems of inequality, and through a reparative, affectionate (perhaps loving?) tie to the other transform those feelings into action for social change. It is likely with this "reparative impulse" belied the work Langer and other Latin American psychoanalysts in Argentina and the Southern Cone countries would engage in—investigating and denouncing torture in government prisons, providing psychoanalytic treatment for activists and their families, and articulating the class and gender determinants of trauma and unconscious rage (see Hollander, 1997; 2010).

The history of psychoanalysis seems to be a history of repetitions—the military's rise to power in Argentina in 1966 paralleled the growth of right-wing sentiments throughout Latin America, congealed in its local form as the Argentine Anticommunist Alliance (or Triple A). The Triple A placed Langer and other psychoanalysts on a death list marked for assassination. Targeted once again, Langer and her family would flee anew in 1974 to Mexico City. During this time, the department of psychology in the University of Buenos Aires was closed, entire staff in the community mental health clinics were fired or killed, and books promoting "subversive" ideologies were burned. The governing military junta had declared that "Marx and Freud are the two main enemies of Western Christian Civilization" (Hollander, 2010, p. 57). One has the impression they read Freud more closely than most.

In a series of lectures and dialogue at the University of Mexico, Langer (1978) articulated the essence of a radical, leftist psychoanalysis—"While we are taught by religion and morality that all men are equal, with the same rights and responsibilities, irrespective of race, class and creed, we are in fact not so" (my translation, p. 57). She argued that being subjected to the lie (*la mentira*) and repression of this truth has consequences for the psyche. To become aware of the means of production and violence that result from capitalist and racist exploitation breeds discomfort and conflict with one's ethical ideals for justice and fairness. This consciousness of oppression, Langer posits, "is a dangerous knowing, because its spread would further incite the exploited toward class struggle. 'Knowing' of the exploitation means placing it in doubt and not accept the capitalist system as 'natural' and, as a result, unchangeable" (my translation, p. 58). Langer uses the word *saber* when she talks of a *saber peligroso* ("a dangerous knowing"). I have made a literal translation as "knowing," but its meaning is somewhat more dynamic in this context. It implies a "knowing in one's mind," free from the repression that would prevent such knowing from entering consciousness. Langer is then talking about "minding" the web of connections (a la Fenichel) that maintain a social system masked by repressive ideology. Psychoanalysis, then, must constantly dedicate itself to "lift repressions and give and acquire consciousness of the [socio-political] situation," even if this means paying dearly for the conflict it enacts with society (my translation, pp. 63–64).

It is against the backdrop of Latin American psychoanalysis' concern with expanding the (critical) political consciousness of the people that I will read the work of Brazilian educator Paulo Freire. We will see that Brazil developed a unique psychoanalytic history, bound at the root with discourses of Blackness and racial reconciliation, yet arriving at strikingly similar concerns to those of Marie Langer and progressive Argentinian psychoanalysts.

PEDAGOGY, BLACKNESS, AND PSYCHOANALYSIS IN BRAZIL

Although psychoanalysis in Argentina was to influence the rest of Latin America in terms of training and theory development, Brazil as mentioned before had its own history with respect to the arrival and cultural assimilation of Freud's work. It would be in the 1920s and 1930s, following Juliano Moreira's initial dissemination of Freud in the turn of the century, that the latter's *Complete Works* would be translated into Spanish, and then Portuguese. With Adelheid Koch's arrival in 1936 we would have the beginning of training analysis as such. But between all of these phases, however, psychoanalysis asserted an influence over the fields of education, sociology, and anthropology in Brazil, one that Afro-Brazilian psychiatrists applied without concern for "Freudian" orthodoxy. And it asserted itself as a focal point of debate between racial science and anti-racist struggle.

Within Brazilian psychiatry, psychoanalysis served unique progressive and conservative tensions. Mainstream Brazilian psychiatry in the 1920s sought to "purify" psychoanalysis of its more critical elements in order to deploy it as a tool of mental hygiene and racial control (Facchinetti & Dias De Castro, 2015). Founded in 1922, the Brazilian League for Mental Hygiene initially focused on using psychoanalysis to cleanse a "diseased and illiterate country" (Russo, 2014, p. 66; see also Rubin, Mandelbaum, & Frosh, 2016). Pedagogy, literacy, and psychoanalysis were joined at the hip in Brazil, as psychoanalysis was deployed as a "civilizing" instrument to dominate and control a multiracial population whose existence evoked anxieties of Brazil's own history of slavery. Up until the abolition of slavery in 1851, Brazil imported more Black slaves than any other country in the Americas (Lange, 2008, p. 10). Much like in the United States, emancipation by itself did not vanquish racial discourse and inequality. When Brazilian White elites discovered that only 40 percent of the population identified as White, they interpreted the predominance of Black, indigenous, and mixed-race Brazilians as the source of Brazil's post-colonial economic and nationalist struggles. Rubin, Mandelbaum, and Frosh (2016) state that this anxiety reflected attempts to construct a new national identity. They write, "As the country was shifting from a slave-based economy to a republican order, the massive contingent of ex-slaves, homeless, sick and malnourished people was seen as a barrier to modernization" (p. 97). Russo (2014) also understands this anxiety as fueling the Brazilian elite's desire to make Brazilian subjectivity "compatible with the teachings of their European masters" (pp. 66–67).

And so the White upper class took upon themselves the project, adopting European ideologies of Black and mixed racial inferiority, of remedying the "disease" they diagnosed as holding back Brazil's prosperity and development. By 1889, policy makers and intellectuals practiced a kind of social Darwinism positing a racial hierarchy (akin to the *scala naturae* of turn of century Europe, or, at his most compliant with colonial anthropology, Freud's theory of primitivity) that would gradually eliminate the lesser races through "natural selection"—*branqueamento* or "whitening" became public policy (Lange, 2008). Depending on one's own identification with the aggressor, one drew on the conventional, oppressive aspects of psychoanalysis, or its emancipatory ones.

Within Brazilian psychiatry there were dissenting voices that challenged the ideology of eugenics and White Supremacy, instead positioning psychoanalysis as a tool for reconciling the tension in Brazilian body-politics between Whiteness and Blackness, European heritage and their Black and indigenous ancestors. Following the teachings of Juliano Moreira and their own readings of Freud, other psychiatrists such as Julio Porto-Carrero and Arthur Ramos resisted the racist orientation of the League for Mental Health. Porto-Carrero and Ramos separately argued that Blackness was not something to be "civilized" out of Brazil's racially mixed heritage. Rather than simply being racist or problematic texts, Freud's works helped them articulate a "search for ancestry and the notion of 'being Brazilian'" (Valladares de Oliveira, 2012, p. 127). In that vein, Porto-Carrero and Ramos argued that all Brazilians needed to engage in an internal sojourn, getting in touch with and accepting their heritage, including their shared Blackness (Russo, 2014; Valladares de Oliveira, 2012).

Arthur Ramos, born in 1903 in Alagoas, Brazil, would prove a critical reader of Freud and a critic of theories of racial inferiority. In 1921 he enrolled at the Faculdade de Medicina in Bahia, where he specialized in psychiatry and forensic psychology, and discovered the work of mulatto psychiatrist Nina Rodrigues. Nina Rodrigues, influenced by Cesaire Lombroso's theories of the heritability of criminality, argued that Black and mixed-race people were prone to mental illness, violence, and anti-social behavior due to their mental atavism as underdeveloped peoples. Ramos would be exposed to Nina Rodrigues thinking through his own interest in population mental health and criminology, but a different turn in his interpretation of Nina's findings. Although the Bahia medical school had been a bastion of Lombrosian theorizing, by 1924 there was a resurgence of students interested in psychoanalysis. Ramos and this new generation of medical students drew on Freud's critique of Lombroso's claim that criminality was racially inherited, arguing that it represented acquired behavior instead. Using Freud, Ramos argued that the perceived "criminality," "primitivity," and "mental atavism" projected unto indigenous and Black populations were instead the product of trauma, poverty, racial inequality, and marginality (Lange, 2008, p. 17; Plotkin & Honorato, 2017, p. 109). Both in Bahia and later in his role as Chief of the Mental Hygiene Service, Ramos conducted research identifying childhood trauma and deprivation as a source of adult misconduct (Lange, 2008).

Ramos identified a kind of "prelogical magical thinking" that could manifest itself among such communities, but rather than being due to their race, he saw reflected in them their oppressive social conditions. The theme of inequality leading to a kind of "magical consciousness" resonates with Freud's thinking on the influence of authoritarian crowds on the psyche in turn-of-century Europe, as well with a distinct Latin American concern with how material deprivation restricts critical consciousness. Psychoanalytic thinking was useful in this regard for Ramos, who drew upon Freud's *Totem and Taboo*, *Group Psychology*, and *Moses and Monotheism*, to normalize and lift up cultural products and experiences common to all human beings—

and all racial groups that comprised the Brazilian body politic (Plotkin & Honorato, 2017, p. 110).

With the publication of his text *The Negro Folk-lore in Brazil* in 1935, Ramos argued that persecution by Whites led post-emancipation Black Brazilians to hide their Macumba and Candomble religious practices within popular song, dance, and culture as a way to "penetrate" and resist White-European culture (for a parallel dynamic in Puerto Rican culture, see Cruz [2005]). For Ramos, Afro-Brazilian culture was a space "of channelization of the 'ancestral unconscious' and moments of updating of collective life" (Valladares de Oliveira, 2012, p. 124). Given the desire for Whiteness by Brazilian elites who identified economic progress with mimicking Europe, Ramos argued that only by becoming conscious of, and accepting, the legacy of slavery in Brazil, and creating space for Blackness and Black identity could the Brazilian people create a more inclusive and just democratic state. This form of Black consciousness required a de-identification and de-centering of European whiteness through a revolutionary education of "depth" that would put Brazilians in touch with their shared ancestral unconscious, "loosening the prelogical binds that have shacked it" (cited in Plotkin & Honorato, 2017, p. 110).

Porto-Carrero and Ramos separately organized their own psychoanalytically informed clinics where low cost and free mental health services were provided to children and adults (Russo, 2014; Valladares de Oliveira, 2012). In their written correspondence with one another, they discussed possible translations of psychoanalytic terms into Portuguese, paving the way for their dissemination and adoption in Brazilian psychiatry (Dias De Castro, 2015). Porto-Carrero also worked on the application of psychoanalysis to education, with the goal of reducing taboos around sexuality and racial integration (Rubin, Mandelbaum, & Frosh, 2016, p. 97). Like Mira y Lopez, Ramos and Porto-Carrero practiced psychoanalysis based on their reading of Freud's writings, yet also sustained a correspondence with the founder of psychoanalysis, sending him copies of their published works (Plotkin & Honorato, 2017, pp. 112; 118). Freud in his replies regretted he could not read Portuguese, but thanked them for their adoption and dissemination of psychoanalytic thinking within their country.

However, Brazil's Great Depression in the 1930s fueled a coup d'etat led by Getulio Vargas, which resulted in a period of authoritarian rule until 1945 (Vargas modeled his administration after Mussolini in Italy), during which Vargas tried to enlist psychoanalysis as part of a pedagogical program aimed as producing "healthy, educated and patriotic youth" (Rubin, Mandelbaum, & Frosh, 2016). In response, new institutionalized forms of psychoanalysis would again alternate between claiming "neutrality" in regard to political conflict in order to "safeguard" itself, and engaging in acts of resistance against control and domination. It was during Vargas' regime that another

Afro-Brazilian from Bahia, one Alberto Guerreiro Ramos, would begin his studies in sociology, later following the teachings of Arthur Ramos (no relation) on psychoanalysis and Blackness.

In the early years of Vargas' government Arthur Ramos was invited by Anisio Teixeira, secretary of education in the Rio de Janeiro school system, to serve as Chief of the Mental Hygiene Service at the Institute of Educational Research in 1933. Although as noted above he contributed to psychoanalytically informed research showing that the behavioral and social problems attributed to Blackness were instead due to marginality and trauma, his work operated under the tensions and demands of Vargas' "civilizing" program (Lange, 2008). Although Ramos' scholarship would lead to a shift in Brazilian academic and public policy circles away from racial theories of degeneracy and the denigration of Black and mixed-race peoples, it also opened the door for a different kind of eugenics project. If the degeneracy associated with Blackness was not inherited but acquired through environmental stressors, then a pedagogical and mental hygiene program could civilize those elements out of them. Paraphrasing Lange's (2008) observations, this implied a shift from a biological *mejorar la raza* to a sociological and psychological one. Illustrating this tension, Ramos wrote psychoeducational guidebooks for parents on how good enough caretaking can be preventative, stressing the role of parental love and empathy—these same guidebooks were provided with illustrations which consistently depicted Black people in a negative light and White people as the ideal, normative, and effective parents (Lange, 2008). Although Ramos was not involved in these illustrations, they showcase how Brazilian anti-racist projects could become distorted and assimilated into a kinder, gentler form of structural racism.

Contributing to this odd and interesting intersection of Brazilian anti-racist movements and their assimilation under Vargas' regime was a nationalizing discourse that sought to eliminate racial differences by essentially muting overt discussions of race (Lange, 2008). For many Brazilian scholars of the 1930s and 1940s, to be anti-racist was to, curiously, render racialized language invisible. This is notable in Ramos' clinical case studies during this period, which minimized the role of race in the patient's difficulties, at times eschewing mention of the patient's race altogether as a way of preventing any quick association between race and mental illness. Did this represent an underlying, perhaps unconscious valuing of Whiteness on Ramos' part, a more benign form of racism? Lange (2008) acknowledges that "one also struggles to find clarity in primary documents" (p. 32). It is important to consider Ramos' work before, during, and after his administrative position in Vargas' government.

Arthur Ramos would cease engaging in clinical and administrative work in 1938, shifting to a greater scholarly focus on racial justice. He visited the United States in 1939, where he engaged in racial justice activism and scholarly collaborations on the Black Diaspora with Franz Boas' disciple and African studies scholar Melville Herskovits, with whom he had started a friendship and written correspondence in 1933. With Herskovits' support, Ramos toured the United States, speaking at conferences and universities about race in Brazil and the question of racial equality. His stay in the U.S. "transformed him into one of the international leaders of the anti-racism and pro-democracy struggle" (Guimaraes, 2008, p. 68). Upon his return to Latin America, Ramos would go on to become the father of Black cultural studies in Brazil, taking a stand against the right-wing nationalism that infected education—that he himself had contributed to, even if unwittingly—and writing a series of political articles on anti-racist anthropology and the rebuilding of democracy post-Vargas (Guimaraes, 2008; Valladares de Oliveira, 2012). Ramos' reading of Freud stayed with him, informing his belief that racial mixing and *mestizaje*, Brazilians would create a "racial democracy" beyond Black or White that would serve as the foundation of a "post-racial world" (Guimaraes, 2008, p. 71). Although well-intentioned and seeking greater integration of Afro-Latinx and mixed-race peoples within the Brazilian body politic, Ramos' racial democracy would be critiqued by later Afro-Brazilian thinkers as masking the underlying racial tensions and inequalities that existed. He would not live to witness these critiques. Like Fanon, he passed away at an early age at 46.

The Great Depression of the 1930s contributed to racial tension, widespread poverty, and rampant inequality, with psychoanalysis serving as both a weapon of control and a tool of liberation by wide ranging interests both in Brazil and broader Latin America. It is in this wider context that I situate Paulo Freire and his work as a teacher and psychoanalytic thinker, who, like other post-colonial descendants of Freud, articulated a psychoanalysis for liberation. In Freire's case, a psychoanalytic pedagogy of the oppressed.

PAULO FREIRE, AFRO-BRAZILIAN PSYCHOANALYSIS, AND FROMM

Born in 1921 in Recife, Pernambuco, Freire experienced poverty and hunger at an early age. This deprivation, along with the death of his father in 1934, deeply impacted Freire. He suffered in school, only able to catch up after his family's financial situation improved. Years later Freire remembered struggling to read during his adolescence with the Great Depression in the foreground, and how this experience framed his relationship to poverty, education, and language:

> I didn't understand anything because of my hunger. I wasn't dumb. It wasn't lack of interest. My social condition didn't allow me to have an education. Experience showed me once again the relationship between social class and

> knowledge . . . When I began to eat better, I began understanding better what I was reading. It was just as [*sic*] this time that I began to study grammar as I loved language problems. (cited in Gadotti, 1994, p. 5)

Freire became enamored with the philosophy of language, and later had the opportunity to study it along with phenomenology and psychology at the University of Recife in 1943. Over the course of his research and education he read and was exposed to intellectual descendants and collaborators of Juliano Moreira, such as Arthur Ramos, Gilberto Freyre, Graciliano Ramos, Lins do Regó, Oswald de Andrade, and Jorge Amado (Freire, 1996, p. 226; Gadotti, 1994, p. 7). Linguistics, psychoanalysis, structuralism, Hegelian dialectics, and sociology all contributed to his thinking about the teacher-student relationship, and the role of dialogue in fostering critical consciousness.

After earning his degree, Freire was appointed director of the Pernambuco Department of Education and Culture. During a time in which literacy was a requirement for voting in presidential elections, Freire was given the task of working with the illiterate poor in order to help them assimilate into the body politic. These marginalized poor, Black and Brown communities would educate Freire on how this represented an act of violence, and organically showed him how literacy fueled political empowerment. Learning from his students-turned-teachers, Freire developed a pedagogical theory and practice that would integrate liberation theology and their Christian Base Communities alongside psychoanalytic thought, Marxism, and post-colonial theory. Later in 1961, he was appointed director of the Department of Cultural Extension at the University of Recife, where he had the opportunity to conduct a large-scale study of his theories on the teacher-student relationship. Based on his pedagogical work, Freire came to adopt the concept of *concientizacao* (*concientizacion* in Spanish) or "critical consciousness" as central to his educational model. Although *concientizacao* is associated with Freire's work, he was always quick to point out that the term actually originated at the Higher Institute for Brazilian Studies, in particular from the work of his colleague the Afro-Brazilian sociologist Alberto Guerreiro Ramos (Freire & Vittoria, 2007).

Alberto Guerreiro (I will use this version of his name to distinguish him from Arthur Ramos), born in 1915 in the state of Bahia like his forerunner Juliano Moreira, was enamored as a boy with Christian existentialist thinkers and their critique of reason and the loss of identity in free market societies. His concern for the distortion of Black identity in the wake of colonialism and rapid capitalist modernization led him in the 1940s and 1950s to train as a sociologist while also drawing heavily on social psychology and psychoanalysis (Alves, 2006; Bick, 2016). His interest in anti-racist thought would also draw him to the work of Arthur Ramos, focusing on the intersection of racism, class prejudice, and the psychological dynamics that impacted race relations. In 1957 Guerreiro would critique Ramos' early work as stereotyping Black Brazilians as "underdeveloped," "primitive" and stuck in the past (Lange, 2008), correcting him with Erich Fromm's thinking.

Guerreiro explored how Brazilian sociology engaged in "imitative thinking," copying and internalizing colonizing modes of knowledge production drawn from Europe and the United States. The answer, for Guerreiro, was nothing short of the liberation of sociology as such (presaging Martín-Baró's [1996] similar call for psychology). Guerreiro saw the "negro problem" in Brazil as a function of the history of colonialism, which marginalized the Black population in order for Brazil to maintain a connection to the European colonizer through the privileging of Latinx Whiteness. Liberation required a critical consciousness of these dynamics, and through that consciousness seek solidarity among all Brazilians. Guerreiro noted the resonance between his and Fanon's work, leading to an interest in Fanon's post-colonial psychoanalysis in the 1950s (Maia, 2014). Joining Fromm with Fanon's thinking, in his 1958 text *A reducao sociologica* Ramos expanded on his model of critical consciousness to analyze the conditions of people in the "Third World," coining *concientizacao* as something that "emerges when collectivities transform themselves into historical beings, able to choose their own destinies" (Maia, 2014, p. 7). Inspired by Fromm, Guerreiro co-founded the *Teatro Experimental do Negro* (Experimental Black Theater), in which he used psychodrama and theater as a form of group therapy to help Afro-Brazilians face their "fear of freedom" due to internalized racism and inequality, and develop a critical consciousness (*concientizacao*) of the internal and external forces that maintained systemic racism (Maio, 2015). This kind of "group therapy" offered a space for Afro-Brazilians to "face their fears and resentments, purging from their personality the racial stereotypes and self-deprecating visions internalized since childhood" (Maio, 2015, p. 611, my translation).

Maio (2015) shares the experience of Afro-Brazilian actress Ruth de Souza who participated in the Experimental Black Theater as a way of working through the racism she faced in childhood. Guerreiro helped facilitate a scene on stage in which de Souza re-enacted an incident in which she was denigrated as "that washerwoman's daughter" by her mother's employers:

> My mother was from the interior [of Brazil]. She was Dona Alaida, a landowner, a respected woman . . . and when we came to Rio [de Janeiro], she became a washerwoman. We were the daughters of the washerwoman, Alaida the washerwoman, I remember that . . . Later I started to cry [during the group therapy experience guided by Guerreiro Ramos] because that is when I discovered I was poor. When I arrived in Rio de Janeiro, I became Black, [though] I did not know that I was Black. When you're a kid you don't pay attention to those things, you know? And I remember this, that discovering being Black

> here in Rio de Janeiro, discovering class differences, was something I did not understand. I was growing up and not understanding very well because why [do] you treat me differently if I'm a person just like you? (p. 611, my translation)

This enactment provided de Souza with a new experience that helped her understand the underlying causes of her experience being devalued as a poor Black girl whose family lost social and economic status in moving from a rural/inland to an urban/metropolitan context. Like many figures in this history of psychoanalysis and social justice, Guerreiro was not a psychoanalyst, nor would be consider himself one or care to. But his use of psychoanalytic ideas, transmitted through generations of Jewish, Afro-Caribbean, and Afro-Latinx scholars led him to engage in a therapeutic experiential practice which "would produce a liberating psychological effect, restoring [Afro-Latinx] self-esteem and confidence in their own creative capacities" (Maio, 2015, p. 611, my translation). To sum, *concientizacao* involves facing one's fear of freedom, a fear installed in the psyche by exploitative and marginalizing social conditions, and expanding the contours of awareness to become conscious of, and then struggle toward changing, those very forces.

By combining a reformulated version of Arthur Ramos' observations on how oppression restricts Afro-Brazilian subjectivity with Fromm's theorizing on the fear of freedom and Fanon's post-colonial call for Black liberation, Alberto Guerreiro became not only a pivotal force in defining *concientizacao*, but also took a number of theoretical steps that Paulo Freire himself would follow—we will see that discovery is always a kind of re-discovery! *Concientizacao*, which Freire learned from Guerreiro, would prove pivotal to his work—"When I heard this word for the first time I immediately realized the profundity of its meaning," Freire remembered, "because I have the strong conviction that education, as praxis of liberty, is a knowledge action, that is, a critical approach to reality. From then on, this word forms part of my own lexicon" (Freire & Vittoria, 2007, p. 112). Hence, although Freire is oft-cited as the originator of *concientizacion/concientizacao*, he was following the language of a tradition that predated him, informed by the routes of Afro-Brazilian interpretations of psychoanalytic, existentialist, and post-colonial theories.

The Brazilian government at the time received Freire's work with enthusiasm, and sought to promote his pedagogy among other marginalized communities. But with the coup d'etat of 1964, the Brazilian Armed Forces—supported by the U.S. government—instituted a military regime that would last until the 1980s. Like Vargas, they would seek to reconfigure education in line with authoritarian ideals. As Freire was an educator focused on raising the formal and political literacy of displaced, poor peoples in the inner cities and slums of Brazil, he framed education as a psychologically transformative and political act—helping people "read the word to read the world" in order to organize for psychological and social transformation. The provisional government saw this as a threat, imprisoning and later exiling Freire as a subversive traitor. He would re-establish himself in Chile, where he would write his major work, *The Pedagogy of the Oppressed.* Exile, conflict, and survival would, in another act of synchronicity, again bring together psychoanalytic voices from across the world.

In the late 1960s, Freire would make a number of visits to Cuernavaca, Mexico, to meet with cultural school theorist and Frankfurt don Erich Fromm, in a series of dialogues arranged by the radical Catholic priest Ivan Illich (Lake & Dagostino, 2013). Over the course of many vibrant dialogues, Freire and Fromm would form a deep friendship discussing how marginalized people come to internalize the ideology of the oppressor, and the challenges involved in decolonizing the mind and rejecting an identification with the powerful. In the back of his mind, Fromm likely recalled how Freud became the very oppressive authority he feared, especially in the rupture with Ferenczi, who had submitted to Freud's authority in order to protect their relationship. In a historical twist of irony the psychoanalytic theories of oppression developed by Freud, and then used by Fromm to critique Freud, would now be used by Freire to breathe new life into Freud. Indeed, it was in hearing about Freire's pedagogical praxis that Fromm remarked, "his blue eyes flashing" as Freire later recalled, that "an educational practice like that is a kind of historical-sociocultural and political psychoanalysis" (cited in Freire and Faundez, 1989; Bingham, 2002; Lake & Dagostino, 2013). Like Guerreiro before him, Freire was influenced by Fromm's psychoanalytic theorizing on the "fear of freedom" as a mechanism that maintained the oppressed's attachment to the oppressor, and elaborated on this insight in the *Pedagogy of the Oppressed.* During his exile in Chile, Freire would also be introduced to another critical post-colonial psychoanalytic voice, when a political activist shared with him a copy of Frantz Fanon's *The Wretched of the Earth.* "I was writing *Pedagogy of the Oppressed*, and the book was almost finished," Freire fondly remembered, "I had to rewrite the book in order to begin to quote Fanon" (Horton & Freire, 1990, p. 36).

Informed by Fromm and the tradition of first generations of psychoanalysts, educated in a cultural milieu textured by Afro-Latinx psychoanalytic thinking from Moreira to Guerreiro, and equipped with Fanon and the African-American, Afro-Caribbean, and existential psychoanalytic lineage that gave birth to him, Freire would create one of the cornerstones of liberation psychology and later multicultural psychology. The child of a five-hundred-year-old wound that refuses to close, it would speak from the margins of history to change its course.

Pedagogy of the Oppressed as a Psychoanalysis of Liberation

In discussing the central concept of his critical pedagogy—*concientizacao*—a group once asked Freire if the oppressed becoming aware of and responding to injustice might not result in their turning to "destructive fanaticism" or the "total collapse of their world" (Freire, 1972, pp. 19–20). Freire responded that critical consciousness is not the same as fanaticism, but makes it possible for people to engage history as "responsible Subjects" seeking self-actualization. Fanaticism or sectarianism, by contrast, distorts humanity's emancipatory energies (p. 22). Freire observed that ultra right-wing movements can evoke a similar destructiveness on the left, noting how activists and revolutionaries can become reactionaries, "falling into sectarianism in the process of responding to the sectarianism of the Right" (p. 22). The pedagogy of the oppressed, essentially a pedagogy of liberation, Freire argues, "is a task for radicals; it cannot be carried out by sectarians" (p. 24). What does Freire mean by this? How is it he can say that liberation can only be carried out by "radicals," but not by "sectarians"? Examining his theory of liberation provides an answer to what is "radical" about liberation, and how a "fanatical" or "sectarian" position can only attempt a facsimile of social justice. It is an answer to Fanon's own struggle with the question of liberation, and also an extension of a line of argument begun by Freud struggle with aggression and the position of the other.

Freire maintained that achieving one's full humanity through recognition—humanization—is a central need in life. A need that is negated by injustice and exploitation, and yet affirmed by the oppressed's desire for justice, and the struggle to restore their humanity (Freire, 1972, p. 28). Dehumanization is a distortion of this yearning, wounding both those who dehumanize and the dehumanized (p. 28). Sooner or later, however, the oppressed begin to rise up to restore their basic humanity. For this struggle to have meaning, Freire argues that the oppressed in seeking their humanity must not become "oppressors of the oppressors, but restorers of the humanity for both" (p. 28). The existential and political task of marginalized people, then, is "to liberate themselves and their oppressors as well" (p. 28). Although oppression dehumanizes both oppressor and oppressed, "[o]nly power that springs from the weakness of the oppressed will be sufficiently strong to free both" (p. 28). Freire's words here are striking—only the *power* that comes from the *weakness* of the oppressed will be *strong enough* to free both. Power from weakness? What could this refer to other than vulnerability? A radical vulnerability on part of the oppressed.

When oppressed people first begin to rise up, they can sometimes be seduced into becoming oppressors or "sub-oppressors" instead of fighting for liberation (Freire, 1972, pp. 29–30). Since their inner world has been structured by their condition of oppression, "Their ideal is to be men; but for them, to be men is to be oppressors. This is their model of humanity" (p. 30). As the oppressed have internalized the oppressed through an adhesion to not only their views, but the position of power that the oppressor inhabit, they are unable to objectivize the oppressive situation, to discover it "outside" themselves. Freire here evokes parts of Freud and Ferenczi's theory of identification with the oppressor when he writes that the oppressed recognizing their existence as opposites to the oppressor does not yet signify a critical consciousness of the need to subvert that contradiction. The oppressed may be seduced by call of power, "not to liberation, but to identification with its opposite pole" (p. 30). *Identification* with the opposite of weakness and vulnerability is power and especially *dominating power*, comes to infect the psyche of the oppressed, finding in the oppressor a model of what it means to be human, and strive to be like them. Echoing Freud's (1917) oft-cited phrase on identification—"the shadow of the object fell upon the ego"—Freire writes, "The shadow of their former oppressor is still cast over them" (p. 31).

The oppressed suffer from a double consciousness, a duality that divides their being. This divide is a function of the conquering oppressor who imposes the contours of his subjectivity on the conquered oppressed, "who internalize this shape and become ambiguous beings 'housing' another" (Freire, 1973, p. 134). Having internalized the oppressor and adopted their "rules for being," the oppressed become "fearful of freedom," citing Fromm (Freire, 1972, p. 31). Freedom for the oppressed would entail ejecting this system from their psyche and replacing it with a new ethic. Until the oppressed discover the "oppressor within" and in turn the depths of their psyche, they will oscillate between a fatalistic attitude and a fanatical one. The fatalistic attitude makes the oppressed wonder if they in fact deserve to have rights, or lack confidence that they can fight for them, having "a diffuse, magical belief in the invulnerability and power of the oppressor" (p. 50). The oppressed feel like objects to be owned by the oppressor, for whom *to be* is *to have*, often at the expense of those who have little to begin with (p. 51). The oppressed embroiled in this fatalistic worldview then takes a complementary position, in which "*to be* is not to resemble the oppressor, but *to be under* him," (p. 51). This foments an experience of total dependence upon a seemingly omnipotent other.

The fanatical attitude, by contrast, can lead to to explosion of aggression outward, not only to the oppressor but toward other oppressed as well, often manifesting as "a type of horizontal violence, striking out at their own comrades for the pettiest reasons" (Freire, 1972, p. 48). This horizontal violence is an enactment of the duality within the oppressed, projected unto others—"Because the oppressor exists within their oppressed comrades, when they attack those comrades they are indirectly attacking the oppressor as well" (p. 48). Here to be is to be like the powerful, to command their power, to exert domination over others, and through that domination, achieve a sense of agency and control. The seductive nature of power, how the oppressed can be transformed into fanatical masses, how they may desire *to have* wealth, capital, and power as the oppressor does, and how to break out of this trap toward true liberation is a central concern of Freire's work. It is critical for him that the oppressed renounce their identification with the oppressor, establishing a psychological distance necessary to see them more objectively as neither gods nor devils, but human beings (Freire, 1972, p. 151). In renouncing an attachment to the fantasy of the oppressor, the oppressed can come to recognize their dialectical relationship critically, and engage in an emancipatory project that is restorative and redemptive of all.

Freire's Stages of Critical Consciousness

Freire's ontology is fundamentally relational in orientation. For him to be human is to be in relation to others and with the world, experiencing them as separate from the self yet able to be known through intimacy and dialogue (1973, p. 3). Recognizing the "otherness" of the world, of other people, and to be receptive to them without submitting or trying to dominate them, constitutes an integrated subject. The tendency toward passive submission versus reactive revolt, and the emergence of one's critical awareness, constitutes different phases in the critical consciousness of the oppressed. He defined these as semi-transitive consciousness, naïve Transitivity (and its corrupted form, *fanatical consciousness*), and transitive or critical consciousness proper.

Semi-transitive consciousness is the stage of fatalism, in which the self submits to a superior and almost magical power who is presumed to dominate over reality. At this stage, the oppressed's adhesion to the values of the oppressor renders those beliefs so natural as to be invisible, unable to locate the oppressor outside of their psyche (Freire, 1972, p. 162, emphasis original). Reality is ordained to be the will of God or the "natural order of things," external and overwhelming forces responsible for their lot in life, and hence unchangeable by the oppressed. A sense of hopelessness and lack of faith in one's own assertiveness predominates, resigning oneself to things "as they are."

As the existing reality is problematized and rendered malleable and capable of change, the oppressed increase their critical awareness of the world, of their dialectical relationship to the oppressor. This signals a shift to what Freire calls transitive consciousness, which leads the oppressed toward increased political and psychological engagement (Freire, 1973, p. 17). Transitive consciousness is a critical consciousness for Freire, and one which pursues liberation. It is characterized by

> depth in the interpretation of problems; by the substitution of causal principles for magical explanations; by the testing of one's "findings" and by openness to revision; by the attempt to avoid distortion when perceiving problems and to avoid preconceived notions when analyzing them; by refusing to transfer responsibility; by rejecting passive positions; by soundness of argumentation; by the practice of dialogue rather than polemics; by receptivity to the new for reasons beyond mere novelty and by the good sense not to reject the old because it is old—by accepting what is valid in both old and new. (p. 18)

Critical consciousness, then, is the dynamic ability to mentalize about society, reality, and the other without falling prey to distortion and one-sidedness. Instead of political polemics and slogans there is reasoned argument and dialogue. Instead of projection there is the ability to perceive the other and establish an intersubjective relation to them. It is in this stance that communication can occur that humanizes each member of the relationship.

"There is," Freire warned, "an initial, predominantly naïve, state of transitive consciousness" (1973, p. 18). Naïve transitivity, which can occur in the course of the shift from semi-transitive to critical consciousness, is characterized by a "over-simplification" of problems, a nostalgia for the "good old days," a lack of curiosity, a negative view of others, by emotional lability and fragility, the tendency toward polemics instead of dialogue, and a persisting tendency toward "magical explanations" for the structure of society. This type of consciousness, Freire argued, is endemic of those who are enthralled in a mass movement, "in whom the developing capacity for dialogue is still fragile and capable of distortion" (p. 18). Although Freire saw this phase as an often necessary one in the process of liberation, he expressed concerned that if it does not progress to critical transitivity, "it may be deflected by sectarian irrationality into fanaticism" (p. 18). If a person falls into this fanaticized consciousness, they will become disengaged from reality, acting "more on the basis of emotionality than of reason," and unable to exert genuine choice and commitments without being reactive.

Freire (1973) theorizes that this emotional lability and rapid shifting in values is due to a diffusion of identity that results from fanaticized, massified consciousness. There is an experience of power and agency that is at the same time brittle and in constant need of repair. Freire writes,

> Men are defeated and dominated, though they do not know it; they fear freedom, though they believe themselves to be free. They follow general formulas and prescriptions as if by their own choice. They are directed; they do not direct themselves. Their creative power is impaired. They are objects, not Subjects. (p. 20)

The identification with the oppressor leads the oppressed to engage in a reversal of tension, taking up the position of dominant power as an attempt at restoring their humanity, even if this power manifests as violence toward an other (whether oppressor or other oppressed). One is in essence saying, "*I* am not the bad one anymore, *you* are!" In identifying with power, they come to desire it, accumulate it, conquer it. Yet while they may have an *experience* of power, they nevertheless remain dominated by the internalized oppressor within them. Hence, they cannot grab hold of the true power that liberates them as subjects in relationship with other subjects.

It is important to reiterate that the naïve transitivity of consciousness Freire identifies is not a phenomenon that occurs among the oppressed in isolation. Rather, it is one type of response the oppressed may have to their conditions of marginalization and exploitation. But more importantly, it is a type of consciousness that is naturally produced by systems of oppression as such. Such a consciousness while potentially threatening to the system in fact reinforces it, by maintaining sectarian divisions between the people which prevent true solidarity and collective movements for change. The oppressor in fact facilitates and participates in this very splitting of the oppressed, both psychologically and communally. "Since it is necessary to divide the people in order to preserve the status quo and (thereby) the power of the dominators," Freire reminds us, "it is essential for the oppressors to keep the oppressed from perceiving their strategy" (Freire, 1972, p. 143). The oppressed must be pit against potential allies, whether across race, class, gender, sexuality, or nationality, in order to weaken attempts at collective action. But it is even better, for the oppressor, when the function and purpose of this division is kept from view. Critical consciousness then must include an awareness of how peoples who share common interests are, by their material and cultural circumstances, placed in economic, political, and psychological conflict with one another.

In order for a shift in consciousness to take place that moves the oppressed from semi-transitive or fanaticized consciousness to critical consciousness, the oppressed must be able to reflect critically upon their internal and external conditions in each stage. For those who are caught in a fanaticized consciousness, this entails reflecting upon the conditions that led to their extreme reactivity, and acting to transform those conditions as well as themselves (Freire, 1973, p. 20). As they are able to tolerate challenges to their more narrow perspective, within a relationship grounded in dialogue, the shift from naïve, fanaticized, or massified consciousness to critical consciousness becomes possible.

Dialogue and Relationality

A dialogue that fosters liberation and critical consciousness must be carried out in communion with the oppressed, regardless of what stage they are in the process of liberation (1972, p. 52). A persistent stance of dialogue opens the path toward true empowerment. Without reflective participation with the oppressed as subjects instead of objects—as Benjamin (1988) might say—the "strong man" or the dominating teacher will instead seduce them "into the populist pitfall and transform them into masses which can be manipulated" (Freire, 1972, p. 52). A drive toward social justice, change and liberation cannot be "implanted" in the oppressed by activist or revolutionary leadership, by educators, or even therapists, but must instead emerge from their own critical consciousness. The answer for Freire is a "humanizing pedagogy," a "permanent relationship of dialogue" between oppressor and oppressed, revolutionary leadership and the people, teacher and student, and (I would add) therapist and patient (p. 55).

Transformative relationships, for Freire, are grounded in love—"When the two 'poles' of the dialogue are thus linked by love, hope, and mutual trust, they can join in a critical search for something. Only dialogue truly communicates" (1973, p. 45). The absence of dialogue reflects a relationship defined by narcissism and arrogance, in which "empathy between the 'poles' is broken. Thus, anti-dialogue does not communicate, but rather issues communiqués" (p. 46). Dialogue for Freire is closely wound up in his definition of intersubjectivity (see 1973, p. 136), which has very close analogues in contemporary relational psychoanalysis (e.g., Benjamin, 1988, see Gaztambide, 2017). Intersubjectivity for Freire is "the encounter between men, mediated by the world, in order to name the world" (1972, p. 76). It involves persons who meet each other not as objects to dominate or be dominated by, but as "Subjects . . . [who] meet to *name* the world in order to transform it" (p. 167).

Dialogue requires love for the world and for others. In naming the world, one is not simply deciphering an objective reality "out there," separate from the relations between self and others. Rather, one is engaging in a creative process of construction and reconstruction (Freire, 1972, p. 77). Domination, its dialectical opposite, "reveals the pathology of love: sadism in the dominator and masochism in the dominated" (p. 78). Dialogue is also characterized by humility, being able to be open to having one's ignorance pointed out by the other, receiving the voice of the other as another I whom I recognize. Only then can I overcome a relation of domination and to create "a relation of communication between Subjects that know, with reference to a knowable object" (1973, p. 136).

Shifting to the context of education, Freire argued that the tensions inherent in the contradiction oppressor-oppressed are also enacted in the teacher-student relationship as a third object. Education then becomes an intersubjective relationship in which teacher and student are mediated by this third—the social, political, and psychological world that grounds the two. The task of the emancipatory teacher, then, is to present this world as a problem for both teacher and student to reflect upon together. To take what is natural and present it as a *problem* to be mulled over is the quintessential task of a problematizing education. Given that the dynamics of oppressor and oppressed become enacted in the pedagogical relationship, when the educator problematizes the world, he makes himself an object to be problematized as well. "Problematization," Freire writes, "is so much a dialectic process that it would be impossible for anyone to begin it without becoming involved in it" (1973, p. 153). Teacher and student, revolutionary leadership and the people, therapist and patient—all are prone to enact relationships of power and domination. In a manner resonant with Ferenczi a half-century earlier—we cannot *help* but enact, in another sense we *have to repeat*, in order to become "involved in it," so that through dialogue we can liberate ourselves from such relationships. It is precisely through this enactment that relationships of domination themselves can be problematized and reflected upon. In this process,

> any step made by a Subject to penetrate the problem-situation continually opens up new roads for other Subjects to comprehend the object being analyzed. Educators who are problematized by engaging in this kind of action "re-enter into" the object of the problem through the "entering into" of the educatees. This is why educators continue to learn. The humbler they are in this process the more they will learn. (p. 153)

The teacher attempts to teach, and in so doing, they inadvertently dominate the student. The student resists the teacher's power, opening up a space for the teacher to reflect on their contribution to this impasse. If the teacher risks an act of love and "re-enters" the problem through the perspective of the students, they show humility and an openness to reconsidering his earlier positions (1972, p. 68). In so doing, a new space is created in which both teacher and student are transformed by their learning.

New subjectivities are created out of this dialogue—"the teacher-of-the-students and the students-of-the-teacher cease to exist and a new term emerges: teacher-student with student-teachers" (Freire, 1972, p. 67). The teacher opens themselves up in loving kindness to be taught by the students, who are now empowered to teach while being taught. Freire argued this intersubjective dialogue is precisely what helps mobilize the oppressed through the stages of critical consciousness, and upon which revolutionary movements and leadership should be modeled. Teachers and leaders in engaging students and the people must create intersubjective relationships in which both are subjects, raising consciousness of our psychosocial reality, while at the same time empowering us to transform it. Influenced by Buberian ethics, Freire describes the difference between domination which turns a conquered *thou* into an *it*, from intersubjective action. The *I* which is dialogical has an awareness of the *Thou* (the not-*I*) as a separate *I* which also "calls forth" and grounds their own existence. "The *I* and the *thou* thus become,"

Freire writes in a relational spirit, "two *thous* which become two *I's*" (1972, p. 167).

Reading critical consciousness through a contemporary lens suggests that what Freire is talking about here is a capacity for mentalization in which we are able to represent (1) a sense of the self, with our own interiority, selfhood, and feeling states, (2) a sense of the other as harboring their own intentionality, and (3) the broader relational and social system that contextualizes the two. Although Freire shifts from oppressor-oppressed to teacher-student in outlining his theory of how socio-political tension is enacted in the pedagogical relationship, there are important implications the reveal themselves if we shift *back* to the oppressor-oppressed relationship with the insights he gleaned from the pedagogical struggle for recognition. These insights further problematize how we consider the oppressor-oppressed relationship itself.

Banking and Problem-Posing Systems of Education as Models of Relationship

For Freire (1972), different pedagogical methods are fundamentally different models of relationship—those that enact societal oppressions and those that challenge them, those that facilitate the emergence of critical consciousness and those that submerge it. He makes the distinction along these lines between what he calls the "banking system" and "problem-posing" approaches to education. The banking system treats the student as a container, a passive receptacle to be "filled" by the teacher. Such a banking system presupposes that a good teacher does a better job at "filling" the receptacle, while submission and meekness as the "receptacle" is "filled" shows the mark of a good student (p. 58). Education is then tantamount to teacher issuing communiqués and making deposits which the students passively accept, memorize, and repeat. This type of relationship creates a split between those have knowledge and those who have nothing, projecting ignorance unto the other (p. 58). By killing curiosity and dominating the mind of the student, the teacher justifies their own existence.

The problem-posing method as a liberationist education "lies in its drive towards reconciliation" between teacher and student, oppressor and oppressed, "reconciling the poles of the contradiction so that both are simultaneously teachers and students" (Freire, 1972, p. 59), and in which the oppressed can apperceive their complicity their oppression, and the oppressor can recognize that in dehumanizing the oppressed, they dehumanize themselves as well. Whereas the banking system serves to "mirror oppressive society," problem-posing presents society as a question, something to be wrestled with and transformed. Those committed to liberation, Freire argues, must reject the entirety of the banking system, and adopt a relational psychology in which human beings are defined by and learn from relationships. Only then can one create conditions under which the human subject can become "conscious of, not only as intent on objects but as turned in upon itself in a Jasperian 'split'—consciousness as consciousness of consciousness" (pp. 66–67). A concientizing dialogue sheds light on one's subjectivity and context through reflection and exploration of other minds, minds which in turn reflect and are conscious of the self. This open, critical, and reflective dialogue then helps oppressed *and* oppressor to develop the ability to critically examine their way of being in the world, and the political structure of the world itself, "they come to see the world as a static reality, but as a reality in process, in transformation" (p. 71).

Love and Vulnerability as Emancipatory Power

Relationships of domination for Freire destroy all participants involved, reducing them to things. The oppressed become a dehumanized "it" by a lack of power or hunger for it, while the oppressors are turned into a monstrous "it," dehumanized by its excess. "And things," Freire writes, "cannot love" (Freire, 1973, p. 11). Vulnerability is the key to breaking out of the cycle of violence. And someone must "go first" (cf. Benjamin, 1988).

For the oppressed, it is important to witness vulnerability in the oppressor, so that a conviction in their ability to both resist *and* humanize them can grow. If the oppressor is able to see their own complicity, recognize that the oppressed have been wounded, and stop making superficial gestures they open themselves up to vulnerability and "risks an act of love" (Freire, 1972, p. 35). Without showing this vulnerability and risking an act of love, the oppressed will continue to alternate between either feeling fearful and dominated, or rising up to resist, destroy, and/or dominate.

Freire also recognized that many readers of Fanon recoiled from his theory of violence, and much like those in power quickly condemn any act of resistance on part of the oppressed—no matter how peaceful or how violent their tactics, no matter how justified. Here Freire notes an interesting paradox:

> It is . . . precisely in the response of the oppressed to the violence of their oppressors that a gesture of love may be found. Consciously or unconsciously, the act of rebellion by the oppressed (an act which is always, or nearly always, as violent as the initial violence of the oppressors) can initiate love. (1972, pp. 41–42)

While the violence of the oppressors and the social structure prevents the oppressed from actualizing their humanity, the oppressed's response—even a violent one—is an attempt at restoring the *right* to be human. In setting limits, demanding equity, and taking away the oppressor's power to dominate, the oppressed restore the oppressor's humanity—the very humanity lost in the act of violence and oppression (p. 42). Within the challenge of the oppressed to the oppressors, we can again hear the plea—no the *demand*—of Levinas' *autrui*: You have injured me, stepped over me, brutalized me, I demand/I entreat/I beg you treat me with justice! It is this act, uttered even in the so-called naïve or fanaticized stage of critical consciousness, that can free the oppressors, should they open their hearts to listen.

At the same time, Freire is aware that the oppressor-oppressed contradiction can become cyclical, lead to back and forth reversals of tension and continue with further violence and disconnection. The oppressor will likely not be responsive to the oppressed's cry for justice. Freire cautions that if liberation is the goal of the oppressed, "they will not achieve their goal by merely reversing the terms of the contradiction, by simply changing poles" (1972, p. 42). Therefore, the oppressed must fight not against the oppressor, but against the contradiction between oppressed and oppression itself, which will be overcome by the creation of a new mode of subjectivity—"neither oppressor nor oppressed, but man in the process of liberation" (p. 42). The oppressed, in order to subvert the rhetoric of oppressor, oppressed, and its reversals, can choose to "go first" by engaging in an act that demands change and condemns the violence of the oppressor, while at the same time, risking an act of love by showing vulnerability—a vulnerability that points not to the oppressor, but the system of injustice, inequality, and violence that mediates the two—the world that calls oppressor and oppressed into being to begin with. From this position, the oppressor is not seen as an enemy, but as another human who is trapped in the contradiction as well. Only then can there be a true dialogue, a "loving encounter of people, who, mediated by the world, 'proclaim' that world. They transform the world and in transforming it, humanize it for all people" (Freire, 1973, p. 115).

The Radical Ethic of a Psychoanalysis of Liberation

We return now to Freire's stipulation that liberation is the work of "radicals," not "sectarians." He believed that only those who become radicalized can risk an act of love, whereas sectarians, although they desire liberation, at the same time harbor a fear of freedom. The sectarian who considers themselves a radical may reject the *content* of the oppressors' values (white is good, non-white is bad), even *reverse* its terms (non-white is good, white is bad), but not the *process* of domination itself. That is to say, they may reject the view that the oppressed are bad, weak, immoral, etc., but make up for those views by viewing the oppressed in overly idealized, all-good terms. From that position, the oppressed are all good, and it is the oppressor who is all bad, and thus must be vanquished. Similarly, other oppressed people who do not hold exactly the same views are similarly seen as just as bad as the oppressor, even equivalent to them. Other oppressed who do not "toe the line" are then seen just as deserving of horizontal violence. In this sense, the oppressed whose consciousness becomes fanaticized maintains an identification with the *position* of the oppressor, with the view that to be (human) is *to have*. This dynamic is akin to the classic salsa anthem, *Quitate tu pa ponerme yo*—"Get out of there, so that I can be there [in the position of the powerful]." One cannot resist quoting Audre Lorde in this context—one cannot use the master's tools to dismantle his house.

True radicals, Freire argues, *reject* this identification with the oppressor in all senses of the phrase, breaking not only with the oppressor's ideology (values, beliefs, etc.), but also the position of the one "who has," "who controls." Instead of engaging in a reversal of terms to dominate the other, the radical revolutionary instead risks an act of love. By being radically vulnerable and taking this risk, radicals humanize the other, inviting the other into a new relationship where together they can explore and understand the contours of their world, a world that splits and pits humanity into haves and have-nots, in order to change it. As between oppressor and oppressed so too between the literate and illiterate—this provides a corrective emotional experience in which they

> would begin to effect a change in his former attitudes, by discovering himself to be a maker of the world of culture, by discovering that he, as well as the literate person, has a creative and re-creative impulse. He would discover that culture is just as much a clay doll made by artists who are his peers as it is the work of a great sculptor, a great painter, a great mystic, or a great philosopher; that culture is the poetry of lettered poets and also the poetry of his own popular songs—that culture is all human creation. (Freire, 1973, p. 47)

And like all human creations, culture, society, and economics become subject to dialogue, negotiation, playfulness, and discovery.

THE LIMITS AND POSSIBILITIES OF FREIRE'S RADICAL PEDAGOGY

Freire's influence throughout the social sciences is profound, impacting education and the birth of liberation psychology, multicultural psychology, sociology, political science, critical race theory, and queer and gender studies—wherever there are activists and scholars committed to social justice. At the same time, there are important critiques that have been made of his work, which also provide a lead in to generating a dialogue between him, Freud, and Fanon.

Gonzalez-Monteagudo (2014) notes that objections have been raised to Freire's generalizing abstractions regarding the "oppressor" and the "oppressed," without reference to particular identities and forms of struggle (e.g., race and racism, gender and patriarchy, sexuality and heteronormativity). Such a "universalizing" stance, while potentially broadening the applicability of Freire's theories, risks neglecting the specific experiences of different marginalized groups. Similarly, scholars like Yang (2014) have called for a repositioning of critical consciousness within an intersectional framework that contextualizes how race and gender identities operate with relative, overlapping, and shifting levels of privilege and oppression. Freire himself, in the latter stages of his career, certainly responded to these critiques by paying greater attention to issues of race and gender, incorporating and growing from his critics (Apple, 2003; Freire, 1996; Gonzalez-Monteagudo, 2014). For example, he discussed how the dynamics of oppression reflect the "ideology of 'whiteness', it is the centre that knows, while the 'periphery' never knows. It is the centre that decides, while the periphery is the object of decisions made by others" (Freire & Faundez, 1989, p. 88).

Indeed, in light of this historical review of Freire's psychoanalytic and intellectual influences, themselves intimately concerned with Blackness and Afro-Latinx subjectivity and interiority, it is *striking* that his foundational works make no mention of race whatsoever. It is important to contextualize this both in his own subjectivity as a light-skinned Brazilian, his pedagogical work, and the racial politics of Brazil. On the one hand, Freire had a clear sense of how oppression in Brazil was "colour-coded." Sharing his own conversations with Freire, American educator Michael Apple (2003) wrote,

> When he [Freire] spoke about the murderous histories of the treatment of indigenous people in Brazil and throughout the world, this sense became even stronger. He and I discussed the "myth of racial democracy" in Brazil and the rapidly growing politics of racial identity that had been taking place among Afro-Brazilian people. For him, this was one of the most important movements in Brazil and elsewhere and he reflected on its meaning for his own sense of a pedagogy of the oppressed. (p. 108)

In their discussion Apple recalls Freire drew on similar points to the ones he made in *Pedagogy of the Oppressed*, that liberation must be forged with, not for the oppressed, leading Apple to state that, "The struggles by Afro-Brazilian people against subjugation were not abstractions to him. He saw them as part of the necessary struggles against domination" (p. 108). At the same time, Apple confirms one's impression from reading Freire that class analysis was a tool he saw as both crucial yet limited.

This would suggest that the obvious empirical reality, that Freire's pedagogical work was with predominantly Afro-Latinx and indigenous communities, was something he was keenly aware of. One cannot help, then, but retroactively read his use of the terms "oppressor" and "oppressed" as indubitably and tacitly *colored* White and Black/Brown as much as they were more overtly discussed in terms of class. Why did Freire not state this explicitly then? One possibility lies in the evolution of racial politics in Brazil. During Juliano Moreira's time in the turn of the century leading up to Arthur Ramos' work in the 1940s there was a shift from Lombroso's overtly racist theories of inherited degeneracy, to a psychoanalytically informed mode of thinking that saw mental illness and social dysfunction as environmentally acquired and universal—in other words, not limited to specific racial groups. As noted above, while Ramos' hope for a racial democracy stressed integration and greater racial equality, the assimilation of this concept in Brazilian body-politics lifted up an idyllic image of harmonious racial integration (exemplified in Gilberto Freyre's work), which also depended on a kind of color-blindness to limit potentially pathologizing ascriptions of degeneracy to racial difference.

This is why Ramos, for example, increasingly limited or erased mentions of race in his case studies in order to prevent an easy association between a patient's race and mental illness. Practicing color-blindness, then, was a strategy for minimizing racial conflict and racial stereotyping. As Alberto Guerreiro Ramos argued in his critique of Arthur Ramos, however, this also had the effect of rendering actual racial inequality and violence invisible, something Freire himself would later openly admit and recognize. For Arthur Ramos and Paulo Freire's respective generations, liberal-progressive anti-racism went in hand with a universalizing tendency whose purpose was to *prevent* denigration of racial others, which inadvertently created other problems in theory and praxis. One cannot *concientize* an oppressive reality which is rendered invisible. In this sense, Ramos, in following Freud's critique of Lombroso, engaged in the same problems as his predecessor. To make the analogy, as noted in an earlier chapter Freud often did not mention the Jewish heritage of his patients in his clinical writing, with the same intention of preventing an easy association between Jewishness and mental illness.

At the same time, part of the strength and applicability of Freire's work to discursive practices as diverse as critical race theory, Latinx studies, pedagogy, multicultural psychology, and liberation psychology lies precisely in his general and non-essentialist discussion of oppressor and oppressed (Mayo, 1993). There is no privileged or universal group, determined in advance, to serve as a primary lens of social analysis nor site of political transformation. Along these lines Freire clarified in a later statement (cited in Mayo, 1993) that one cannot reduce all forms of oppression, as is in vogue in a certain strain of Marxist thought, to the contradictions of class struggle. As Freire took on different roles and positions as a career educator, his overt emphasis shifted from illiterate campesinos living on the margins of major urban centers, to poor Brazilians of African descent, to people of color in the U.S., to dispossessed women facing a "double labor" in Brazilian cities (Mayo, 1993). In each context Freire re-read his theories through the immanent experiences of the communities he served, and so too have different ethno-racial communities across the world read and re-read his work through their own local experience, effectively extending and transforming it in turn.

However, there is a critique more central to Freire's pedagogy and world-view, aimed at his "utopian" vision of society. Freire's conception of the eventual "victory of the oppressed" has been recognized to be too linear and utopian, mired in mechanistic Marxist notions of the rebellion of the proletariat (Gonzalez-Monteagudo, 2014). As observed by Simpson and McMillan (2008), some of Freire's critics, especially among leftist-progressive circles, "seem charred by his radical and uncompromising love, a love that seeks to humanize even the dehumanizer" (Simpson & McMillan, p. 4). Does this not place the oppressed in a vulnerable position of further subjugation, providing some form of care-taking to the very oppressors who have traumatized and dehumanized them? Is it not asking too much of the oppressed to perform this "labor," when the oppressor either refuses or (as Freire himself claims) is unable to do so? It is at this juncture that a dialogue across generations of psychoanalytic thinkers is called for, bringing together divergent and convergent strands of theorizing on culture and society, oppression and liberation, from Freud to Fanon to Freire. It is in taking stock of their thinking across generations that we will be positioned to examine how these routes lead into Martín-Baró's liberation psychology.

Chapter Six

"To Recognize Ourselves In Our Reality"

Liberation Psychology as Political Mentalization

In his opus *The Psychoanalytic Theory of Neurosis*, Otto Fenichel (1945) took a moment near the end of his work to deviate from his encyclopedic review of theory and technique to address something he found quite curious. "It is strange," he remarked, "that two absolutely contradictory judgments can be heard in respect to neuroses" (p. 588). He found that some believed neuroses and mental illness to be a direct result of social and economic deprivation, "that it is not surprising that people who lack food and shelter become 'nervous.'" Others argued that neuroses and psychotherapeutic treatment are "a kind of 'luxury of the idle rich' and that a workman has other things in his head than to be nervous." Such debates, one recognizes with much chagrin, have not changed much in over a half century. "Both statements are wrong," he clarified, "and, in their clash of opinion, betray only the general emotional resistance against an unprejudiced study of the neuroses." The "enormous extent" of neuroses in society did not recognize class differences. At the same time, "This statement does not contradict the thesis that the neuroses are socially determined. It only illustrates the fact that morality, in spite of extremely different living conditions, is not too different in the different classes of the same society" (p. 588). Fenichel here seems to address a contradiction at the heart of liberal debates around oppression, psychology, and mental health, one which resurfaces time and again.

Is it only, for example, that social, cultural, material, economic, and political deprivation that impacts rates of mental illness and distress among communities of color? Or, as Patricia Gherovici is fond of saying "tongue and cheek," are marginalized communities "too busy" being poor to have an unconscious? Furthermore, if both the poor and the rich, or people of color and White people, struggle with trauma and mental health issues, it is argued, then social, political, and economic forces must be irrelevant to mental health. What this kind of debate obfuscates is that it is not merely the marginalization of an oppressed group that is the problem.

What liberation psychology teaches us, from Freud to Martín-Baró, is that the problem is a social and economic *system* that by oppressing some, ends up destroying all. And it is out of that dehumanization that, perhaps ironically, communities on different sides of a social antagonism can come to share in a similar type of neurotic "morality"—what Erich Neumann (1990) would have termed the "old ethic" of creating a scapegoat which functions as an obstacle to fulfilling an idealized world, an ethic which then demands the destruction and purification of that obstacle. Indeed, Fanon (1952/2008) would have concurred with this analysis when he wrote, "The Negro enslaved by his inferiority, the white man enslaved by his superiority alike behave in accordance with a neurotic orientation" (pp. 42–43). This chapter will first summarize and integrate the underlying psychodynamic theories of inequality, critical consciousness, and liberation of the preceding chapters, and draw on liberation theology, the psychology of humiliation, and research on attachment theory and inequality to understand how this scapegoat system works to distort both oppressor and oppressed. With this clarification in hand, I will conclude by showing how these ideas influenced the life and work of the founder of liberation psychology, Ignacio Martín-Baró.

A PSYCHOANALYTIC PSYCHOLOGY OF LIBERATION

If we turn to the structure of Freud, Fanon, and Freire's theories of oppression and liberation, we find—again, following Tate's (1996) classic paper on Freud, race, and psychoanalysis—a fascinating tripartite structure of sociopolitical antagonisms. In Freud, and also Fenichel, we find a psychoanalytic analysis of how ruling White European elites maintain their position of domination relative to the White European working class by providing them with a ready-made other—the non-White, "Black" Jew. By displacing economic hatred, envy, and hostility along racial lines, a system of economic inequality is maintained through the creation of a racial other which then solidifies identification between the White working-class and the ruling White upper-class. In Fanon, we find not only a binary antagonism of colonizer and colonized, but also a similar tripartite tension between the colonized Black/African, the colonizing Whites and especially working class Whites, and the White bourgeois caste. By remaining "in slumber" via enthrallment to the White bourgeois, the working-class continues to "play footsie" with the powerful by oppressing or being indifferent to the plight of the Black and Brown colonized people of the world. Lastly, Freire provides us with a extensively delineated model comprised of oppressor, oppressed, *and* the sub-oppressors who participate in the reproduction of a system of exploitation and domination. A model that, as covered in the previous chapter, was built upon and tacitly addresses racial tensions in Freire's Brazilian society.

Such a psychoanalytic reading of race and class suggests that racism serves at least three interconnected functions: (1) dominate, exploit, and control the minds and bodies of Black, Brown, and other non-White peoples through the cultural and economic mechanisms of racial otherness, (2) dominate, exploit, and control the minds and bodies of the White working class by mobilizing fear and anger toward a racial other, and (3) maintain a system of rampant racial and economic inequality. I will expand further on this point in my conclusion, but suffice it to say for now, the history we reviewed in chapter 1 suggests a very complex relationship between race and class.

It is not simply that racism is a tool for class domination. Rather, if we remember how earlier European mythologies of Blackness and Aryanness were used to mark the boundaries between "Aryan princes" among the ruling class in comparison to the "blackened" White European peasants, we can see how class is intimately textured by prototypical notions of race. With the advent of colonialism, the introduction of Black and Brown bodies in the conflict of White bourgeoisie and working class, a displacement of sorts occurred—"*You* are not really Black," the ruling powers clarify to their poor, "*they are.*" And so the rulers and their poor participate in the unholy communion of Whiteness—"This is our body . . ." This history, seen through the prism of psychoanalysis, suggests that class is perennially textured by race, much as race, and specifically anti-Blackness, is wielded as a weapon of class domination and capitalist exploitation. Racial justice activist Scott Nakagawa (2012) once wrote that "anti-Black racism is the fulcrum of White Supremacy." This analysis suggests that anti-Blackness and racial discourse are, along the lines suggested by Karl Marx (see Anderson, 2017; Jeannot, 2007; Singh, 2016), just as easily *the fulcrum of capitalism*.

At the same time, reading Freud and Fanon through Freire, we find that just as the terms oppressor, oppressed, and sub-oppressor can reflect antagonisms such as White ruling class, people of color, and White working-class, it is important to recognize that these are not the only possibilities. The model could just as easily reflect dynamics within subaltern communities, such as Latinx communities (oppressed) in relation to White supremacy and the White ruling class (oppressor). Among Latinxs, for example, may arise contingents of—let's say—White middle-upper class Latinxs or even working-class Latinxs who identify with the White upper class, and become sub-oppressors in relation to darker-skinned and poorer members of the Latinx community. Extending this argument further, one expresses concern in relation to the Black and Latinx middle-upper class who identify with the White/Capitalist bourgeois as the only possibility for political interpellation and inclusion, becoming sub-oppressors by enacting policies and discourses which harm the Black and Latinx poor.

Of course, these psychopolitical conflicts are not limited to race and class. The various ways in which capital—and its erstwhile cultural mechanisms such as gender, sexuality, race, etc.—can splinter, divide, and turn communities against one another should give pause for concern in our contemporary political landscape. A liberation psychology is then a psychology of how political polarization and inequality harms oppressed communities and the well-being of nations. In order to highlight the implications of this theorizing for our world today, and clarify the connection between Freud, Fanon, Freire, and Martín-Baró, I will now turn to examining the trauma of shame and humiliation as affects central to the psychology of political violence and polarization. In tandem, I will also unpack the psychopolitical implications of critical consciousness through the perspective of attachment-based mentalization theory. By drawing on contemporary theorizing on shame, political action, and trauma, we will find ample context for the genius of Martín-Baró's work, and for the legacy of psychoanalysis in informing liberation psychology.

LIBERATION THEOLOGY, SOCIAL JUSTICE, AND THE PSYCHOLOGY OF SHAME

Gustavo Gutierrez (1971/2006), one of the pioneering figures of liberation theology in Latin America, spoke of the importance of balancing "the universality of God's love and God's predilection for those on the lowest rung of the ladder of history. To focus exclusively on the one or the other is to mutilate the Christian message. Therefore every attempt at such an exclusive emphasis must be rejected" (p. xxvi). For Gutierrez, the poor and oppressed deserve this preferential option *not* because they are morally superior or more pure than others, but because they have been victims of oppression. I read this to be a *de*-idealizing stance on the part of liberation theology, to hesitate on impinging some sense of ultimate goodness upon oppressed peoples. Liberation theology, and the liberationist movements descended from it, must take precisely such a discourse which is self-critical and "aware of itself," preventing a premature jump to superficial activism, preserving communities from falling into "fetishism and idolatry, as well as from a pernicious and belittling narcissism" (p. 10).

Gutierrez (1971/2006) concludes that, "The universality of Christian love is, I repeat, incompatible with the exclusion of any persons, but it is not incompatible with a preferential option for the poorest and most oppressed"

(p. 160). He clearly entertains a kind of dialectics, between serious commitment to the poorest and must vulnerable, and at the same time, de-centering that very central value by allowing space for some notion of universality. However, as I have discussed in this book so far, hatred, anger, and humiliation that result from oppression are real affects that must be contended with as part of any emancipatory discourse or social movement. Given Gutierrez's recognition that, "*Indigent, weak, bent over, wretched* are terms which well express a degrading human situation . . . The climate in which poverty is described is one of indignation" (p. 165), we must in turn further delineate the relationship between shame and humiliation to social justice.

To sharpen my discussion of shame, humiliation, and anger, I will draw on Jones (2008), who has articulated a compelling psychodynamic model from which to think about the relationship between these affects and social transformation. Although he wrote primarily with religion and religiously motivated terrorism in mind, I also find his work highly applicable to this book's concerns. Jones wrote that there are five components which operate in tandem to turn a social group toward violence:

> (1) profound experiences of shame and humiliation either generated by social conditions outside the group and potentiated by it or generated from within the group, (2) splitting humanity into all-good and all-evil camps and the demonizing of the other, (3) a wrathful, punitive idealized deity or leader, (4) a conviction that purification requires the shedding of blood, and often (5) a fascination with violence. (p. 70)

Jones is quick to caution given his object of study—religiously motivated terrorism—that "not everyone from an oppressed or occupied community joins a suicide campaign" (p. 118), and I am certainly not trying to make that comparison here. What I want to do is borrow the language of shame to talk about how marginalized and oppressed communities can experience humiliation, and how feelings of shame serve psychopolitical purposes.

Groups that experience humiliation due to their social conditions—for example, low income African-Americans subject to disproportionate policing practices, Latin American immigrants separated from their families and kept in cages, Palestinians treated like terrorists at Israeli checkpoints, Jews victim to violence within their houses of worship—can then have those feelings either regulated or exacerbated by a social movement or religious affiliation. The splitting of the world into all-good and all-bad groups, with the demonizing of "the other" need not depend on radicalization by an extremist group. As Fanon noted, this splitting on part of the oppressed often reflects their existential-material situation, serving as *a natural response to the splitting of their oppressors*.

These emergent groups, whether religious or sociopolitical in nature, may provide idealized precepts to those who face oppression: a revised and idyllic history, values, and traditions that uplift rather than denigrate the community; a belief in an eschaton in which the "last will be first," redemption is assured, and the unjust will face their due; a charismatic leader who advocates for change; etc. For Jones (2008) it is not the idealization of aspects of the community that is a problem, but whether those idealized objects, figures, and values *also* become a source of shame and humiliation (p. 122). Absolute purity, whether religiously, ideologically, or politically is demanded, with submission to the values of the community a necessary price of membership, with communal exile as the alternative.

As Jones (2008) describes in his model, the more such groups hold the belief that purification of the oppressed requires the shedding of blood, and the more they become fascinated, even obsessed, with violence as a necessary mechanism to achieve their goals, the more likely then the predilection toward violence and the justification for terrorism and extremism. But terrorism and militant violence are extreme forms of this kind of fanaticism. And often, I would argue, not necessary for the kind of violence that someone like Freire envisioned. The horizontal violence he identified and was critical of need not be physical or even fatal. The wielding of power, and especially the taking of a position of power over an other through identification with the oppressor, is psychologically and politically violent enough.

Jones (2008) describes how religion, and I would add, even movements for social change, can contribute to a cycle of scapegoating which promotes and magnifies humiliation. At the same time, these very movements can also be powerful sources of transformation and liberation. Jones' vision for this possibility is worth quoting at length:

> We should also note that religion may mute and transform that humiliation rather than reinforce it, as the Dalai Lama is trying to do with the Tibetans under Chinese occupation and as Martin Luther King attempted to do with the humiliation of African Americans in the face of American racism. Clearly a different psychology—a different view of the divine, a rejection of splitting and dichotomizing, a conscious muting or transformation of aggression—is at work in those who seek to transform humiliation rather than magnify it . . . the ability to empathize with a victim decreases the use of violence. So religions that seek to move those feeling humiliated away from violence work to encourage compassion and empathy for the other, even the other who is a source of social or economic humiliation. (pp. 122–123)

Jones follows Rene Girard's psychoanalytic anthropology of the "scapegoat system" in arguing for methods of solidarity "based on an identification with the violence-victim" rather than with the perpetrators (p. 155).

Jones (2008) points to the tradition of the Jewish prophets and their unceasing critique of ceremonial and sacrifice in favor of justice. Echoing Freud's own attraction to the ethic of the prophets, Jones argues that traditions "that connect us to a transcendental or sacred reality that critiques and relativizes our egotism and its acquisitive desires are the only way out of the mimetic cycle of rivalry and violence" (p. 156). This implies developing discursive practices, organizing tactics, effective policies, individual and communal therapeutic approaches, and activist methodologies that serve "to replace shame and humiliation with realistic humility, to overcome splitting and demonization with an acknowledgement of human commonality, [and] to evoke experiences of forgiveness and compassion rather than abjection and condemnation" (p. 170). These values have long been a component of liberation psychology, and resonate with other social justice methodologies such as restorative justice (see Watkins & Shulman, 2008). However, they deserve further clarification. It can be said that the wounding, humiliation, and injury that result from oppression reveals a socio-systemic *failure in mentalization*. This in turn also impacts the ability of the oppressed to mentalize about their psychological, interpersonal, and societal reality. In order to further flesh out these ideas I will describe recent thinking in attachment theory which has taken a turn beyond the caregiver-infant dyad toward the social, systemic, and communal sphere.

ATTACHMENT THEORY, RACE, AND POLITICS

Attachment theory, originated by the psychoanalyst John Bowlby and expanded upon by Mary Ainsworth and other investigators, is one of the juggernauts of contemporary developmental and clinical psychology research, with widespread influence in public policy as much as clinical intervention. As explained by Duschinsky, Greco, and Solomon (2015), the influence of attachment theory has been felt as much in the laboratory and the clinic as it has in the political economy of gender. They note how attachment theory has been employed to politically conservative ends as a way to police mothers and families, emphasizing psychological factors for well-being while obfuscating the role of socio-economic and systemic factors—Bowlby's remark that it is "fortunate for their survival that babies are so designed by Nature that they beguile and enslave mothers" (cited in Duschinsky, Greco, & Solomon, 2015, p. 181) notwithstanding. Following Deleuze and Guattari, however, they also argue for the deployment of attachment theory for progressive politics. They cede the point that the activation of the attachment system in an infant—the pull toward the mother or primary caregiver as a "haven of safety"—can be read as an "ontologically 'conservative' vector," but push back that this conservatism "is in turn a vector for the possibility of becoming (as) an individual at the molar level of the child, a vector of the process of returning-to-oneself-as-an-other" (p. 184). While there is a need for a "line of sight" toward the caregiver (attachment theory itself does not require it be strictly a biological mother), there is also a need for a "pull outward," the caregiver functioning as a secure base from which the infant can individuate by going out to explore the world. Attachment theory, then, doubles as a theory of the intersubjective negotiation of needs between parent and child, as opposed to a model of radical dependence that demands the mother's constant availability, with all the economic and social implications that this would entail.

Dalal (2006) also critiques and repurposes attachment theory from within a relational psychodynamic and political point of view, outlining a "theory of difference" which can be applied to different dimensions of identity, but within the bounds of his article, with race and racism as his focus. Dalal describes the basic components of attachment theory—the biologically driven need to connect, to belong, to find some secure base for the development of the self. "Attachment theory tells us," he elaborates, "that one does not have a choice about whether to attach or not, we cannot help but attach, however vile or neglectful the base is" (p. 18). When we experience disruption in attachment with an unavailable, shaming, or distant other, we can often respond with aggression and protest, avoidance and self-soothing, or even fall into an obsessive, hypervigilant states, which are also "found readily in descriptions of racist phenomena" (p. 19).

Dalal (2006) cites Felicity de Zulueta's account of racism from precisely such an attachment perspective:

> Racism . . . begins, as all acts of dehumanization, by a distortion of perception . . . This cognitive process *originates* . . . from the experience of abuse which the infant or child attempts to ward off by identifying with the aggressor . . . *the seeds of . . . racism . . . are sown in the emotional words of the abused and traumatized.* (de Zulueta, 1993, p. 244; cited in Dalal, 2006, p. 19, italics added)

Dalal notes Zulueta's argument that racist beliefs are *only* possible when developmentally injurious templates of dehumanization are already present. To put it another way—a child who faces abuse, adversity, and mistreatment from their caregivers is more susceptible to adopting racist beliefs. Dalal here rightly criticizes this naïve developmental tilts. While acknowledging that trauma early in development could certainly contribute to a desire to "make good" on the injuries of one's childhood by becoming aggressive toward people of color, this is neither necessary nor sufficient to account for racism itself.

In this way I agree with Dalal's overall criticism of a developmental tilt in the psychoanalytic analysis of racism, while at the same time, cannot help but appraise how, from a phenomenological perspective, de Zulueta's perspective dovetails with those of liberation psychology—racism as a form of *dehumanization* that results from a distorted view of the other, a view that originates from one's own experience of dehumanization by the powerful, which is warded off in order to maintain an identification with them. Relatedly, there is evidence that as inequality increases, so too do rates of child maltreatment (Eckenrode et al., 2014). Perhaps there *is* some mechanism whereby inequality impacts one's schemas of self and other by disrupting attachment relationships in childhood themselves. Conversely, childhood trauma need not be a prerequisite for this process. Being subjected to marginality, dispossession, inequality, and violence, and then told that the cause of your suffering is the racial-ethnic other (the Jew is taking your money, the Black is benefiting from your tax dollars, the Latinx is taking your jobs, etc.), is, if not sufficient, a tried and true formula for the powerful to exert their domination throughout the century.

Although attachment theory has been extensively studied and validated cross-culturally, Dalal (2006) asks us to go beyond a multicultural ethic of merely "respecting differences," and contextualizes attachment theory within "the problematic of power" (p. 20). Power and social relations texture the parent's capacity to *mentalize*—that is, to hold a picture of the child's thoughts and feelings and then reflect back this reality to the child. Dalal unpacks how the child derives their sense of self through the parent's mentalizing function (or lack thereof), and that this function is impacted by social discourses that privilege "desired" identities and denigrate "undesirable" ones, such as the case of Afro-Caribbean and Latinx families who express subtle favoritism for the male, light-skinned child. Dalal is adamant on this point—it is not just an image of the child that is reflected back, but an *attitude* formed and constrained by social discourse, yet formed by the caregiver's own unconscious. It is these pre-reflective attitudes or organizing principles, operating outside of awareness, that allow consciousness to take form, and make up the nature of the social unconscious as such (p. 23).

Hence, the self the infant develops in the attachment relationship to the caregiver is intrinsically textured by society (as Lacanians might argue), rendering social categories of identity (race, gender, class, etc.) as integral to the sense of a "true me." This leads Dalal (2006) to conclude, "*then it follows that in attaching to persons we are also, of necessity, attaching to categories, however subliminal our sense of them might be*" (p. 25, emphasis original). This is why attacks on our social identities, even those identities that operate outside of conscious awareness, feel like attacks on our sense of self. In the same way that we cannot not-attach to others in forming relationship, so too we cannot not-belong in developing our social identities. And in the same stroke as we "belong" to one thing, Dalal reminds us, we "do not belong" to another, and don't allow others to "belong to us." This binds experiences of attachment and social belonging to "the negation of something and someone" (p. 25). Such differences similarly mark a distinction between "haves" and "have-nots," with attending emotional valences of idealization and denigration.

Dalal, in line with much developmental and clinical thinking, sees more benign forms of attachment as resulting from the capacity for empathy, which is central to mentalization. Racism, by contrast, functions as a paradoxical "keeping in touch/distancing" that betrays a different, we might say disorganized, form of attachment. "If we go down this road then," Dalal wonders, "could we say that hate too is a form of attachment?" (p. 34). In reflecting on how a hateful attachment to blackness took form over the course of centuries, Dalal remarks,

> It is surprising to discover how recent so many of these associations are. The association of black with dirt was first recorded in 1300 AD, with death in 1400 AD, immorality in 1552 AD, with evil in 1581 AD. Eventually, things that can have no colour like the negative emotions start being called black from the 17th century onwards. This last point is a particularly telling one. What it is showing is that as the world is becoming increasingly colour coded, so is the psyche. (p. 29)

His conclusion is that depending on time, place, and politics, Blackness "gets attached to a thing *in order* to cathect it with repellence, with the converse being true of whiteness" (p. 29). This leads Dalal to an interesting and, perhaps, idiosyncratic definition of racism—"*racism is the manufacture and use of the notion of race*" (p. 32, emphasis original). If so, who is manufacturing it? And more importantly, for what purpose? Whose needs and purposes are served by this reproduction of race, this trans-historical denigration of Blackness? What *function* does it serve within the psychic and political economy?

Epistemic Trust and Inequality

In a recent piece on mentalization and political trauma, Lorenzini, Campbell, and Fonagy (2018) articulate a series of research and theory-based arguments that inadvertently connect with a hundred years of thinking in liberation psychology—which makes sense given that attachment theory, like liberation psychology, has important roots in psychoanalysis. They define mentalizing as "the capacity to understand other people and oneself in terms of possible thoughts, feelings, wishes, and desires" (p. 403). This is an ability built up over the course of one's early attachments to primary caregivers, as well as subsequent attachments throughout the lifespan. We depend on other's ability to mentalize our inner state in order to nurture our own. When the individual's relationships become repeatedly disrupted, as in cases of trauma, there is a "closing off of the mind to the possibility of accessing other people's minds as *safe and reliable* sources of knowledge about how to navigate the social environment" (p. 403, emphasis added), which I would argue, includes navigating our interpersonal *and* political environment. The extent to which our mind is open to the other, and able to mentalize them as a safe and reliable source of knowledge reflects what Fonagy and others have called "epistemic trust."

Trauma, abuse, and mistreatment have been found to be related to reduced ability to reflect and mentalize, in turn eroding epistemic trust (Lorenzini, Campbell, & Fonagy, 2018, p. 406). Lorenzini, Campbell, and Fonagy note the importance of the *other's* ability to mentalize in our recovery—"we are far more likely to learn from and listen to someone else if we feel that that person has recognized our agency and subjectivity. We are more likely to adopt a position of epistemic trust toward someone if they appear to be able to mentalize us" (p. 406). Receiving empathy, recognition, and understanding from the other in turn opens up our capacity to empathize, recognize, and mentalize, increasing our trust toward them. Under conditions of chronic and repeated trauma, we protect ourselves by developing a form of epistemic vigilance and mistrust. Although helpful in preventing us from trusting others who are untrustworthy and potentially dangerous, the crystallization of epistemic mistrust renders "the subject unable to learn from the social context, and this perpetuates maladaptive relationship patterns" (p. 406). Thus, one of the outcomes of political trauma is to essentially isolate minds—individuals as well as entire communities—from one another such that mentalizing dialogue cannot take place. The inability to trust socially and politically can then play a role in perpetuating mutually reinforcing maladaptive cycles that leave us unable to perceive our political situation accurately, and alongside others, build relationships and alliances to effect political and economic change.

Acknowledging the attachment literature's focus on caregiving relationships, Lorenzini, Campbell, and Fonagy (2018) ask,

> But, what if that family is operating within a wider social system characterised by high levels of violence and threat, particularly if the violence and threat emanate from entrenched social and political institutions? In such circumstances, it may not be possible to regard neighbours, school teachers, and even relatives as trustworthy. (p. 407)

As a survival mechanism, the "epistemic channel" between caregiver and child, teacher and student, community leaders and constituents, etc., might be used to communicate a need for epistemic vigilance. This might take an explicit form, for example, when parents tell their children "don't talk to strangers." Or when African-American parents have "the talk" with their children about police brutality and being Black in America. But this communication may also take implicit forms, in the subtle ways that parents express anxiety, anger, and fear toward certain "others," affect that is then mentalized by the child as a cue to exhibit epistemic vigilance toward that object. These explicit and implicit cues, in turn, may reflect broader social antagonisms. It is important at this point to recall a fascinating point Fonagy, Luyten, Allison, and Campbell (2017) made in an earlier article on epistemic trust and socio-political context. They reviewed how a history of adversity can impair the capacity for epistemic trust, leading to a stance in which one is unable to respond to new information from the environment, developing a rigid cognitive-emotional stance, citing Wilkinson and Pickett's (2009) work on inequality and mental health.

The point Fonagy and colleagues make in regard to mentalization, epistemic trust, and inequality requires some unpacking of Wilkinson and Pickett's work. In a pioneering series of books (Wilkinson & Pickett, 2009; 2019) as well as a updated review article (Pickett & Wilkinson, 2015) and recent follow-up book (Wilkinson & Pickett, 2019), they compared the Western developed countries in terms of their relative level of inequality, what they also call the "inequality gradient." They documented how countries with widening wealth inequality fared much worse in prevalence of negative social, medical, and mental health outcomes. Examples include worse outcomes for life expectancy, infant mortality, academic performance, homicides, percentage of the population in prison, teenage births, obesity, mental illness including drug and alcohol misuse, social mobility, and germane to Fonagy's work, level of trust. When they conducted mediator analyses of the relationship between inequality and psychosocial outcomes, they found that these were mediated by social capital—the degree to which people are involved in their communities and draw on social supports—and the level of mutual trust between people. In essence, Wilkinson and Pickett argue, inequality leads to worse psychosocial outcomes not only through the obvious systemic damage it renders, but primarily through the erosion of the capacity for trust and empathy between individuals and communities.

Wilkinson and Pickett (2009) note that if one were to simply assess the relationships between gross income and psychosocial factors, these relationships disappear, which implies that it is not average income that drives these outcomes (e.g., whether one is rich or poor), but the degree of inequality itself. This relates to their second point, that although there is much evidence for the negative medical, social, and psychological outcomes associated with being trapped in utter poverty and destitution, these negative outcomes affect social classes across the board. To be clear—they do not argue that the richest and poorest are *equally* miserable, but rather that in countries where there is a wider wealth gap *everyone* suffers. Although the poor do very poorly (forgiving the redundancy) as a result of marginalization, the rich in more unequal countries also face worse outcomes in well-being. In this sense, inequality distorts and wounds everyone, including those who are "at the top."

In explaining their findings and the results of their mediator analysis, Wilkinson and Pickett (2009) argue that greater inequality heightens one's social evaluation anxiety, increasing the importance of one's status on a given hierarchy. Getting a sense of where one "sits" on this hierarchy relative to "the other" becomes increasingly central as inequality widens. In sum, they write,

> Changes in inequality and trust go together over the years. With greater inequality, people are less caring of one another, there is less mutuality in relationships, people have to fend for themselves and get what they can—so, inevitably, there is less trust. Mistrust and inequality reinforce each other. As de Tocqueville pointed out, we are less likely to empathize with those not seen as equals; material differences serve to divide us socially. (p. 56)

Inequality corrupts social relations and gets inside our skulls, so to speak, by creating a litany of social divisions framing different configurations of haves and have-nots, which are crafted in terms of rich and poor, White and non-White, men and women, straight and LGBTQ, able and differently abled, and so on. This creates a prime environment for one to ask—who is the cause of this division? Who has taken my job, my opportunity, my partner, my future? In an environment of epistemic mistrust, the voice of the powerful answers: "It was the other! They have humiliated you and taken what is rightfully yours. But do not fear, *be like me and all will be restored. You will be great again.*"

Critical Consciousness and Political Mentalization

Returning to Lorenzini, Campbell, and Fonagy (2018), they argue that when others in our environment are unable to mentalize us, in turn impacting our ability to mentalize ourselves, those aspects which are unable to find a home in consciousness come to comprise our "alien self, which disrupts self-coherence" (p. 408). In a context of political repression, inequality, and violence, this alien self can produce what they call a "totalitarian object," which is not experienced as separate from the self (note the parallels with Freire). The totalitarian object "strives to control and own the other to impose a rigid ideology" (p. 408). This internalized object "can be idealized and identified with, because it is thought that this object is also a source of safety, self-importance and (false) wholeness" (p. 408). This alien self which has been structured by the environment into a totalitarian object is not able to receive corrective feedback due to the individual's epistemic mistrust, which is "carefully manipulated by totalitarian authorities through propaganda, persecution of creative endeavours, and through the prohibition of assembly" (p.

408). This totalitarian object, furthermore, thwarts "exploration and creativity, impede constructive dialogue and blur the borders between internal and external reality, in a state of 'psychic equivalence' . . . [representing] a dogmatic truth" (p. 408). In the absence of an external, different perspective that can facilitate working through traumatic experience, the totalitarian object isolates individuals and entire communities from communing with one another, engaging in a productive dialogue which can allow the trauma and its source to be mentalized and transformed.

Following the work of Chilean psychoanalyst Juan Pablo Jimenez, who experienced violence and torture during the civil war and unrest of the 1970s, Lorenzini, Campbell, and Fonagy (2018) argue that overcoming experiences of oppression involves coping "with the ambiguity of the way we interpret the world . . . to work though the position of victim, we inevitably find the aggressor within us" (cited in p. 410). Wrestling with the internalized oppressor means becoming aware of and verbalizing one's "alien totalitarian object, to tolerate self-incoherence" (p. 410) while pushing toward a new, liberated, and more pluralistic sense of self. Shifting from the socio-political to the clinical, Lorenzini, Campbell, and Fonagy argue that the role of the therapist is to build a relationship in which the patient "feels his/her subjective experience is being thought about so that he/she can begin to trust the social world again" (p. 412). This is less a matter of didactic teaching than it is "rekindling" an evolutionary capacity for learning from others, which Lorenzini, Campbell, and Fonagy curiously (from a Freirean point of view) call "natural pedagogy."

Lorenzini, Campbell, and Fonagy's (2018) clinical recommendations hold important political relevance from a liberation psychology perspective. They argue that good therapy is a circular process,

> when the patient is once again open to social communication in interpersonal contexts previously been blighted by epistemic hypervigilance, he/she shows increased interest in the therapist's mind and the therapist's use of thoughts and feelings, which stimulates and strengthens the patient's capacity for mentalizing. Improvements in mentalizing or social cognition may thus be a common factor across different effective interventions: they share in common this benign virtuous cycle arising from the experience of two minds working together in a mutually mentalizing way. (p. 414)

I argue this process parallels Freire (1973) when he refers to how the progressive teacher's attempt to understand and elucidate the problem-situation from the student's point of view continually "opens up new roads" for the student to mentalize (the other, the relationship, society, etc.).

From a mentalization and psychoanalytic point of view, this is the critical insight of Freire's work, descended as it is from Ferenczi's original clinical experimentation, "The relaxation of the patient's hypervigilance . . . enables the patient to become open to social learning more widely" (Lorenzini, Campbell, & Fonagy, 2018, p. 414), where we can also replace patient with student, the oppressor, the oppressed, the other, and so on. The critical counterpart to this process, of course, is the clinician, educator, and activist's own mentalizing capacity, who "consistently seeks to build, and critically to re-build, a perspective in his/her own mind of what might be happening" (p. 415) in the patient's qua student's qua other's mind. For Freire, when the student questions the teacher's knowledge this signals a breakdown in mentalization. By showing humility in response, the teacher then is able to "re-enter into" the problem through the "entering into" of the student. To put it in attachment terms—the teacher restores the relationship by mentalizing the student's perspectives, thoughts, feelings, and knowledge. As for a mentalizing therapist, so too, for a mentalizing teacher and a mentalizing activist—"The humbler they are in this process the more they will learn" (Freire, 1973, p. 153). Freire (1973) similarly argued that when two "poles" of a dialogue—teacher and student, therapist and patient, oppressor and oppressed—are "linked by love, hope, and mutual trust, they can join in a critical search for something" (p. 45), whether that something is the innermost contours of the self, the dynamic interplay of their intersubjective relationship, or the intersecting matrix of relationships that make up our political economy.

Important to note in these considerations is that when we lose our capacity to properly mentalize and shift to attacking, blaming, or "speaking for" the other, we lose our "mentalizing capacity perhaps even in the context of political trauma, *identifying with the totalitarian object*, thwarting the other's agency and subjectivity" (Lorenzini, Campbell, & Fonagy, 2018, p. 416, my emphasis). When we are unable—whether as individuals, a community, or a political system—to provide mentalizing spaces, this instigates the "shutting down of epistemic trust, rendering individuals incapable of trusting their social world, hindering in turn the capacity to understand and work through their position of victim (or perpetrator) of violence" (p. 417).

I would like to take this examination of attachment, mentalization, and epistemic trust one step further. When we become mired in this inability to trust the other, and explore the various centripetal and centrifugal ways we enact positions of victim and perpetrator, oppressor and oppressed, we also become *unable to mentalize about our position in the socio-political system, how the political economy operates, and how the powerful enact divisions of oppressor and oppressed which serve to maintain the system of inequality itself.* This ability to mentalize about our own affective and political experience as well as the other's, and how the broader socio-political system necessitates and produces this distinction between self and other, is what Freire (and Guerreiro Ramos before him) referred to as *concientizacao* or critical consciousness, and what I would define, following Fonagy and his associates, as a kind of *political mentalization.*

I am using political mentalization to refer to how humanizing dialogue can, through empathy, create a sense of self as an agentic being with thoughts, feelings, beliefs that are also political, cultural, and social. When we experience that kind of subjectivity and reflection from an other, and are able to trust and mentalize that other as well, we then bring into focus the broader social, economic, and political world in which we exist. Under conditions of rampant inequality, political mentalization questions a system of difference whose *primary purpose* is to distract from and obfuscate the very system of oppression that gave rise to it—and in fact *depends* on it.

Questioning the system then involves a series of dialectical considerations not only of my self, but in turn the other: (1) empathy and understanding of the subjectivity and experience of the other, (2) a representation of the socio-systemic *context* from which the other's subjectivity arises, and (3) an analysis of the social, cultural, and political economy that gives rise to the very antagonism between my self and the other to begin with. This critical consciousness or political mentalization brings into sharp focus how experience arises from the socio-cultural systems that impact our collective well-being, and our individual role—even complicity—within those systems.

Sustaining and surviving this tension between self and other, holding and tolerating both love and hate (Freud) within a murderous encounter (Fanon), allows not only a socio-political and intersubjective third that brings this conflict into view (Freire)—which in turn gives us the opportunity to mentalize it—but also a novel, creative, and third solution beyond the impasse of do'er and done-to, oppressor and oppressed, domination and submission. As Alschuler (2007) writes, "*Liberated consciousness means holding the tension of psychic opposites, where the opposites are images of ethnic groups in conflict*" (p. 80, emphasis original). We might extend these opposites in tension to other dimensions of identity as well—gender, sexuality, class, ability, nationality, etc. This "third way out" is not so much an integration between these poles, so much as the ability to hold them, and the world they emerge from, in tension. With this clarification of Freud, Freire, and Fanon's ideas through a contemporary lens, we turn to the last stop in our historical journey—the life and work of Ignacio Martín-Baró.

MARTÍN-BARÓ FROM SPAIN TO SAN SALVADOR

As noted in Chapter 1, the Spanish crown in its hunger for land and gold funded Columbus' journeys and the colonialism that ensued from it, turning Spain into a global superpower. But its wealth and prominence waned with competition from other nation states, as well as revolts from its holdings overseas. Centuries-long conflicts over the crown between different monarchic families (the Bourbons, Hapsburgs, Carlists, etc.), the land-owning nobility, and the Catholic Church bled the common man and woman, whether it was through their labor or their service in war. As the established monarchic and nobility system was perpetually thrown into crisis by infighting among the powerful, the waxing and waning of power opened a window for progressive forces seeking a different world for the common people.

Challenges to the crown and the land-owning oligarchs took place in the 1850s, 1870s, 1910s, and 1920s, with failed attempts to introduce land reform and policies aimed at the redistribution of wealth. Each attempt "provoked reactionary efforts to stop the clock and reimpose the traditional balance of social and economic power" (Preston, 2006, p. 18). By 1917, Spain was an increasingly polarized country, made up of landowners and corporatists on one side and urban and landless laborers on the other, with the exception of the smallholding peasantry and small farmers. With landslide electoral victories by a republican-progressive coalition in 1931 seen as a referendum on the monarchy and the existing economic and social system, the king at that time, Alfonso XIII, fled the country, paving the way for the advent of the Second Spanish Republic. With full parliamentary control, the alliance of socialists and liberal democrats drafted a new constitution establishing freedom of speech and assembly, voting rights for women, and increased autonomy to the different cultural and linguistically distinct regions of Catalonia, Galicia, and the Basque Country.

At the same time, in order to limit the power of the landed nobility and the Church, the new constitution restricted the nobility's land rights and political influence, pressed for better wages and improved working conditions, and imposed greater controls upon the Catholic Church's property ownership and involvement in education. Through both legislative and cultural means, the left-leaning government challenged the religious and monarchic right, whether by legalizing divorce, expanding women's civil rights and involvement in political life, or limiting governmental funding for the church. These radical economic, social, and cultural changes made the landed classes realize "that the Republic's commitment to improving the living conditions of the poorest members of society inevitably threatened them with a major redistribution of wealth" (Preston, 2006, p. 41).

Despite attempts by liberal Republicans to appease the wealthy with legislation aimed at protecting property and capital, the oligarchs and industrial forces began to mobilize cultural, economic, and later military forces in order to destabilize the republican-democratic order. Whereas socialism and anarchism had spread among workers in major cities, the big landowners mobilized the staunchly Catholic peasantry and small farmers with a combination of financial credits and the promise of protecting "traditional values" in exchange for an anti-socialist position. A tactical opportunity presented itself in the fact that the new legislation meant to limit the Church's political and economic power in Spain "failed to take into account the sensibilities of

Spain's millions of Catholics" (Preston, 2006, p. 53). A formidable counter-coalition of wealthy industrialists, conservative Catholic popular support, and right-wing military led by General Francisco Franco represented a fierce right-wing backlash leading up to the Civil War in 1936. General Franco represented not only a military coup seeking the return of the monarchy, but also the restoration of Catholic authority and conservative values, all the while exploiting economic and cultural frustrations of rural communities who felt threatened by the rapid social changes taking place in Spain, as well as fear of their holdings being threatened by a "Jewish-Masonic-Socialist" plague.

In 1936 a failed military coup led by a contingent of fascists and Nationalists against the Republican government inspired a wave of violence against Catholic laypersons and the Church that included extrajudicial killings, a period leading up to the end of the Civil War that was termed the "Red Terror" (Ruiz, 2012). Using the language of antifascist activism, communities that experienced centuries of oppression under prior monarchic and military regimes erupted into the streets, persecuting, policing, torturing, and brutalizing Catholic clergy and laypersons seen as sympathetic with the fascist rebellion. Violence in the name of "revolutionary justice" overwhelmed Republican attempts at maintaining order, as Preston (2006) details,

> Some violence was certainly an expression of popular outrage at the very fact of the military coup and its attempt to destroy the advances made by the Republic. Acts of revenge were directed at the sections of society on whose behalf the military was acting. Thus, hatred of an oppressive social system found expression in the murder or humiliation of parish priests who justified it, Civil Guards and policemen who defended it, the wealthy who enjoyed it and the employers and landlords' agents who implemented it.

While some acts were performative and non-violent, such as the burning of property records and land registries, these were overshadowed by lynchings, murder, looting, and sexual assault. Due process was replaced by "revolutionary tribunals" enacting a kind of righteous vengeance. Preston (2006) noted that while these extra-juridical acts by the populace invalidated the Republic's claim to be a defender of democracy against fascism, "the atrocities in the Nationalist zone did nothing to diminish its standing even in British and French government circles, let alone in Berlin or Rome" (p. 234).

Franco's coordinated military coup in mid-late 1936 unleashed a wave of violence throughout Spain. There were massive casualties in the frontline battles between Nationalist forces supported by Nazi Germany, Italy, and Portugal and Republican forces supported by the Soviet Union, Mexico, and the International Brigade, but also pogroms and further mass killings within their respective territories. Franco's forces regularly bombed civilian centers, carried out mass killings and torture in the name of traditional values and "law and order." On the ground level, an eye for an eye reigned supreme—rage, envy, humiliation, vengeance, and greed made all of Spain blind.

After Franco's victory brought the civil war to an end in 1939, the hundreds of thousands killed in the conflict were augmented by hundreds of thousands more in what became the Nationalists' own "White Terror," assassinating, imprisoning, and executing dissidents until Franco's death in 1975 (Preston, 2013). With the support of Mussolini's Italy and Hitler's Nazi Germany, Franco enjoyed a long and absolute reign. His claim of "neutrality" during World War II was porous, as he was fond of sending political dissidents into the hands of the Nazis for manual labor. Sometimes the Nazis would capture Spanish exiles and refugees and send them back to Spain where they would be executed. The Catalan, Galician, and Basque regions were decimated. All the while singing anti-capitalist tunes, Franco's regime "dutifully served their masters by disciplining the urban working class within the corporative syndicates and drumming the peasantry into the rural *Hermandades* [brotherhood militias]" (Preston, 2006, p. 322).

The Death and Rebirth of Psychoanalysis

Many leftists, even those mindful of the Red Terror executed by fringe elements of the Spaniard left, still regard the Spanish Civil War with a sense of nostalgia as the "last bastion" in the fight against rising fascism in Europe. Paul Preston (2006), a recognized historian of the war, once reflected that, "There remains something intensely tragic about Italian and German refugees from Mussolini and Hitler finally being able to take up arms against their persecutors only to be defeated again" (p. 6). Franco shared in the racism and anti-Semitism of the Nazis, often praising those values among the 15th-century Spanish monarchs as they spread their hatred over the Atlantic (Payne, 1987). The Nationalists themselves had likened their coup with the Christian *Reconquista*, expelling the "Moors" (e.g., Jews, Marxists, Socialists, etc.) from Spain through racial and cultural cleansing. Once in power, they would make the humiliation and exploitation of the vanquished absolute, justifying their violence through a combination of Catholic doctrine—the wicked Republicans must "expiate their sins"—and social Darwinism. "The defeated were denounced as degenerate," Preston (2006) explains, "their children were taken away and military psychiatrists carried out experiments on women prisoners in search of the 'red gene.' In prisons, massive efforts were made to break not only the bodies of prisoners but also their minds" (p. 310)

We covered in previous chapters how different progressive psychoanalysts and psychoanalytic thinkers had fought in the Spanish Civil War, and later fled to Latin America or France. Emilio Mira y Lopez and Francois de Tosquelles were committed Socialists and Catalonians who fought for economic equality and Catalan independence and against the fascist forces, while Marie Langer and her husband Max were Marxist physicians providing medical and psychiatric assistance on the Republican side as part of the International Brigade. Sandor Eiminder and other Jewish psychoanalysts had fled Hungary and later Germany's turn to fascism, only to find their newly adopted home set on fire. As most psychoanalytic psychiatrists in Spain had supported the Second Republic, and had worked in its publicly funded hospitals and institutions, they had no choice but to either escape or be exiled, if not killed in the violence that followed (Druet, 2012).

With psychoanalysis destroyed, this created space in Spanish psychiatry for a religiously based alternative supported by the new regime (Druet, 2012). Supporters of Franco's regime in psychiatry celebrated his victory and the "new spirit" that would define mental health from then on, purging Freudian influences and replacing them with a new "national psychiatry rooted in a Christian tradition" (p. 61), designed to not contradict Catholic dogma. The new mission of psychotherapists would be to "teach the patient how to be sane" (p. 61). Despite support from the state for this new "Christian" therapy, some resisted the new dogma. In 1939 two Catalan medical students, Pere Folch Mateu and Pere Bofill Tauler, founded a group called "Erasmo," where like-minded progressives and members of Spanish regional groups could get together in each other's homes, read Freud and psychoanalysis, and discuss their opposition to Franco's regime. Although their primary purpose was not Catalan independence, the intersections of psychoanalytic thought, practice, and social justice continued in Spain, if only in darkness.

Just as World War II spread psychoanalysis, like a refugee, across the globe, so too did the Spanish Civil War spread its seeds. After the war Langer ultimately fled to Argentina, where she would cross paths with Mira y Lopez, making a profound influence on psychoanalysis in Latin America, whereas de Tosquelles escaped to France where he would later meet and then mentor Frantz Fanon. Yet another Marxist psychoanalitic thinker, a Basque priest by the name of Jesus Arroyo Lasa, would leave Spain for El Salvador, ultimately procuring a faculty appointment at the Universidad CentroAmericana of San Salvador. In Latin America he would be exposed to Paulo Freire and his work, and go on to mentor another young priest from Spain, a child of the Civil War who would give his life for justice.

A Bridge to the Future: The Life and Work of Ignacio Martín-Baró

During the transition from dictatorship to democracy after Franco's death in 1975, the Spanish populace would engage in *el pacto del olvido*, the "pact of forgetting" to repress the traumas of the fascist regime. But long before the end of Franco's rule many were already engaged in a tacit—Ferenczi would have called it hypocritical—pact of silence. From 1939 until 1975, those loyal to Franco settled into an odd kind of "peace" after the war, praising his restoration of law, order, and religion while everyday assassination, disappearances, vigilante violence, and executions operated in the background. It was in 1942, in the shadow of this strange new world that Jose Ignacio "Nacho" Martín-Baró was born in the city of Valladolid, the same city in which Christopher Columbus died, still convinced he had discovered a "new route" to India.

Martín-Baró was the fourth of his siblings, born to Francisco "Paco" Martin and Alicia Baro, a devoted Catholic family loyal to Franco's regime in the post-civil war era. His father Paco, a renowned writer and poet, penned ballads praising the heroism of the Nationalist army and extolling the virtues of the dictator's ideology (Portillo, 2012). Paco was very close to his son, supporting his interests in music, the arts, literature, and later, his decision to join the priesthood, writing a poem offering to be the godfather of Nacho's clerical vows. Indeed, in much of his work as a writer and poet, Paco expressed deep affection and love for Nacho. His Catholic faith and concern for his son's upbringing led him to enroll Nacho in the Jesuit school of San Jose for his early studies (De la Corte Ibañez, 1998).

It was in San Jose that Nacho was exposed to the Jesuits and their passion for education, humanism, and an applied faith that was as much ethical as it could be political. However, his family's Catholic conservatism and loyalty to Franco would become a source of conflict for him. Although his immediate relationships were full of love and care, he sensed something was not quite right in his world. As he grew older, he began to question his family's values, leading to clashes over Franco's regime and the social dissociation it engendered. At the age of 17, possibly as way of getting distance from a world that increasingly made less and less sense, Martín-Baró formally entered the Jesuit order in 1959.

Martín-Baró moved to El Salvador to continue his clerical training, a country he would years later adopt as his own. From El Salvador, Martín-Baró was transferred to Ecuador and later Colombia where he attended the Javeriana University. "It was there," biographer and psychologist Nelson Portillo tells us, "that Nacho found his true intellectual calling—psychology—and combined it masterfully with his studies in philosophy" (Portillo, 2012, p. 79). Martín-Baró became enthused with humanistic psychology and psychoanalysis, writing a review of Carl Rogers' approach to psychotherapy which informed his undergraduate thesis, "To be and to suffer" (Martín-Baró, 1964). Particularly taken with Viktor Frankl's work, Martín-Baró wrote to him about his experiences working with indigenous and Afro-Colombian communities, "This experience left a deep mark on Nacho as he tried to understand the social roots of fatalism among disenfranchised people from the perspectives of logotherapy and existentialism" (Portillo, 2012, p.

79). Frankl encouraged Martín-Baró to pursue his studies in psychology, a brief mentorship via the written word that would prove meaningful.

Martín-Baró would travel to Frankfurt, Germany in the 1960s to initiate his Jesuit theological studies, coinciding with the enrollment with other figures of liberation theology, such as Jon Sobrino. He travelled back and forth between El Salvador and Europe, becoming ordained as a Jesuit father while working as a translator. Of note, Martín-Baró translated psychological and psychoanalytic works such as Pierre Flotte's *L'histoire et L'inconscient—The Unconscious in History*—which was published in Spain in 1971 (Portillo, 2012, p. 80). Having completed his training as a Jesuit, Martín-Baró was invited by Basque Jesuit and liberation theologian Ignacio Ellacuria to continue his studies in El Salvador. Based on their acquaintance and later friendship, Martín-Baró enrolled at the Universidad Centro Americana (UCA) to begin an undergraduate degree in psychology, where he would later serve in the faculty and administration until his death in 1989. Portillo (2012) relates how,

> At UCA, Nacho was mentored by Jesús Arroyo Lasa, a Basque Jesuit who had studied applied psychology and psychoanalysis in Innsbruck [Austria] and was an enthusiast of Marxist social psychology. Authors like Paulo Freire and Herbert Marcuse and the like became referents for Nacho thanks to Father Arroyo. (p. 80)

Arroyo was a psychoanalytically oriented priest who was also an advocate of liberation theology (see Arroyo Lasa, 1990), as well as a scholar of Paulo Freire's work. In his 1973 text, *Paulo Freire: Su ideología y método* ("Paulo Freire: His ideology and method"), Arroyo called for a "social psychology of depth," (p. 54) and furthermore, a "depth sociology" (p. 97), reading the psychoanalytic implications of Freire's theorizing.

Following Freire, Arroyo (1973) argued that dialogue is the most powerful weapon for "proclaiming" the world, "where the false revolutionary is distinguished from the truly radical" by enacting a praxis of reflection and action, love and humility, faith and hope (p. 50, my translation). These qualities depend on an *experience* that transforms

> not just ideas and ideals, but, what is more important, the world of affect, and not only those conscious affects, those we manage day to day in reference to the external world, but the unconscious level that takes form as the emotional structures, the motivational ones, the condensed energies that work in the shadows of the unconscious. (p. 53, my translation)

In turning to this social psychology of depth, Arroyo called attention to the "social unconscious" by drawing on mechanisms of identification and affect that—as we have shown—formed part and parcel of psychoanalytic approaches to the analysis of culture and society. Dialogue, social critique, and participation in politics, prior to being moral and ethical challenges, were primarily psychological in nature.

It is here that we likely find Martín-Baró's earliest exposure to Freire and also Fanon, in the work of his mentor Jesus Arroyo. Expanding on his own Freudo-Marxist interpretation of critical consciousness, Arroyo (1973) wrote that "*Concientizacao* is an unmasking . . . a process from which emerges what is good and bad from our past" (p. 99), specifically referring to our collective past, revealing histories of abuse, injustice, bitterness, and humiliation perpetrated by "regimes inspired by their classist, racist, and economic interests" (p. 103). Critical consciousness means reflecting upon one's historical and socioeconomic context while integrating the "good" and "bad" objects that exist within and outside oneself. This process is impaired by the identification with the "repressive aggressor" (p. 105) which is internalized within the oppressed, in effect "conquering their unconscious" (p. 105). The "paranoid politician" knows they are easily controlled as "in the reality of their unconscious, the very same resides with all their pathology and oppressive power" (p. 105, my translation). This internalized oppression is no abstract mentalistic concept; it has resounding political impact, yielding to profound ambivalence toward social change and others who could be allies of solidarity in enacting that change,

> they [the oppressed] respond to their psychosocial ambivalence: they allow themselves to rebel against the official authority, and, at the same time, to submit in a sick way to another authority. And the consequences? One dictatorship is traded for *another*. To come? A revolt of half-measures . . . Solution? At this moment, the *psychosocial therapy* represented by the Freirían method. (pp. 106–107, my translation, emphasis original)

The desire for freedom and the attachment to the oppressor results in precisely this ambivalent, conflictual mode of political relating. One that can only be resolved through a kind of political therapeutics, a methodology of dialogue. Anything else risks a type of incremental reformism, maintaining and identifying with the very systemic forces that brought us to the brink—instead of waking up, we succumb to an even deeper slumber.

Appraising his mentor's work, Martín-Baró (1971) wrote a review of Arroyo's *Reflexiones sobre Psicología Social* ("Reflections on Social Psychology"). In it Martín-Baró discussed the "symptoms of our marginalizing social reality": "marginalized consciousness—real or imagined—psychic envy and possession neurosis" (p. 211, my translation). In a context of inequality and rapid polarization, groups alternate between a tremendous anxiety to have, possess, and dominate while others experience envy over their power, both reflecting two forms of marginalized consciousness. Drawing on psychoanalytic jargon, Martín-Baró reflects based on Arroyo's work that

> to become conscious implies more than a new experience, but a return to our human roots, that is to say, to the "Hispanoamerican *it*" [*ello hispanoamericano*]. This liberating return is only possible . . . through love. Because "only love, in the final analysis, redeems and liberates. Everything that promotes liberation has reason to do so insofar as it is imbued with love and arrives at praxis in the virtue of love itself." But this supposes an unmasking [*desenmascarar*] of false revolutionary attitudes, so paranoid in their *raison d'etre* much like the prevailing authorities, and like false charity full of secrecy and neurotic exculpation. Social liberation has to come through blood, not that of the other, but one's own. (p. 212, my translation)

The "unmasking" of consciousness and the lies of consciousness then finds itself transmuted from Freud through Fanon and Freire to Arroyo and now Martín-Baró, signaling a psychological and sociopolitical process of "returning" to and reconnecting with ourselves, but especially our collective histories of trauma. Following Fanon, this does not mean a return to an idealized, crystallized past, but a wrestling with ambivalence, and in that wrestling, finding (in a Latin American context) our *it*. Tolerating and resolving this ambivalence, as much for Freud as Arroyo and Martín-Baró, requires an act of love. A love which renounces the desire to possess, to dominate, to draw the blood of the other. Instead, it offers up our own.

Mentalizing La Mentira: Polarization and Ideology in Liberation Psychology

Exposed to Freud, steeped in Freire, and informed by Fanon, Martín-Baró received a Fulbright scholarship to earn a master's and later a doctorate from the University of Chicago. I will now turn to some of his key ideas, to illustrate the culmination of the tradition identified in this text. Writing in a neo-colonial context of civil war and political repression in Latin America, Martín-Baró (1995) was cognizant of the impact of sociopolitical polarization on the populace—a society whose members stop engaging with one another, turning to violence "to solve its problems, both large and small, is a society in which the roots of human relations are diseased" (p. 112). As ethnic, racial, class, and other political groups become displaced toward emotional extremes,

> A critical split is produced in the framework of coexistence, leading to a radical differentiation between "them" and "us," where "they" are from the outset the "bad guys," and "we" are the "good guys." The rivals contemplate each other in an ethical mirror that inverts characteristics and values, to the point that what is reproached in "them" as a defect is praised in "us" as a virtue. (pp. 112–113)

This splitting, projection, reversal, and polarization distorts the members of a society and "in the end, implicates the whole scope of existence" (p. 113). People, ideas, and actions no longer have any inherent value, but are judged based on whether they represent "us" or "them," to what extent they forward "their" or "our" political cause. "Thus" Martín-Baró warns, "the basis for daily interaction disappears . . . the assumptions of coexistence themselves are being put on trial" (p. 113). Martín-Baró did not have access to the internet when observing this phenomena, which are no less resonant. Do we not hear the echoes of a divided society today? How much less antagonistic does it appear? Or should we say, how much more?

Under such conditions reality itself loses meaning, giving way to the power of *la mentira*, "the lie" (harkening back to Langer). The lie corrupts the working of institutions and intentionally deceives in public discourse (this or that is "fake news," etc.), creating an ambiance of "distrustful falsehood." "Almost without realizing it," Martín-Baró (1995) writes,

> we have become accustomed to institutions being exactly the opposite of what they are meant to be: those responsible for guaranteeing our safety are the main source of insecurity; those in charge of justice defend abuse and injustice; those called on to enlighten and guide are the first to deceive and manipulate. The lie has come to permeate our existence to such an extent that we end up creating an imaginary world, whose only truth is precisely that it is a false world, and whose only pillar of support is the fear of reality, which is too "subversive" to be tolerated. (pp. 113–114)

Who is our enemy? Who is our friend? Can we trust the government? Our institutions? What is up? What is down? And if this news network said this, then what of that *other* news network? What if *we* are the enemy, and they in the right? Impossible. Intolerable. *Inconceivable*. We come to fear the other's truth—even the possibility there is some *germ* of truth—and fear this reality we have muddled with the lie.

In a provocative essay on how right-wing ideologies assault all that challenges them as "fake news" (to use again a contemporary phrase) titled *La verdad de la mentira*, "The truth of the lie" (my translation), Martín-Baró (1976) expands on the psychological violence we suffer under conditions of rapid polarization and ideological colonization,

> This matter of the lie is something quite serious. It could be said that from so much lying things end up appearing somewhat true, or at the very least, uncertain: We all know they are not true, but we end up thinking that perhaps they are not false, finding ourselves living in the world of ambiguity (where rumor blooms and manipulation reigns) . . . Even though reality does not change by sheer force of words, we end up changing our understanding of it. That is to say, *we end up diluting our consciousness*. And little by little we become

> habituated to living in a world of half lies and half truths, alienating us more and more. (p. 1, my translation, emphasis added)

We can see, then, that with the political splitting and ideology of the lie there is an egregious failure in political mentalization. We are barely able to understand ourselves, our wants, our material and existential conditions, our needs, and so are unable to understand the other, their wants, the experiences and realities that lead them to be how they are. Much like the failure of interpersonal mentalization marks a rupture in a relationship, so too the collapse in political mentalization signals a rupture in the social order that impairs our ability to have a joint dialogue about the problems we face. It is out of this rupture, however, that a site of truth may be found.

Here is where Martín-Baró (1976) identifies the role of the psychologist in deciphering this truth. He argues that a psychologist knows that

> Lying is a way of projecting a truth: the truth of what *is* in each case and, it follows, what it is *feared* to be. The lie compulsively proclaimed and publicly institutionalized seems to proclaim a sad truth: the fear of being our very selves, *to recognize ourselves in our reality*. Fear because—we are sure—the reality would imply that we have no need for such a product, that such an organism is harmful and we would have to begin resolving certain problems that are going from bad to worse. But recognizing this would seem odd: it would appear to be the lie in the truth. All of this is a "subversive joke." And that is no stereotype. (p. 1, my translation, emphasis added)

By tearing apart the truth contained in the lie, and how even lies can have the trappings of truth, the psychologist, and we might add, the activist organization, the agent of change, etc., can help restore our capacity to mentalize politically by reflecting and restoring our sense of our own reality and self-experience, and aid us in reaching out toward the other and comprehending their experience. By struggling through the web of lies to reach the other, we can begin to acknowledge—and mentalize—about the calamity we are both caught up in. In this way, we restore a sense of our shared humanity, and "connect the dots" to understand the world we must transform together.

This brings us face to face with the central challenge of liberation psychology, "to construct a new person in a new society" (Martín-Baró, 1995, p. 121). *Concientizacao*—concientizacion, critical consciousness, or political mentalization are not mere cognitive maneuvers or beliefs, nor simply the representation of a "true" objective reality. Rather, it is the inventive and imaginative negotiation of models of relatedness that, through wrestling with the other, continually creates, negates, and re-creates the world into—to paraphrase the words of the Zapatistas—a world where many worlds exist. The formulation of this thinking makes sense not only in terms of Martín-

Baró's psychoanalytic lineage, but also reflects his own life world as both the child of a civil war, and the victim of another.

Transubstantiating Love and Hate: Martín-Baró's Legacy

In 1979, amid rising food prices and widespread socioeconomic inequality, civil war broke out in El Salvador between the U.S.-backed government and the Socialist-Communist Farabundo Marti National Liberation front (FMNL). Many Catholic priests who identified with liberation theology stood on the side of not just the rebels, but also the everyday poor and indigenous peoples clamoring for change, exercising a preferential option for the poor and downtrodden. Voicing this charge, in February of 1980 the Archbishop Oscar Romero wrote a letter to president Jimmy Carter calling for an end to U.S. support of the right-wing military forces. The visibility of clerical support for the rebels drew the ire of paramilitary groups, who in retaliation declared the motto "Be a patriot, kill a priest" (Portillo, 2012). A month later Romero was gunned down while celebrating mass, along with several parishioners, priests, and nuns.

Martín-Baró himself was accused of being a subversive communist by more conservative psychologists. In some circles, his progressive stances earned him the moniker "Nacho, the Red One," a name that would mark him and his peers as enemies of the state. He and other liberation theologians experienced bombings and the threat of the war spilling into the streets just outside their residence at the UCA. Martín-Baró was overwhelmed and felt incredible terror and helplessness. Still, he did not cease speaking against injustice and inequality. While he traveled and held numerous visiting professor positions in Venezuela, Puerto Rico, Spain, and Costa Rica, he refused to take a post outside of El Salvador despite pleas from friends and family to leave the country. He was remembered as once saying to an American colleague, "For you in America, it is publish or perish. For us, it is publish *and* perish." In his last visit to Spain in 1989, his brother Carlos witnessed a man torn by war, death threats, and repeated exposure to trauma, "with several medications on top of the nightstand" (Portillo, 2012). Martín-Baró continued to talk and write about the psychological impact of war and inequality on the polarization and deterioration of communal bonds in Salvadoran society, up until the night of his death.

On the night of November 16, 1989, Martín-Baró was on the phone with his sister Alicia, who could hear gunfire piercing the darkness around his home. Just outside the UCA, a decisive battle was being waged between the military junta and the FMNL as the country recoiled from eight years of war and open conflict (De la Corte Ibañez, 1998). As midnight struck with the sky alight by bombs and fire, Coronel Guillermo Benavides of the armed forces ordered the U.S.-trained Atlacatl batallion to storm the UCA and kill the Jesuits hidden inside. De la Corte Ibañez (1998) details the coronel's chilling orders: "Gentlemen, we are being played on all fronts. It is either us or them. These are the intellectuals who have guided the guerilla for a long time . . . [you know] where the Jesuit fathers sleep and I want no witnesses" (my translation).

Ignacio Martín-Baró knew that death had come for him; he was already dressed by the time the government forces breached the campus. Thirty soldiers crossed the exterior walls of the UCA and tore through the area looking for the priests. Martín-Baró was the first to step out and open the gate leading to the Jesuits' residential quarters. He greeted them with righteous indignation—"*This is an injustice, you're all thugs!*" He took two strikes from the butt of a soldier's rifle and was dragged out into the lawn with his friends and colleagues. They stood defiant, inerrant in their belief in a God who stood on the side of the oppressed until finally, the AK-47s roared. With the morning dawn, the military vehicles of the first infantry brigade patrolled the surrounding city of San Salvador, blasting on their loudspeakers, "Ellacuria and [Martin] Baro have fallen. Let's keep killing communists!" (De la Corte Ibañez, 1998, my translation).

The route carrying the spirit of social justice from psychoanalysis through Freud, Fanon, and Freire to Martín-Baró and liberation psychology had been displaced, exiled, killed, and repressed time and again, and yet it continues to return. Because you cannot kill an idea.

Ideas are bulletproof.

Conclusion

"A Preferential Option"

In recovering the historical memory of psychoanalysis and liberation psychology, we have traveled from Vienna to El Salvador and back again, tracing the roots and routes of a tradition created and found, lost to time but growing gradually in darkness only to re-emerge time and again. This tradition reflects a way of thinking psychoanalytically about culture and society, as well as a series of relationships—Freud, Ferenczi, and Fenichel, Sullivan and Ellison, Wertham, Wright, de Tosquelles and Fanon, Fromm and Freire, Moreira, Ramos, and Guerreiro, Langer and Hollander, Arroyo and Martín-Baró. Each one is a turn, a chapter, a link in a chain, a root rising from the earth to form routes bridging generations of psychoanalysts and psychoanalytic thinkers wrestling with oppression and its impact on the psyche, their gaze raised toward the incomplete futurity of liberation—a dream continually born, killed, and reborn in the transitional space between fantasy and reality. Not between truth and falsehood, but emergent in an indeterminate space where a new world can rise over the embers of the old. A world that—in the words of Zapatista subcomandante Marcos—can fit many worlds.

I will begin this conclusion by outlining some of the historical assertions of this text, and what they tell us about psychoanalysis and social justice, and the history of psychoanalysis and liberation psychology. Then I will shift to an analysis of the political implications of this history, through a dialogue with Karl Marx as well as one of his descendants, activist and scholar Asad Haider (2018). Scrutinizing the challenges of contemporary politics in North America from the perspective of a psychoanalytic liberation psychology will in turn require addressing the dangers and promises of a social justice pedagogy. Relaying the pedagogical implications of psychoanalysis and liberation psychology means defining what kind of dialogue is most conducive to promoting change—with particular attention to training in mental health fields such as psychology, psychiatry, and social work. Lastly, as many of the ancestors explored in this book from Freud to Ferenczi to Fanon were either psychotherapists or engaged in therapeutic applications of analytic thinking (e.g., Guerreiro Ramos and the Black Experimental Theatre), I will discuss some of the clinical implications of this history for contemporary practitioners working across lines of race, class, gender, and sexual orientation.

It might seem strange to conclude a book on the intellectual and social history of psychoanalysis and liberation psychology with commentary on contemporary political activism, pedagogy, and even clinical work. But what is the point of recovering this history if not to learn from it? If not to adapt our praxis in light of its genius and its flaws? If not to nourish ourselves with its roots and routes, and bind our wounds with its bits and pieces? If we do not learn from it, we are more likely to repeat its mistakes and lose sight of its insights.

A PEOPLE'S HISTORY OF PSYCHOANALYSIS

I began this book by raising the question of whether psychoanalysis was, since its inception, antagonistic to issues of social, racial, and economic justice, and whether there was any relationship between psychoanalysis and liberation psychology. Relatedly, I brought up the concern that psychoanalysis was if not indifferent to issues of social justice, then irrelevant to the concerns of oppressed, marginalized, and colonized peoples. In concluding this review, I reach the following conclusions.

Firstly, psychoanalysis was the product of a historically oppressed ethnic minority group—Jewish men and women living, existing, surviving, and resisting a venomously anti-Semitic world. This very same world made a series of racist associations between Blackness and Jewishness that would inform the thinking of the first generation of psychoanalysts which they themselves, including Freud, reflected upon and theorized about. Furthermore, as members of a historically marginalized group, many of this first generation held a wide range of leftist political views critical of the existing social, cultural, and economic system. These two realities, their Jewish identity within an anti-Semitic world and their social democratic and socialist beliefs, informed the development of psychoanalysis as such.

Secondly, we examined how Freud and his inner circle reflected upon their Jewishness and its relationship to Blackness in a way that contextualized racial discourse as a tool of social control, division, and domination. In Freud, Ferenczi, and Fenichel's writing, we saw that they thought clearly and cogently about culture and power, race and economics, the psyche and society. They did not seem to repress or dissociate issues of culture. Quite the contrary, cultural and social tensions informed the development of clinical theory, which in turn textured how clinical theory could shed light on sociopolitical dynamics. Through their dialogues in their scholarly writing, their personal correspondence, and their clinical work, they developed a complex and nuanced theory of how the oppressed—across racial lines—internalize and introject an identification with the wealthy and powerful, through which they can experience a semblance of power by becoming "like the master" in relation to other oppressed peoples. They also constructed a theory of how affect becomes socially structured, creating a split between feelings of anger and hatred toward the other and love and affection toward that which represents the "self" (e.g., the in-group). Freud's definition of social justice as owning our desire for power, for aggression toward the other, for domination, and renouncing these wishes out of an affective tie with the other—a reparative identification with the victim of our desires—would reverberate with later developments of the role of love and the passions in liberation psychology.

Thirdly, psychoanalysis served as a relevant and powerful tool for psychosocial healing and political activism among scholars and clinicians of color. The first person to adopt and disseminate psychoanalysis outside of Vienna was the Afro-Latinx psychiatrist Juliano Moreira, who inaugurated a tradition of drawing on psychoanalysis to subvert racist discourses in Brazil. Richard Wright's library was filled to the brim with books written by Freud, Ferenczi, and Fenichel, among others, and drew freely on analytic thinking in his writing and advocacy. Wright, Ellison, and Wertham founded the first psychoanalytic outpatient low fee clinic in Harlem. Frantz Fanon, Arthur Ramos, Alberto Guerreiro Ramos, and Paulo Freire engaged in psychoanalytically informed therapy, applied group therapy and psychodrama, and analytically informed pedagogy that created liberatory spaces for their communities. From Harlem to El Salvador, psychoanalysis proved not only a therapeutic method, but also a tool for critiquing oppressive racial, economic, social, and cultural structures. For these people of color and their allies, psychoanalysis belonged to the people, and was drawn upon in the consulting room, on the battlefield, and in the streets.

Lastly, we traced an intricate genealogy from Sigmund Freud to Ignacio Martín-Baró, revealing the influence of psychoanalysis and psychoanalytic thinkers on Harlem Renaissance novelists, Afro-Caribbean and Latin American post-colonial scholars, and Spanish and Latin American social psychologists. Through these relationships, we also discovered the working and re-working of a theory of internalized oppression, splitting and sociopolitical polarization, and the resulting horizontal violence that maintains systems of exploitation by turning people who might have common interests against one another. By discerning the evolution of this theory, we have a clear picture of how tensions and debates within psychoanalytic theory developed through the influence and work of people of color in North and Latin America and the Caribbean, ultimately informing Martín-Baró and the birth of liberation psychology (see Figure C.1). It is also important to underscore that these liaisons reflected a series of dialogues and collaborations between Jewish, Spaniard, Basque and Catalan, Latin American, African-American, and Afro-Caribbean peoples who were able to recognize one another through shared experiences of trauma, loss, and oppression, bound together in their resistance to a system built on racial and economic exploitation.

The concern for "the other," in all its meanings and implications drew these men and women to one another, and to the wound that mediated them. We must evoke Dussel with Gherovici for a moment. The advent of the colonial era posed a question, the answer to which would decide whether to pillage the Americas, Africa, and the known world—were the Amerindians human? Did they have a soul? What about the Black, the Jew, the woman, the queer, the ill, the child, the poor, the widow, and the stranger? Psychoanalysis in the lips and souls of the women and men surveyed in this book

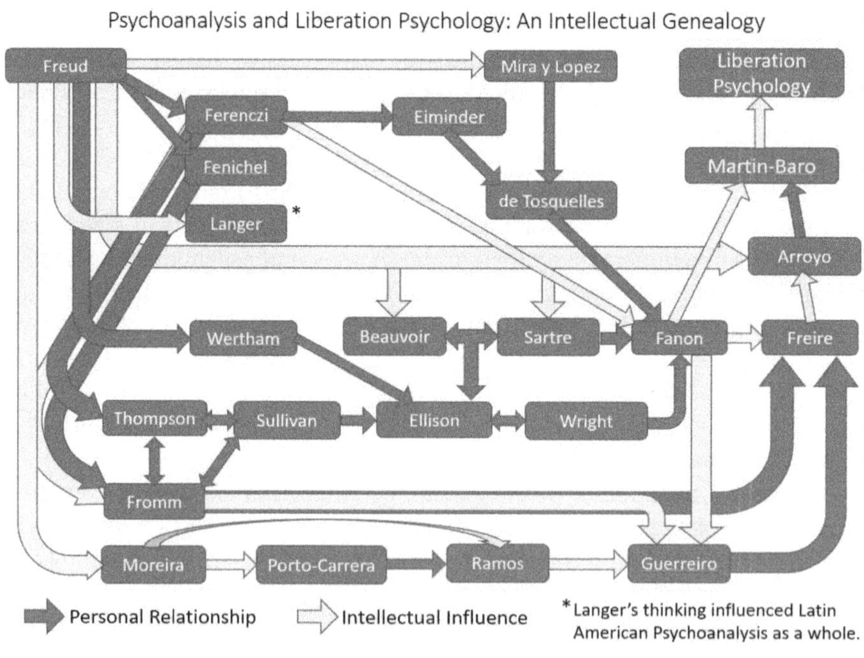

Figure C.1. Psychoanalysis and Liberation Psychology: An Intellectual Genealogy.

answered—Yes we are, and yes we do. The bigger question is who decides whose souls to mind? Do we mind the soul of the other? How is our minding or mentalizing defined by social, economic, and political forces? Without question, the psychological is always political.

This history has important implications for contemporary North American multicultural psychology. To the extent that multicultural psychology takes liberation psychology—and its trinity of Freire, Fanon, and Martín-Baró—as its foundation, and draws on concepts such as internalized oppression, horizontal violence, identification, and unconscious racism, it is then drawing on what are fundamentally *psychoanalytic* concepts, *psychoanalytically informed* thinkers, and a *psychoanalytic* ethic. And by ethic we refer to a concern for who or what is being left out, repressed, dissociated, and marginalized in psyche as well as society. Historically speaking, psychoanalysis has made multiple and resonant contributions to multicultural psychology, post-colonial theory, and cultural studies. Recognizing this history and these contributions does not by itself "wipe the slate clean"—the sins of psychoanalysis are many and they should continue to be counted. What this book argues is that there is more to psychoanalysis as a theory, practice, and ethos that is highly relevant to marginalized communities and social justice struggles.

The Post-Colonial Legacy of Sandor Ferenczi

A surprising finding of this study is the ubiquitous and far-reaching influence of Sandor Ferenczi. Although Freud may have been the founder of psychoanalysis, and the originator of concepts like identification, internalization, and splitting (and their socio-cultural applications) it was Ferenczi who developed and refined them into a theory that defies clear assignation as purely "clinical" or "political." As was shown, his elaboration of introjection and internalization emerged from his observations of how feelings around class, gender, sexual difference, and trauma are "taken inside" the psyche. These clinical observations then informed his later work on how trauma can lead to an identification with the aggressor, who then colonizes the mind of the victim. The oppressed struggling with the oppressor within is a theme that was most clearly formulated by Ferenczi, and informed Freud's thinking as well. This line of thinking reverberated throughout generations of liberation psychology, both directly and indirectly (see Figure C.1).

Ferenczi mentored Sandor Eiminder, who analyzed Francois de Tosquelles who then read Ferenczi's work and his concept of introjection. De Tosquelles taught and mentored Frantz Fanon, who became fascinated by Ferenczi's writings and sought any translations of it he could find, informing not only his clinical work but his post-colonial theorizing. Fanon's own writings would enrapture Paulo Freire, who rewrote *The Pedagogy of the*

Oppressed from the ground up to be able to cite him. Ferenczi also analyzed Clara Thompson, who then conveyed what she learned in their analysis by analyzing Harry Stack Sullivan, who consulted with Ralph Waldo Ellison. Ellison collaborated closely with his friend and colleague Richard Wright, who had many of Ferenczi's books in his personal library. Wright corresponded with Fanon and informed his thinking. Lastly, Erich Fromm admired Ferenczi, defending him in print against Ernest Jones' accusations of madness. Fromm highly valued his "Confusion of Tongues" paper, further elaborating his ideas around identification with the aggressor from a social and political point of view. It was these same ideas that Fromm used to critique Freud's own identification with power. Through the dissemination of Fromm's work worldwide and his tenure at the National Autonomous University of Mexico, he further disseminated Ferenczian thinking to a wider context in the global south and Latin America in particular. It was ultimately in Mexico, with Ivan Illich's intervention, that Fromm would connect with Paulo Freire, in whom he recognized—I think—a Ferenczian sensibility. Martín-Baró depended on both Freire and Fanon in his articulation of a liberation psychology, and in it we find echoes of Ferenczi's critique of social and psychological and hypocrisy in Martín-Baró's assault on the "the lie" that distorts our reality.

The breadth of innovation and creativity exhibited by each of these scholars is not reducible to Ferenczi. But they do reveal a sprawling web of influence, dialogue, extension, and recreation of his ideas. Each generation and each thinker reviewed in this text, however, made them their own, speaking to their community's struggles and needs, and baptizing psychoanalysis in the rivers of their experience. This is not to say that psychoanalysis was the only tributary flowing into liberation psychology. But it is an important and central one.

RACE, CLASS, AND DIALOGUE: IMPLICATIONS FOR POLITICS, PEDAGOGY, AND PSYCHOTHERAPY

This book has outlined a people's history of psychoanalysis, informed by the legacy of economic exploitation and racial oppression beginning with the advent of colonialism. Through each phase of this history, we saw a repeated pattern in the societies these psychoanalytic thinkers existed—economic and social crises gave rise to increased polarization, racism, and right-wing fascism. Crises that Karl Marx was familiar with.

Marx observed in the tumult of the 1860s the rise of racist attitudes from the British working class toward the Irish minority in their midst, and toward Ireland as a colonial territory itself. The Irish immigrants were seen by British workers as providing a form of "cheap labor" that caused competition and a drop in wages, and so subjected them to discrimination and exclusion. For Marx, however, this racist trend reflected the British working class's identification with the ruling class itself (Anderson, 2017, p. 29). These observations led Marx to write that the British viewed the Irish

> similarly to how the poor whites of the Southern states of North America viewed black slaves. This antagonism among the proletarians of England is artificially nourished and kept up by the bourgeoisie. *It knows that this split is the true secret of the preservation of its power.* (MECW 21: 120, cited in Anderson, 2017, p. 29, emphasis added)

Divide and dominate—this was the truth of ruling class and the system they designed. Marx initially believed that when the British proletariat eventually liberated itself from exploitation, this would in turn liberate the Irish in turn. After witnessing how British workers became mired in their racism, he reversed his position. He criticized attempts by other socialists to frame the suffering of the Irish as a "distraction" from true class struggle. "The English working class will never accomplish anything before it has got rid of Ireland," Marx wrote, "*The lever must be applied in Ireland.* This is why the Irish question is so important for the social movement in general." (MECW 43: 398, cited in Anderson, 2017, p. 29, emphasis added). Only British solidarity with the Irish, and the Irish liberating themselves from oppression and colonization, would in turn free the British as well. This insight that class action, and more broadly any kind of political action, must have a praxis from the point of view of the other, including the most excluded and racially oppressed (let us remember, Irish and Jewish people of this period *were coded non-white*), would color Marx's assessment of the conditions of Black people under American slavery.

W. E. B. Du Bois (1935) in *Black Reconstruction* drew attention to how Marx applied a similar standard in his analysis of Black slavery leading up to and during the Civil War. Marx did not think dismantling slavery by itself would destroy capitalism, but reasoned that it would create better conditions for class solidarity across racial lines. In *Capital* Marx ([1867–1875] 1976) wrote that in America, "every independent workers' movement was paralyzed as long as slavery disfigured a part of the republic. Labor in a white skin cannot emancipate itself where it is branded in a black skin" (p. 32). A similar remark can be made about contemporary capitalism in the U.S. and abroad—any substantive anti-capitalist working class movement is inert and ineffective so long as White Supremacy distorts the subjectivity of Whites and especially working class Whites—contorting the American Dream into an American Nightmare. But maybe it always was so, and the wish for a "dream" was itself a defense against the reality of that nightmare.

In the *Poverty of Philosophy*, Marx outlined the centrality of anti-Black slavery to capitalism,

> Direct slavery is as much the pivot upon which our present-day industrialism turns, as are machinery, credit, etc. Without slavery there would be no cotton, without cotton there would be no modern industry. It is slavery that has given value to the colonies, it is the colonies that have created world trade, and world trade is the necessary condition for large-scale machine industry. Slavery is therefore an economic category of paramount importance. (MECW 38: 101–102, cited in Anderson, 2017, p. 35)

For this reason Marx experienced great excitement in hearing about Black rebellions and abolitionist resistance leading up to the Civil War, interpreting slave uprisings in the U.S. as a "signal" for worldwide anti-Racist, anti-Capitalist struggle (Marx and Engels, 2016: 17; MECW 41: 4, see Anderson, 2017, p. 35). Marx spent his efforts spent reporting on the Civil War for British periodicals and newspapers, while helping organize and supporting British workers protesting Great Britain's attempts to enter the war on the side of the South, leading to a remarkable example of international solidarity across the Atlantic (Jeannot, 2007; Anderson, 2017).

In writing about the Civil War and the system of Black slavery that led to it, Marx noted the discrepancy between the "narrow oligarchy" who were actual slave holders and the "many millions of so-called poor whites." Like Freud, Marx compared them to Roman plebeians during the period of Rome's economic decline—"Only by acquisition and the prospect of acquisition of new Territories," he wrote, "is it possible to square the interests of these poor whites with those of the slaveholders, to give their restless thirst for action a harmless direction and to tame them with the prospect of one day becoming slaveholders themselves" (Marx and Engels, 2016, p. 46; MECW 19: 40–41, cited in Anderson, 2017, p. 35). This is why, similar to Nakagawa's (2012) argument (mentioned in the previous chapter), anti-Blackness and other forms of racism have served as the lever or fulcrum of capitalism (see also McWilliams, 1948). Although these observations provided the material basis for what Marx would later call the "false consciousness" of poor whites, this consciousness was anything but false, betraying a lack of nuance and interiority that psychoanalysis aimed to correct.

As we have seen throughout this book, the dynamics Marx analyzes here reflects well-established unconscious dynamics of identification, introjection, desire and domination through which even exploited groups become active participants in the even more violent oppression of other groups by enacting the subjectivity of their masters. I bring in Marx in this conclusion because he has, in essence, haunted this text since the beginning—he was read by the first generations of social democratic and socialist psychoanalysts seeking social change in their turn-of-the-century world, used by liberation theologians in Latin America to re-interpret the Judeo-Christian bible in light of "God's preferential option for the poor and oppressed," and drawn on by Black voices from the Harlem Renaissance to the Caribbean and Latin America to understand the economics of anti-Blackness. As Jeannot (2007) argued, understanding the relevance and resurgence of Marx over the years lies in "the recognition that Marx must be thought of first and foremost as a philosopher of liberation, who takes his stand with the self-activity and self-development of every freedom struggle" (p. 78). With Marx as with Freud, there is a history and a tradition of marginalized peoples and peoples of color engaging with these "dead old white men" to dialogue with them, critique them, and go beyond-them-yet-with-them toward liberation.

Paulo Freire's case (2010) is illustrative. In a rare video interview he described how his faith in Christ moved him to work with people in the favelas and rural areas of Pernambuco, communities who faced hunger and economic hardship as he did in childhood. Freire spoke with his heart on his sleeve about his integration of Marx and Christianity during an interview, talking about his first experiences teaching literacy in poor communities in the favelas:

> It was their hard facts that drove me to Marx . . . [the] hard facts of the people of the slums, the negation of their being as a person, the tendency to those adaptations that we spoke of before, that almost inert state in front of the negation of freedom, all of it drove me to Marx . . . the more I read Marx, more and more I found a type of objective basis to continue as Christ's comrade. So the reading that I did of Marx . . . never suggested to me that I cease finding Christ in the corner of the favelas. I stayed with Marx in the world, looking for Christ in the transcendent. (Freire, 2010)

In my own way—my own Christian background notwithstanding—my reading of Freud also led me, perhaps ironically, to Marx. And the more I read Marx and the liberation theologians who cite him, the more centered I became in my reading of Freud. Freud, as progressive psychoanalytic thinkers from Fenichel to Ellison to today have recognized, *deepens* Marx. Dialectically speaking, one must also take the stance that Marx in turn *deepens* Freud. And we, those of us who speak from our own positionalities as people of color, women, and LGBTQ peoples, *deepen* both Freud and Marx by—to return to an idea popular during my time at Union Theological Seminary—immersing them within our experience.

In recovering our historical memory as a field of mental health practitioners, researchers, and advocates, these ideas have incredible import for psychologically informed social justice work today. I will outline these implications first in terms of politics and coalition building in the United States context, social justice pedagogy (especially around issues of race, class, gender, and sexuality), and psychotherapeutic clinical work.

Identification with the Oppressor as an Obstacle to Social Justice Politics

The psychoanalytic theories of oppression reviewed in this book support a view long-held in progressive circles—the identification between the exploited and their exploiters along the lines of a *perceived shared identity*, and the material privileges associated with it, results in envy, aggression, and violence becoming displaced to another oppressed group which is triangulated as a site of domination and empowerment, destroying the possibility of shared solidarity and transformative social change. Harkening back to DuBois' critical insight that, "The emancipation of man is the emancipation of labor and the emancipation of labor is the freeing of that basic majority of workers who are yellow, brown and black," Ignatin and Allen (1967) chastised the Progressive Labor Party in America for its failure to draw on Marx's insight that so long as Black people are not free, the White worker will never be free. In their oft-circulated pamphlet "White Blind Spot," they argued how the U.S. ruling class made an ideological and implicit (to not say unconscious) "deal," at one point they refer to it as a "the sweetheart agreement," with the White working-class (p. 27).

"The terms of the deal," worked out over the course of three hundred years of settler colonialism and rabid capitalism, were as follows:

> you white workers help us conquer the world and enslave the non-white majority of the earth's laboring force, and we will repay you with a monopoly of the skilled jobs, we will cushion you against the most severe shocks of the economic cycle, provide you with health and education facilities superior to those of the non-white population, grant you the freedom to spend your money and leisure time as you wish without social restrictions, enable you on occasion to promote one of your number out of the ranks of the laboring class, and in general confer on you the material and spiritual privileges befitting your white skin. (Ignatin & Allen, 1967, p. 27)

Ignatin and Allen make the point that fighting for racial justice *is* fighting for economic justice, just as fighting for economic justice *must depend* on fighting for racial justice. They make the analogy that demanding for a "larger slice of the pie" for the working class does not by itself actually influence how that slide is then distributed *within* the working class, since the ruling class "has always utilized every concession won from it to *increase* the gap between white and black, thus turning even a victory of the working class into a cause of greater division" (p. 28). Working class politics without a robust anti-Racist agenda then creates a "back door" for wealth inequality as such, which impairs the effectiveness of anti-capitalist projects, hence maintaining the current distribution of wealth (take the case of "red lining" in the wake of the New Deal in America, for example). In that sense, it is insufficient to say that racism is the "back door" of capitalism. Rather, racism is the grotesque gaping maw through which ravenous capitalism triumphantly marches in. Such gates must be closed and sealed shut. Perhaps we do have need for a wall after all.

Ignatin and Allen (1967) make the case that working class Whites must renounce (note the echo with Freud) the White privilege that maintains the material base for "the split in the ranks of labor," and "join the Negro, Puerto Rican and other colored workers in fighting white supremacy," as the most urgent issue facing the working class. In exchange for beginning to dismantle White Supremacy, White workers, "*together* with the rest of the workers will receive all the benefits which are sure to come from one working class (of several colors) fighting together" (p. 29). Ignatin and Allen caution against any "naïve staging" of a racial justice struggle without a class struggle and vice-versa, or making a clear delineation between the two. Rather, engaging in such solidarity will expose "white chauvinism . . . as the weapon of the oppressor, thus preparing the working class for the assumption of power" (p. 29). The concept is fascinating—by disarming the (White, wealthy) oppressor from using White skin privilege to divide and dominate the poor, a path is created for a racial coalition to enact broad, systemic change, wresting power away from the dominant.

In our contemporary American political landscape, however, there are multiple tools of systemic splitting between social groups. Haider (2018) has written on how the dominant ideology of political interpellation in the United States is to convince its citizens (often at the level of normative unconscious processes, see Layton, [2006]) that there is no alternative to a neo-liberal capitalist system. "In this flat, hopeless reality," Haider writes, "some choose the consolations of fundamentalism. But others choose the consolations of identity" (2018, "Identity Politics"). White supremacy proves to be the example *par excellence* of this turning to identity as a compensation for the deprivations of inequality. But it is not the only one.

Smash the Cookie Jar

Drawing on Judith Butler's psychoanalysis of the formation of "the subject" within the neo-liberal state, Haider (2018) notes how identities are formed in accordance with certain requirements. The term "subject" betrays an ambivalence of meaning—being an agent capable of exerting power on the one hand, and also being "subjected," subordinated, under the control of external power. "The liberal form of politics" Haider clarifies, "is one in which we become subjects who participate in politics through our subjection to power" ("Identity Politics). It is a crystallized, fossilized notion of identity that then "locks us into the state, [which] ensures our continued subjection." Haider's answer by way of Butler is to "refuse"—I would clarify, *renounce*—those types of identity not only correlated with the disciplinary power of the neoliberal state, but also *identified with it*. My Freudian twist on Haider's words involves not just a rejection of "identity" as a foundation for thinking about social justice, but quite specifically *any identity formation that depends on an unconscious identification with the powerful, through which I can then wield institutional, systemic, and coercive power against others, including other marginalized groups*. My psychoanalytic clarification aside, I will follow Haider's definition of identity politics as "the neutralization of movements against racial oppression," and in turn wealth inequality. Identity politics, as defined by Haider, then emerges as an adaptation to our current social and political system that also advances the political and economic interests of race, class, gender, and sexual orientation elites.

Dovetailing with the psycho-politics articulated in this book, identity politics can become "tethered to a formulation of justice that reinscribes a bourgeois (masculinist) ideal as its measure" (Haider, 2018, "Identity Politics"). By coding demands for justice from marginalized groups within the language of identity politics, "the white male identity is enshrined with the status of the neutral, general, and universal." To put it somewhat facetiously—one starts to seek what is in the (White, Male, Upper-class, Heterosexual) cookie jar, rather than smash it and release its contents for everyone. Although White Supremacy and different forms of White nationalism function as the prototypical form of identity politics, there is the danger of racialized non-dominant subjectivities to *identify with this very kind of subject formation*. We already saw, for example, not only Freud's analysis of how suppressed (White/poor) classes can identify with the power and aim to be White, but how Freud himself, in seeking a White, Male, middle-upper class identity also enacted a turn against women, LGBTQ people, and other sub-altern racial groups (other Jews and people of color). We also saw Fanon's analysis of how colonized (including Black) people can become violent against and marginalize other colonized people through an identification with European male bourgeois Whiteness. In my analysis of Fanon we saw how even he, despite his emancipatory genius, *also* performed a Black male and heterosexual form of identity that subjected LGBTQ people and women of color to exclusion. The tacit and quite overt ways that identity politics can corrupt social justice causes cannot be understated.

When movements for racial justice base their methodologies in identity politics and lose their "grounding" in organizing for structural change, the "bourgeois masculinist ideal rushes to fill the void" (Haider, 2018, "Identity Politics"). There may be a pull for educational and professional attainment, careerism, economic mobility, protection from harassment, and the re-inscription of a meritocracy ("I didn't earn this position because of my race/affirmative action," and so on). Social change then becomes equivalent with "inclusion in the bourgeois masculinist ideal . . . inclusion in the structure of society as it is means forfeiting the possibility of structural change" (Haider, 2018, "Identity Politics"). But this is not what identity politics was initially deployed to do, and unfortunately reflects an assimilation of its emancipatory energies within capitalist modes of knowledge production.

Haider (2018) reminds us of the historical origins of the term "identity politics" in the work of the Combahee River Collective (see Taylor, 2017), a group of Black lesbian feminists who in 1974 realized that many single-issue political organizations often center the most privileged members of a constituency, who then marginalize the less privileged members in a form of internal subordination. For example, a LGBTQ rights group may center White males, whereas a racial justice movement may center cis-heterosexual men of color, etc. In order to address these gaps, the members of the Combahee River Collective developed their own brand of identity politics as a way of organizing and building relationship around issues that impacted LGBTQ women of color. In other words, this meant building a broad coalition across differences with economic, racial, gender, and sexual orientation-focused justice movements. Each intersection of identity then provided another angle of intervention through which by fighting to liberate LGBTQ Black women the members of the Collective would in turn *fight to liberate everyone*. In a sense, the focus seemed less on the intersection of identity and more on the intersection of oppressive systems, and the various communities harmed by them.

This is a far cry from identity politics today, which operates with a much narrower, as opposed to emancipatory, vision of intersectionality that calls for the privileging of the identity "with the most intersecting lines" as being the "most injured," and in turn most deserving "in the juridical framework to which politics is now reduced, both discursive and institutional protection" (Haider, 2018, "Contradictions"). Jousting with other marginalized groups in an "Oppression Olympics" earns access to crumbs from the master's table, a nibble from a cookie in the cookie jar. This form of activism, Haider observes, often results in a separatist and exceptionalist perspective, "rejecting even the minimal gesture toward coalitions implied by the term people of color." Separatist ideology, which Freire would have called "sectarian," prevents the building of relationships, coalitions and alliances among marginalized people, "the kind of unity that could actually overcome their marginalization" (Haider, 2018, "Contradictions").

From the perspective of a separatist, sectarian type of identity politics police brutality and colonialism become "Black" or "Brown" issues while the cost of living, the collapse of the housing market, and access to healthcare become "white issues," as if people of color did not suffer wage inequality, were not victimized by predatory mortgage loans, or did not struggle with disproportionate barriers to medical and mental healthcare. Even more granular forms of splitting take place, in which it is argued that Black activists should focus on police violence and "Black" issues, whereas LGBTQ activists should focus on marriage equality and "gay" issues, and Latinx activists should focus on immigration and "Latin issues." As if Afro-Latinxs did not suffer police violence, LGBTQ people of color did not struggle with being refugees in their home countries and denied asylum, and Black people (especially LGBTQ Black people) did not struggle with socio-economic conditions that render legal marriage an almost untenable economic privilege. Do each of these dynamics—this splitting—not comprise a different "sweetheart agreement" between marginalized communities and a White elite liberal class?

I want to clarify that I do not believe that White identity politics and the identity politics adopted by marginalized communities within the United States context are the same, or even equally problematic. I am also empathically *not* equating, for example, racial justice movements with identity politics as such. But, following Freud, Fanon, Freire and their descendant Martín-Baró, we have to deconstruct the lie—*la pura mentira*—that a reified, fossilized form of identity politics presents the only methodology for meaningful change. It risks a "sweetheart agreement" in which the existing economic and political order remains untouched in exchange for vapid gestures of diversity, inclusion, and representation on the system's—not our—terms. Recalling Freire, "To make capitalism more human is an impossible dream in which angelic spirits or incorrigible deceivers are devoted" (1996, p. 188). We must also seriously scrutinize how identity politics represents not only a form of self-defense of the oppressed within neo-liberal market capitalism, but also an unconscious ideological formation.

Haider (2018) correctly traces this back to how the subject, following Butler, "is tied up with a 'passionate attachment' to power . . . [which represents] an arbitrary repressive authority but also the models of selfhood" (2018, "Racial Ideology"). Freud and Fanon clearly analyzed how the White working class, in their identification to the ruling class, attempt to hurt people of color only to damage their own interests. So too Fanon and Freire showed how even people of color and other marginalized groups can, through an identification with repressive authorities, consciously attempt to rebel against Whiteness, but through their unconscious identification with it, wind up harming other oppressed groups as well as themselves. Martín-Baró in turn pointed to how political polarization envelops us in a web of lies in which it becomes impossible to discern friend from foe—no sense of common good is possible, no emancipatory coalition is tenable, only a thrashing in the dark, from which those who set up and spread *la mentira* benefit from the obfuscation of shared realities.

Remember, once again, our brief review of the history of colonialism in the Americas. Although there certainly was a history of alliances between indigenous peoples and escaped Black slaves, there was also a history of horizontal violence and identification with power. Free and escaped Blacks did venture into Native American territories and fight them in order to assist the expansion of American Empire, in the hopes that by procuring land they could generate capital, and with capital, assert the demand for civil rights and citizenship. Conversely, Native American nations did own and trade Black slaves who were forced to till the land and generate wealth, in the hopes that the capital raised could be used to assert native sovereignty. In Latin America, Brazil as a case in point (though we could add Puerto Rico as another example), Blackness and indigenous heritage were marginalized and pushed into greater *blanqueamiento*, an "enwhitenment" that was fantasized as helping accelerate economic development on par with Europe. Similarly, Fanon shows how in post-colonial African states the desire to mimic European capitalist practices led to the marginalization of different African ethnic, national, and tribal groups. In each of these examples identification with Whiteness per se may or may not have been present, as it also seems that anti-Black (and anti-Native) sentiment is possible *without* an idealization of Whiteness. But still, an identification with capitalist projects and policies, including a desire for recognition, drive oppressed people into punching down or sideways instead of up.

To repeat—White identity politics and the identity politics practiced by people of color and other oppressed groups are not the same nor do they occupy the same level of problematic subject formation. Nor does identifying the problems with identity politics in this context an attempt to "blame the victim." These forms of politics, however, present a problem in their ability to neutralize substantive efforts for societal and systemic change. They also demand an analysis of the tactics, strategies, and methods we employ, and a serious interrogation of whether those methods meet emancipatory racial, economic, gender, and sexual justice goals.

Breaking Out of the Impasse: Toward Insurgent Universality

Haider (2018) calls for an ethics conversant with that of the Zapatistas when he writes of the desire for "a world with no borders, a world with no detention, a world in which humans move freely and welcome every stranger" ("Universality"). Haider calls for an "insurgent universality" from below, "which says that we are not passive victims but active agents of a politics that demands freedom for everyone . . . I fight for my own liberation precisely because I fight for that of the stranger" ("Universality"). Stating it effusively and in a way that reverberates with Freire, Haider writes that insurgent universality is not handed down from an abstract universal above,

> It is created and recreated in the act of insurgency, which does not demand emancipation solely for those who share my identity but for everyone; *it says*

> *that no one will be enslaved.* It equally refuses to freeze the oppressed in a status of victimhood that requires protection from above; it insists that emancipation is self-emancipation. ("Universality," emphasis added)

Let us recall Freire's dictum—the primary task of the oppressed is to liberate themselves and other oppressed peoples, including the oppressor and sub-oppressor as well. This requires not a forgetting of wounds and sins. Rather, it asks us to risk an act of love—mentalizing even those who do not mentalize, let alone humanize us. But following the path of what I have called political mentalization, in mentalizing and humanizing even this other who is a source of our displacement we may create spaces for the mentalization of all. In order to build a coalition for social change and convince others to breach their "sweetheart agreement" with the elite class, we must be willing to rip apart our own. And in doing so, we incarnate the words cited in Immortal Technique's song "The Harlem Renaissance" (see Chapter 4)—we're looking for love from the wrong people. Why not love each other and make sure we are *all* protected?

Haider's argument for an insurgent universality parallels Fanon's (1952) critique of the Negritude movement as a kind of post-colonial identity politics. Rather than retrieving an uncomplicated and idealized view of Black identity from the past of Black peoples, Fanon argues that instead one must "recapture . . . the whole past of the world" (p. 226). Even more strongly, he states:

> Every time a man has contributed to the victory of the dignity of the spirit, every time a man has said no to an attempt to subjugate his fellows, I have felt solidarity with his act. In no way should I derive my basic purpose from the past of the peoples of color . . . I was committed to myself and to my neighbor to fight for all my life and with all my strength so that never again would a people on the earth be subjugated. It was not the black world that laid down my course of conduct. My black skin is not the wrapping of specific values. (pp. 226–227)

Fanon saw himself as responsible not only for the Black struggle, the anti-Colonial struggle, but also the working class struggle, and so too I would add, we must see ourselves responsible for the LGBTQ struggle, the feminist struggle, the immigrant struggle, etc., *regardless* of whether we share in their specific identity memberships. To reduce solidarity to identity for Fanon would be to "encase" human beings, whose "destiny [is] to be set free" (p. 230).

So too Freire (1996) in the latter stages of his career, articulated how the fight for liberation should not be restricted to a single category of analysis, whether gender, race, or class. "It is a fight to overcome obstacles to the humanization of all," he wrote "It is a fight for the creation of structural conditions that make a more democratic society possible" (p. 160). Not a perfect society in which no sexism, racism, or class divisions exist, but one which recognizes that human beings are limited and capable of great evil as well as love and fairness. In fighting for liberation, one can neither minimize the role of gender, race, or class, nor allow any one angle of analysis to demean another. Intersectionality for Freire, much like for the Combahee River Collective, is an analysis of the intersectionality of systems—"I cannot discount the struggle of women or the struggle against white oppression, but I also cannot afford to discount the role of class . . . in understanding racism and sexism. I cannot for the sake of my tactics in my own struggle" (p. 160).

From a policy point of view, I harken back to Carey McWilliams' (1948) analysis and proposal.[1] Drawing on a social and psychoanalytic analysis of American anti-Semitism in the 1930s and 1940s he concludes, similar to this text, that anti-Semitism much like anti-Blackness operates as a "mask for privilege," hiding the power and wealth of the elite class and mobilizing the White American working-class toward racist action to maintain the multifaceted system of inequality. He argued that a campaign to eradicate racism must be organized on two levels—"a general attack on the socio-economic conditions that breed the disease; and a special campaign to eliminate all forms of discrimination based solely on race, color, or creed" (p. 223). This necessarily entails an economic policy which brings the economy "under conscious democratic controls and must be made to serve a major purpose of all social organization—namely, to enlarge the areas in which co-operation rather than competition is the norm" (p. 224).

A social system built on social antagonisms, political polarization, and splitting is maintained by their reproduction. Hence, different economic arrangements in the distribution of wealth are called for, side by side with a robust anti-Racist program. Such a program must serve to ensure the equitable distribution of wealth and services to marginalized communities, and also provide pedagogical interventions to fight racial bias and foster a dialogue on how racism and other "isms" create an opening for wealth inequality and increasingly predatory forms of capitalism (to the extent there exist such things as "less predatory" forms). But working to reduce racial bias, for McWilliams (1948), goes beyond mere "cultural exchange groups" for sensitivity or tolerance, or displaying a hyper focus on the quirks and peculiarities of prejudice. Rather in like with Freire's work, a pedagogical program aims to demystify the function of racism to divide communities that might otherwise have a shared cause, and direct their attention toward the "real scapegoat" (pp. 241–249). By real scapegoat he means not yet another group to be denigrated, split, and defended against—but the very system of inequality, division, and conflict that mediates the antagonistic relationship between different social groups. A contemporary example of this kind of program in the United States is Haney Lopez's (2019) research on using political messaging that explicitly links race and class, pointing out to average voters how racism is used to divide Whites and People of Color in order to benefit the wealthy. This requires of necessity a critical pedagogy.

A Pedagogy of Liberation is a Pedagogy of Oppressor and Oppressed

In order to bridge the political polarization that divides us, we need to create spaces for dialogue that build epistemic trust between different communities, but especially those with histories of mutual mistrust and unequal violence—white working class people and Latinx/Black/Asian/Native American working class people, for example. As Freire teaches us, any pedagogical program, even progressively oriented ones, that depend on a banking method of education will either result in reproducing relations of domination or evoking a natural response of resistance in part of those being "educated." A problem-posing or dialogical approach is indicated, not just with historically oppressed communities (e.g., poor people of color) in developing political mentalization of their psychological and socio-economic conditions, but also toward those sub-oppressor communities (e.g., poor white people) who while privileged by their material and psychological relationship to the oppressor, also suffer within systems of inequality and stand to benefit from a more just society.

A couple of important points: let us remember Wilkinson and Pickett's (2009; 2019) research showing that while the poor and marginalized suffer the brunt of negative social outcomes in more unequal societies, inequality also leads to poorer outcomes to the upper end of the wealth spectrum as well—everyone becomes sick in a sick society, including those invested in maintaining and spreading the disease. As a result, while the poorest and most vulnerable communities would be the most benefited by greater equity (poor, displaced LGBTQ people of color), greater equity would also benefit the health and well-being of more socially well-off groups. A related point is that while my focus in this book has been on race and economics, the same argument can be made in regard to gender and sexual orientation antagonisms. Cis-heteropatriarchy is obviously most deadly, damaging and deleterious to trans-women and LGBTQ people, *but* it also requires the domestication, domination and distortion of cis-heterosexual men and their humanity in order to invest them in the maintenance of misogynist, heteropatriarchal structures.

The purpose of a pedagogical-dialogical project, following liberation psychology, is not merely to uplift the oppressed and convince the oppressor to be aware of and divest themselves of their privileges—it is to subvert the cyclical enactments that maintain racist, sexist, LGBT-phobic, and capitalist social, cultural, and economic formations. To put it succinctly, it is to subvert the oppressor-oppressed dialectic itself through the delineation of a space of eros, recognition, and solidarity. A space in which we can mentalize not only about one another's feelings, inner life, and beliefs, but how those subject formations arise from conditions of historical-material wounding, injury, and trauma that are the very symptoms of (racial, gendered, economic, sexual) inequality. A pedagogy of liberation does not "belong" to the oppressed, but it cries out from the negative space of non-being for recognition, restitution, and justice. As Fanon states, a cry that demands to be treated humanely and restores humanity to the other.

Freire (1996) addressed how a faux-progressivism drawing on the banking system of education can undercut social justice pedagogy. He states as a dictum, "We must not adopt a progressive discourse and then engage in a reactionary practice" (p. 160). He gives the example of a professor who fights against gender discrimination, but in their pedagogy "behaves in such an authoritarian manner that students have little room to be intellectually adventurous" becoming relationally both oppressor and oppressed, "that is, incoherent . . . [the] struggle against sexism loses its strength and becomes inconsequential babble" (p. 161). In such an enactment of power and domination, the professor is presented with two options: "to cynically accept authoritarianism and falsely continue the antisexist struggle, or to revise his or her relationship with the students in order to continue honestly the antisexist struggle" (p. 161). For Freire, the true antidote to this incoherence is humility, the ability to accept one's missteps as an educator, and endeavoring to repairing their relationship with their students, dying to their "ego" in order to "be reborn as true progressives" (p. 163). One must be progressive with respect to relational *process* as well as *content*.

Speaking for a moment from an empirical point of view, we have evidence that such an approach is not only possible, but effective. Randomized controlled trials and process-outcome studies provide evidence that intergroup dialogues, a contemporary pedagogical methodology grounded in Freire's work, are effective at raising critical consciousness and commitment to action through dialogue between oppressor and oppressed groups over above didactic instruction or mere debate about social issues (Gurin-Sands et al., 2012). Intergroup Dialogues places an emphasis on building relationships within and across groups, developing a critical consciousness of group identities and inequality, and increasing a commitment to social justice action. Groups of students from historically marginalized and privileged backgrounds are guided by facilitators to share their perspectives, actively listen and engage in empathy and perspective taking, and discuss how social structures can be changed. The facilitators' role is key, in that they help normalize the expression of emotion, and support members in reflecting back the feelings and thoughts of others—even others from a more privileged group. In essence, members are supported in their ability to mentalize politically. As we saw in Chapter 6, political mentalization allows for the creation of epistemic trust, the opening up of one's mind to the other, which then facilitates the exchange of ideas about one's psychological, social, and political world.

Part of the efficacy of these interventions is due to what is called intergroup contact theory (Pettigrew & Tropp, 2008). Intergroup contact theory states that prejudice and discrimination result from groups of people not having enough accurate knowledge, having high levels of out-group anxiety, and have less empathy and perspective taking toward the out-group. By itself this theory risks operating in a decontextualized, ahistorical manner without reference to the specific systems and structures of oppression, exploitation and inequality that exist in the world. However, it captures perfectly some of the symptoms that result from an ideology of domination, polarization, and social control that serves the interests of the powerful. The research conducted under this theory also shows that when people are divided by ideological and social forces, the ability for dialogue becomes impaired. Increased opportunity for contact then helps provide a more accurate and three-dimensional perspective on an out-group, reduced anxiety toward the other, and again, and increased ability to mentalize the other's experience and point of view.

However, mere contact between historically oppressed, sub-oppressor, and oppressor groups without attention to the quality of the interaction or without a program aimed at identifying the antagonisms that preclude solidarity is not sufficient, and can even be harmful. While positive and dialogical intergroup contact does lead to change in biases, prejudice, and perception of inequality, *negative* and aversive contact actually worsens prejudice and a avoidance of system causes at a higher rate (Stephan, 2014). This is why a dialogical, empathic, mentalizing approach is so important, as it helps inoculate pedagogy from being derailed and inadvertently reinforcing biases, which in turns maintain the status quo. But taking a politically mentalizing stance should not be confused with coddling or privileging the oppressor's or sub-oppressor's feelings. Quite the contrary, as feminist relational psychoanalyst Jessica Benjamin (1988) has written, to halt the cycle of domination "the other must make a difference." The oppressed "must claim their subjectivity and so be able to survive destruction," offering the oppressor "a new possibility of colliding with the outside and becoming alive in the presence of an equal other" (p. 221). Political mentalization entails surviving the dominating other's attack and still being able to reflect about their feelings, fears, and circumstances without retaliation. In doing so, the dominating other is functionally disarmed and then challenged to reconsider their earlier impressions—put into a position where now *they* must mentalize.

Recent research supports this notion, showing that at the end of racial intergroup dialogues group members' emotional engagement, awareness of racial privilege and inequality, and ability to engage in empathic perspective taking increased while their avoidance of difficult dialogues decreased. Interesting, however, there were no significant changes in the experience of or level of conflict. Furthermore, the perception that other group members were engaged in the dialogue predicted post-intervention increases in empathic perspective taking and awareness of racial privilege and inequality (Muller & Miles, 2017). Researchers interpret the lack of changes in perception of conflict as validating the assumption that conflict, confrontation, and challenging perspectives is a "necessary and expected component of intergroup interactions." Empathy, perspective taking, and emotional engagement—all hallmarks of mentalization—are not sentimental gestures aimed at providing comfort to the comfortable. Rather, they are assertive interventions that communicate that the other's violence has not destroyed my mind, and while I can create space in it for their humanity, I will not let them trample my own. *That* is a both a display of true revolutionary power, and an attempt to restore decency, justice, and equity.

A recent and ingenious example of political mentalization outside of the university can be found in Broockman and Kalla's (2016) groundbreaking study. They examined the impact of empathic perspective taking, of "imagining the world from another's vantage point" (p. 220) to engage in active, reflective, conscious processing of the other's experience, on voters' attitudes toward transgender rights. The canvassers in this study knocked on doors to speak with potential voters about trans rights by engaging in a series of strategies to facilitate dialogue, taking anywhere from 10 to 20 minutes. Canvassers first asked voters about their views and reflected their experiences back to them, and after defining the term "transgender," invited the voter to engage in "analogic perspective-taking." The canvasser would ask the voter about a time they had suffered discrimination, judgement, or some bias, and then encourage them to see if their experience "offered a window" into the experiences of trans people. The interaction would then end by asking the voter to describe if and how the exercise had changed their views.

The intervention was successful in reducing homophobia and transphobia among those surveyed, and increasing support for a non-discrimination law, lasting long after the canvassing took place. The case examples of successful dialogue are illuminating. One case involved a voter who was a military veteran and initially "unsympathetic" to trans issues. When invited to tell a story about an experience of discrimination he faced, he talked about how he was denied employment due to suffering PTSD. When the voter shared he felt that potential employers stereotyped him based on this one aspect of his identity, he then expressed thinking about what it would be like for a trans person if they were not hired because of their identity and "realized that he and such a transgender person would be similarly situated." In another example, the voter expressed he would not support transgender rights legislation out of fear that "predatory men using the law as an opportunity to enter women's bathrooms." When the canvasser expressed curiosity about his fear, he responded, "I'm from South America, and in South America we don't like fags." When the canvasser disclosed she was gay in a friendly, non-retaliatory manner, the voter expressed interest and curiosity in turn. They discussed their love for their respective partners, and how much "that love helps them overcome adversity. Gustavo tells Virginia that his wife is a disabled person." The voter disclosed that his partner had a disability, and that "God gave me the ability to love a disabled person," concluding that "taking care of one another is why love matters." The canvasser again reflected how much this resonates for her, and framed how anti-discrimination laws are about precisely that—"They're about how we treat one another." After he concluded there was no reason to be afraid of sharing a bathroom with a transgender person, the voter disclosed he was probably mistaken in his original position. When asked if he would vote in favor of banning anti-trans discrimination, he answered in the affirmative.

The cases from Broockman and Kalla's (2016) study are insightful and evocative. Mentalizing about one another's experience, thoughts, and feelings established epistemic trust and allowed for an exchange of views, values, and ideas. In that exchange, it is not only that the voters could see themselves in the other's shoes. In the case of the voter who was a war veteran, he situated himself in relation to trans people as both victims of discriminatory hiring practices that exclude those who are different. In the case of the South American voter, he was able to see himself and LGBTQ people as having a loving relationship that could be threatened if laws impaired their ability to care for their loved ones. The latter's insight that "taking care of one another is why love matters" speaks to central political, pedagogical, and even clinical ethic of this book—when we stop seeking love from our mutual oppressor, we can start loving each other, and make sure that everyone is taken care of.

A Psychotherapy From the People

Freud, Ferenczi, Fenichel, and Fromm were theorists, cultural critics, but also clinicians and psychotherapists. Fanon read Ferenczi and was intimately informed by him in his clinical work, and indirectly in his politics. Freire was an educator, but as Benjamin (1988) has observed, there is much affect in the relationship between teacher and student, affect that evokes powerful parallels between therapeutic and pedagogical relationships. Freud, Fanon, Freire, and Martín-Baró would all agree—love, to paraphrase Lacan, is a sign that healing, revolution, and transformation are taking place. Learning from the routes of their influences led us to connect psychoanalytic theories of liberation with attachment theory, and its extension, Fonagy's theory of mentalization. This connection allows us to integrate a theoretical and phenomenological psychoanalytic tradition with attachment theory as an empirically derived body of work. Of course, attachment theory historically speaking evolved from psychoanalysis, and there are also contemporary forms of research-based psychodynamic therapies and concepts. But integrating these theories in turn helps us bring together a broad array of empirical and theoretical considerations (e.g., intergroup contact theory, theories of trust and inequality, etc.) under one overarching framework (mentalization). Given the broad clinical interest in attachment theory from a psychoanalytic point of view, this also allows us to make a direct and explicit connection between the concerns of liberation psychology and psychotherapeutic work.

Psychoanalysis is fundamentally a theory of relationships and a theory of affect—how we regulate emotion and how it drives our behavior. But it is also a theory of mind and a theory of consciousness. More precisely, it is a theory of those thoughts that come to be associated with "negative" affect, and how they come to be dissociated from consciousness in order to maintain a tie with certain relationships—a theory of the *unconscious*, of what is and is not allowed within the bounds of conscious awareness. Thus Freud's initial dictum of psychoanalysis as a form of treatment, to make the unconscious conscious. A hundred years later, our understanding of psychoanalysis and psychotherapy has evolved, and with it how we frame what it is therapy accomplishes—providing a corrective emotional experience to rework our unconscious object relational schemas of self and other, to get in touch with warded off affect, to better manage and regulate feelings we feel ashamed or fearful of, to reflect in a deeper, more flexible way about ourselves in relation to others, and others in relation to us.

But the making of what is unconscious, tacit, unspeakable, verboten, and outside of our awareness *conscious*, to *concientize* it, has also evolved. We learn to understand ourselves, our inner life, our experiences more deeply, while also learning to understand and think deeply about the other—to see the other as a separate and complex site of agency (Benjamin, 1988). But psychoanalysis has also evolved yet further beyond this two-some of self and other, patient and therapist, bringing in the dimension of the "social third" (Altman, 2009). Or rather, recognizing that it has always been there, hidden in plain sight. With this shift in contemporary psychoanalysis, the connection with liberation psychology becomes obvious. Any therapist—certainly any psychoanalytically oriented one—works to mentalize deeply and coherently about their own internal state, feelings, thoughts, contradictions, and beliefs, as well as mentalize about the patient's inner world in all their profundity and depth. In mentalizing with the patient using reflections, questions, exploration, and interpretations, the patient's world is broadened to include a more complex permutations of self and other. Often through the survival of crises, ruptures, and enactments in the therapeutic relationship.

Related to the establishment of epistemic trust is another insight that can be drawn from Freud to Fanon to Freire—the ways in which even oppressed people can alternate between identification with the perpetrator and the victim of oppression. Addressing this splitting and dissociation of self-states, including socio-culturally mediated ones, becomes part and parcel of psychoanalytically informed culturally competent clinical work (Tummala-Narra, 2016; cf. Yeomans, Clarkin, & Kernberg, 2015).

The therapeutic relationship then becomes a space in which patient and therapist transform, rework, and reorganize their self-experience, within a new, emergent system—the relationship certainly *is* a system in and of itself. But it is not a self-encapsulated one, not a micro system existing in outer space somewhere. The relationship exists within a matrix of social, cultural, economic, and political antagonisms that call it forth to begin with. It is in many ways, a *symptom* of that very system. Psychotherapy is a structural response to a deficit of egregious inequality, an attempt to repair the symptoms of a structural failure. Looking back over our history, it always has been. The question becomes whether we reflect deeply, whether we actually allow ourselves with our patients to actually mentalize politically about this world of interlocking systems and structures, in order to imagine a different world, a different set of relationships. As Lynn Layton (2006) has argued, part of the function of normative unconscious processes is to destroy attempts to *link* intrapsychic, relational, and intersubjective dynamics in psychotherapy with the broader political, economic, and racial crises of our world.

I am reminded of an anecdote shared by psychoanalyst Ricardo Ainslie in the documentary *Psychoanalysis in El Barrio* (Christian et al., 2016), of when he was in analysis in Mexico during the conflicts of the 1970s and 1980s. Ainslie described being on the couch talking about a relationship dynamic in his life, associating and exploring his self-experience, when his analyst turns to him in his chair, exclaiming, "*Pero no ves que estamos en plena revolución?!*" "*But don't you see we're in the middle of a full blown revolution?!*" Delivered with some humor certainly, but this intervention exemplifies therapist inviting patient to reflect on their shared social crisis. To become conscious of a political and social upheaval that ultimately impacts our relationships and being in the world. The specific technique and tact involved in such an intervention is up for debate, but more and more important it becomes that clinicians think not just about cultural competence or diversity in their work, but also of equity, justice, and restoration. There is too much at stake not to.

As a clinician, Fanon (Fanon & Geronimi, 1959) was aware of how "The *a minima* master/slave, prisoner/gaoler dialectic" of oppressive social relations can be enacted within the therapeutic relationship. For him it is every therapist's responsibility to make the relationship a space in which the oppressor-oppressed dialectic "is radically broken . . . the doctor-patient encounter forever remains an encounter between two freedoms. That condition is necessary for all therapy, but especially in psychiatry" (p. 497).

The Liberation of Psychoanalysis

And what of psychoanalysis today? There are a number of important lessons to be drawn from this history for psychoanalytic theory, practice, and training. Lessons which can revitalize contemporary psychoanalysis itself. Firstly, a clear distinction between a "clinical" psychoanalysis and an "applied" or socio-political psychoanalysis does not seem supported in the original works of the first and second generations of psychoanalysts, let alone their descendants in the genealogy explored in this book. The relationship between clinical observations and social and cultural critique seemed dialectical in nature. Second, although I noted Ferenczi's influence throughout generations of progressive thinkers, one cannot discern a formal "break" or distinction between a "Freudian" or a "Relational" line. Quite the contrary, many of the figures of this book read and borrowed liberally from Freud, Ferenczi, Fenichel, Fromm, Klein, and others (in Ramos' case, even Jung!). They did not perceive or potentially care for the distinction between a "one person" or "two person" psychology. The whole of psychoanalytic thinking was drawn upon as sources of inspiration for anti-racist, anti-capitalist, and anti-colonial work. Thirdly, for clinicians who engaged in psychotherapy like Juliano Moreira, Arthur Ramos, and Frantz Fanon, it is important to note that they essentially taught themselves how to conduct psychoanalytic psychotherapy, either by reading Freud and Ferenczi's works, or in Fanon's case, with some clinical training and supervision. They did so, however, without care or concern for psychoanalytic institutes, analytic authority, or an "analytic establishment" as such. The case of Brazil and Argentina are illustrative in that with the arrival of "trained" analysts and the institutionalization of psychoanalytic training there was an erasure of the analytically informed clinical work and activism of Moreira, Ramos, and to an extent Langer's generation. Conversely, Langer herself did pursue the completion of her analytic training and a personal analysis. Although Fanon would not live to fulfill his dream, he did display an interest in undergoing a personal analysis and formal analytic training.

These points raise a number of issues regarding the state of psychoanalytic training. If these figures in psychoanalytic history, including the people of color among them, did not really mind or care for analytic training, then why should people of color interested in psychoanalytic thinking do so today? Especially when one considers the financial and time investment involved, and how these can exclude candidates from historically vulnerable populations. The answer, dialectically speaking, may lie not so much in upending the structure of analytic training wholesale—the frequency of sessions for personal analysis or analytic cases, etc.—but in allowing for greater flexibility in how analytic training is pursued. Not in dismantling the frame of analytic training, but in being open with it. Relatedly, all analysis should by definition be considered applied in nature. Patients and therapists do not exist in a vacuum, but function and relate within a broader sociopolitical world. By extension, psychoanalytic clinicians must be trained to think with their heart in the therapeutic relationship, and their feet marching in the streets advocating for social justice and equity. There is no theoretical or clinical precedent, historically speaking, for the illusion that our work can be disaggregated from the issues that affect our societies. If we truly ground ourselves in Freud or Ferenczi (or both!), then let us learn from their mistakes and take to heart their example that individual psychology is always already social psychology (Freud, 1921).

The natural objection may be raised, even among psychoanalytic practitioners, that in our existing economic system psychoanalysis and psychoanalytic training is too expensive and costly for poor and diverse communities. In the North American context managed care, it is often said, controls reimbursements and the length and quality of treatment. The reimbursements themselves are found wanting. These are certainly real issues that cannot be ignored. But if we only remember our history, we realize that the first generation of analysts developed innovative systems for redistributing wealth and resources. Every psychoanalyst contributed at least 4% of their income to fund free clinics. The analytic free clinics charged those with means and subsidized treatment for those who lacked, without compromising the integrity of treatment. Something like this is worth bringing back at a collective level beyond one's individual practice. But much more important is the fact that the early analysts advocated for welfare reform to include mental health issues. When will psychoanalysts not only talk about managed care and reimbursement, but start advocating for comprehensive healthcare reform? For a system and a society in which all can have access to mental health care, including long-term treatment? This would require us to get off the couch and into the streets.

Lastly, I want to advocate for the inclusion of the thinkers discussed in this book in the canon of psychoanalysis and psychotherapy teaching and training. With the publication of Khalfa, Young, and Corcoran's translation of Fanon's clinical writings (2018), we now have the opportunity to expose future analytic candidates and students of psychotherapy to his post-colonial psychoanalysis *and* his approach to psychoanalytic therapy. There is also much that can be learned from Freire's work about humility and relational responsiveness in psychotherapy, group work, and community activism. The novels of Ellison and Wright, infused with analytic ideas, provide a different but more experiential window into the dynamics of desire. By reading Freire and Fanon alongside Freud and Ferenczi, we stand to deepen the diversity of our tradition, and expanding our repertoire of ideas spanning clinical, communal, and societal applications of psychoanalysis.

CODA: AN ETHICS OF TRUTH AND JUSTICE

In wake of the violence over the Western Wall between Jews and Palestinians in 1929, Freud received a request from the Jewish Agency's Dr. Chaim Koffler. The letter, sent to prominent European Jews, asking Freud to lend his voice in criticism of British policy regarding access to the holy site and Jewish immigration to Palestine. In his response to Koffler, Freud wrote

> I cannot do what you wish. I am unable to overcome my aversion to burdening the public with my name and even the present critical time does not seem to me to warrant it. Whoever wants to influence the masses must give them something rousing and inflammatory and my sober judgment of Zionism does not permit this. I certainly sympathize with its goals, am proud of our University in Jerusalem and am delighted with our settlement's prosperity. But on the other hand, I do not think that Palestine could ever become a Jewish state, nor that the Christian and Islamic worlds would ever be prepared to have their holy places under Jewish care. It would have seemed more sensible to me to establish a Jewish homeland on a less historically burdened land. But I know that such a rational viewpoint would never have gained the enthusiasm of the masses and the financial support of the wealthy. I concede with sorrow that the baseless fanaticism of our people is in part to be blamed for the awakening of Arab distrust. I can raise no sympathy at all for the misdirected piety which transforms a piece of an Herodian wall into a national relic, thus offending the feelings of the natives. Now judge for yourself whether I, with such a critical point of view, am the right person to come forward as the solace of a people deluded by unjustified hope. (Cited in Yerushalmi, 1991, p. 13)

Freud cannot be called "anti-Zionist"—he wished for the liberation of the Jewish people from oppression and marginalization across the world, and believed they should have a home of their own where they can be protected and feel safe. But he cannot also be called a staunch Zionist per se.

Although he considered himself "a good Jew who has never renounced Judaism" he could never ignore his bias against religion, "including Judaism, which differentiates me from my fellow Jews and makes me unfit for the role you would like to assign to me" (cited in Chemouny, 1988, p. 127). He similarly expressed that despite his relentless criticism of religion he considered what was left of his Jewishness to be "a very great deal, and probably its very essence." That "very essence" we have covered in this book as the resources that allowed the Jewish people to survive countless persecutions, all the while maintaining that central ethic of the prophets—to love the poor, the widow, the orphan and the stranger. Remembering that they too were once strangers, enslaved and oppressed, in the land of Egypt. And as strangers, to value a life of truth and justice. But walls should not divide us—they should house us and create a scaffolding for the roof above. Beneath it should be nothing but laughter, the breaking of bread, the brewing of good coffee.

Freud believed in freedom for the Jews and the right to establish a home for their persecuted, displaced people. He *did not* object, and in fact expressed pride "of our University in Jerusalem" and felt "delighted with our settlement's prosperity" in Israel. He believed his people should have a home. But, in line with his psychoanalytic ethics of social justice, he did not believe a Jewish home should result in Palestinian homelessness. As Rose (2017) observed, "What Freud will not join in, or put his name to, is mass identification . . . national identity raised to a pitch . . . his distrust first arises from being the target of mass hatred as a Jew. As a Jew he dreads the mob, as a Jew he pulls back from national passion" (Chapter 2, "Displacement in Zion"). Like all things in this book, such "national passion" breeds mistrust which leads to cyclical, repetitive, enduring violence. Victim then becomes perpetrator begetting victim and birthing perpetrator anew in a whirlwind of tears, trauma, and tragedy. Still, time moves forward. People forget the historical and material reasons for the conflict, remembering only pain and loss with the trauma frozen in place.

Kill or be killed. *Lex talionis*. *Screw* unto others as others have screwed unto you. "They" are the source of "our" pain. "We" are innocent. "They" must be vanquished. Haven't we suffered enough? You criticize *our* violence but what about *theirs*? *What about* . . . and round and round it goes. Freud was right. We repeat instead of remember. Ferenczi was also right—in a sense we *need* to repeat. Fanon, too, was right—we repeat because our bodies will us to. And Freire had it right all along—we will not be free if we simply engage in a reversal of terms, each turn dancing to the tune of *Quitate tu, pa ponerme yo*.

"Oh my body," Fanon calls us back, "make of me always a man who questions!" Whenever our body lifts our hand to wound, to cleave, to injure, to destroy, to kill—let us turn to it with curiosity. Let us ask it questions—Why do you rise, oh hand of mine? Do you not remember we were once orphans? Should we let you come down with all your fury, and render orphans unto these? Do you remember? It is important you never forget, because the cry that calls out to you without knowing if it comes in peace or waging war, coming to accept or reject you, shake your hand or injure you, kiss you or kill you—that very same cry that cries out "Don't kill me! Have compassion for me! I am a daughter! I am a son! I am a mother! I am a father!"—listen to it closely. For that cry is yours.

"Bullshit!" You exclaim. "What about them!? The White person, the Black person, the immigrant, the Jew, the Palestinian, the straight, the gay, the man, the woman, the rich, the poor, the Hatfields, the McCoys—what of *their* violence? How do I trust them after all they have done? How dare you make us one and the same?!"

You are right. You are not the same. History, context, power, inequality—all of these things matter. But calling foul over "who goes first" will not get us out of this impasse. Of course somebody started it. We have the receipts. But as Ferenczi might say our hands are not clean. To repeat Dussel (1985), "To approach in justice is always a risk because it is to shorten the distance toward a distinct freedom" (p. 17). The only way to wash these hands is to put them down. Let me be clear—to choose to do so. When we keep them raised, ready to strike, we fear this freedom and the other on the other side of whom lies the unknown we fill with our unconscious. And we humans have come to fear that.

I am Latinx—I am Puerto Rican. The White man is my other and I have feared him. I am his other and he fears me. Some would argue it is not my responsibility to educate him. Freire would argue it is my primary task to free both myself and him. Fanon would remind me to not let him off the hook and demand humanity from him. Freud would interpret my hatred and my love, ask me to hold both while letting love rise above. To turn toward what we ignore, to attend to what evokes trembling, to be vulnerable toward the other I fear will hurt me, to privilege those things and those people that are cast out of my awareness—all of these represent a choice, a return, an option. A preferential option for the repressed.

NOTE

1. Carey McWilliams' work was pointed out to me by psychoanalyst Nancy McWilliams, who was his daughter-in-law. Of note, he drew on Fredric Wertham's psychoanalytic writings on race and capitalism within his own analysis of the use of anti-Semitism as a "mask for privilege."

Bibliography

Ahad, B. S. (2010). *Freud upside down: African American literature and psychoanalytic culture*. Chicago: University of Illinois Press.

Alschuler, L. R. (2007). *The psychopolitics of liberation: Political consciousness from a Jungian perspective*. New York: Palgrave Macmillan.

Altman, N. (2009). *The analyst in the inner city: Race, class, and culture through a psychoanalytic lens (2nd ed.)*. Hillsdale, NJ: Analytic Press.

Alves Soares, L. A. (2006). *A Sociologia critica de Guerreiro ramos: Um estudo sobre um sociology polemivo*. Rio de Janeiro: CRA-RJ.

Anderson, K. B. (2017). Marx's intertwining of race and class during the Civil War in the United States. *Journal of Classical Sociology*, *17*, 28–40.

Apple, M. W. (2003) Freire and the politics of race in education. *International Journal of Leadership in Education*, *6*, 107–118.

Aron, L. (1996). *A meeting of minds: Mutuality in psychoanalysis*. New York: Routledge.

Aron, L., & Starr, K. (2012). *A psychotherapy for the people: Toward a progressive psychoanalysis*. New York: Relational Perspectives Book.

Arredondo, P., & Perez, P. (2003). Expanding multicultural competence through social justice leadership. *The Counseling Psychologist*, *31*, 282–289.

Arroyo, J. (1973). *Paulo Freire: Su ideología y metodo*. Zaragoza, Spain: Editorial Hechos y Dichos.

——— (ed). (1990). *Universidad y cambio social: Los Jesuitas en El Salvador*. Mexico City, MX: Magna Terra.

Bacciagaluppi, M. (1993). Ferenczi's influence on Fromm. In L. Aron & A. Harris (eds.), *The legacy of Sandor Ferenczi* (pp. 185–198). New York: The Analytic Press.

Basauri, V. A. (1997). *Orígenes y fundamentos de la psiquiatría en España*. Madrid, Es: Editorial Libro del Año.

Beaty, B. (2005). *Fredric Wertham and the critique of mass culture*. Jackson: University Press of Mississippi.

Benjamin, J. (1988). *The bonds of love: Psychoanalysis, feminism, and the problem of domination*. New York: Pantheon Books.

———. (2004). Beyond doer and done to: An intersubjective view of thirdness. *Psychoanalytic Quarterly*, 73, 5–46.

Benveniste, D. (2012). Siegfried Bernfeld in San Francisco: A conversation with Nathan Adler. *Fort Da: The Journal of the Northern California Society for Psychoanalytic Psychology*, 18, 1–15.

Bergner, G. (1995). Who is that masked woman? Or, the role of gender in Fanon's *Black Skin, White Masks*. *Publication of the Modern Language Association*, *110*, 75–88.

Bernstein, R. J. (1998). *Freud and the legacy of Moses*. Cambridge: Cambridge University Press.

Berti, G., Forcadell, S., Serra, L., & Sol, M. (2012). El pensamiento desde la frontera: de Tosquelles a Guattari. In G. Berti (ed) *Felix Guattari: Los ecos del pensar entre filosofía, arte, y clínica*. Barcelona, ES: Haka Books.

Bick, M. (2016). Guerreiro Ramos's intellectual trajectory in the U.S. as seen through his writing. *ILHA: Revista de Antropologia, 18*, 229–253.

Bingham, C. (2002) On Freire's debt to psychoanalysis: Authority on the side of freedom. *Studies in Philosophy and Education, 21*, 447–464.

Borossa, J. (2007). Therapeutic relations: Sándor Ferenczi and the British independents. In L. Caldwell (Ed.), *Winnicott and the psychoanalytic tradition* (pp. 141–164). London: Karnac Books.

Brabant, E., Falzeder, E., & Giampieri-Deutsch, P. (1993). *The correspondence of Sigmund Freud and Sándor Ferenczi, volume 1: 1908–1914*. Cambridge, MA: Belknap Press.

Breger, L. (2000). *Freud: Darkness in the midst of vision*. New York: Wiley.

Brickman, C. (2003). *Aboriginal populations in the Mind: Race and primitivity in psychoanalysis*. New York: Columbia University Press.

Brookman, D., & Kalla, J. (2016). Durably reducing transphobia: A field experiment on door-to-door canvassing. *Science, 352*, 220–224.

Brunner, J. (1995). *Freud and the politics of psychoanalysis*. Cambridge, MA: Blackwell.

Buchen, T. (2012). "Learning from Vienna means learning to win": The Cracovian Christian socials and the "antisemitic turn" of 1896. *Issues in Contemporary Jewish History, 3*, 215–226.

Bulhan, H. A. (1985). *Frantz Fanon and the psychology of oppression*. New York: Plenum Press.

Burston, D. (1991). *The legacy of Erich Fromm*. Cambridge, MA: Harvard University Press.

Chemouny, J. (1988). *Freud et le sionisme*. Paris, Fr: Solin.

Cherki, A. (2006). *Frantz Fanon: A portrait* (N. Benabid, trans). Ithaca, NY: Cornell University Press.

Christian, C., Reichbart, R., Moskowitz, M., Morillo, R., & Winograd, B. (2016). Psychoanalysis in El Barrio. *PEP Video Grants, 1*, 1.

Cone, J. (1970). *A black theology of liberation*. New York: Lippincott.

———. (1975/1997). *God of the oppressed*. Maryknoll, NY: Orbis Books.

Cox, A. (2018). *The bone and sinew of the land: America's forgotten Black pioneers & the struggle for equality*. New York: Public Affairs.

Cruz, S. (2005). *Masked Africanisms: Puerto Rican Pentecostalism*. Dubuque, IA: Kendall Hunt Publishing.

Dagfal, A. (2012). Psychoanalysis in Argentina under Peronism and Anti-Peronism. In J. Damousi & M. B. Plotkin (eds.), *Psychoanalysis and politics: Histories of psychoanalysis under conditions of restricted political freedom* (135–163). Oxford: Oxford University Press.

Dalal, F. (2006). Racism: Processes of detachment, dehumanization and hatred. In K. White (ed.), *Unmasking race, culture, and attachment in the psychoanalytic space: What do we see? What do we think? What do we feel?* (10–33). London: Karnak Books.

Danto, E. A. (2005). *Freud's free clinics: Psychoanalysis & social justice, 1918–1938*. New York: Columbia University Press.

———. (2007). The Berlin Poliklinik: Psychoanalytic innovation in Weimar Germany [Spanish]. *Revista de la asociacion Psicoanalitica de Buenos Aires, 29*, 633–659.

———. (2009). "A new sort of 'Salvation Army'": Historical perspectives on the confluence of psychoanalysis and social work. *Clinical Social Work, 37*, 67–76.

———. (2012). "Have you no shame"—American redbaiting of Europe's psychoanalysts. In J. Damousi & M. B. Plotkin (eds.), *Psychoanalysis and politics: Histories of psychoanalysis under conditions of restricted political freedom* (213–231). Oxford: Oxford University Press.

———. (2016). Trauma and the state with Sigmund Freud as witness. *International Journal of Law and Psychiatry, 48*, 50–56.

De la Corte Ibanez, L. (1998). Compromiso y ciencia social: El ejemplo de Martin-Baro (Unpublished doctoral dissertation). Retrieved from http://www.uca.edu.sv/facultad/chn/c1170/testo.html on June 7th, 2019.

Delion, P. (2014). Tosquelles and Oury, because it was them . . . *Chimeras*, *84*, 20–28.

De Macedo, H. O. (2019). *Clinical lessons on life and madness: Dostoevsky's characters*. New York: Routledge.

Dias De Castro, R. (2015). Correspondência de Julio Porto-Carrero a Arthur Ramos: a Sociedade Brasileira de Psicanálise e a preocupação com a tradução dos termos psicanalíticos, décadas de 1920 e 1930. *Historia, Ciencias, Saude-Manguinhos*, *22*, 1451–1465.

Diaz-R. Labajo, M. A. (2016). *El exilio cientifico republican en Argentina: Contribuciones e impacto de los médicos, biomédicos, y psicoanalistas españoles en la ciencia argentina (1936–2003)*. Salamanca, ES: Ediciones Universidad de Salamanca.

Doane, R. (2004). Ralph Ellison's sociological imagination. *The Sociological Quarterly, 45*, 161–184.

Drescher, J. (1997). From preoedipal to postmodern: Changing psychoanalytic attitudes toward homosexuality. *Gender and Psychoanalysis*, *2*, 203–216.

Druet, A. (2012). Psychoanalysis in Franco's Spain (1939–1975): Crónica de una "agonía" anunciada. In J. Damousi & M. B. Plotkin (eds.), *Psychoanalysis and politics: Histories of psychoanalysis under conditions of restricted political freedom* (pp. 57–78). New York: Oxford University Press.

Du Bois, W. E. B. (1935). *Black reconstruction: An essay toward a history of the part which Black folk played in the attempt to reconstruct democracy in America, 1860–1880*. New York: Harcourt, Brace, and Company.

Duschinsky, R., Greco, M., & Solomon, J. (2015). The politics of attachment: Lines of flight with Boldby, Deleuze and Guattari. *Theory, Culture & Society*, *32*, 173–195.

Dussel, E. (1985). *The philosophy of liberation* (Aquila Marrinez & Christine Morkovsky, Trans.). Maryknoll, NY: Orbis Books.

———. (1996). *The underside of modernity: Apel, Ricoeur, Rorty, Taylor, and the philosophy of liberation*. New York: Humanity Books.

Eckenrode, J., Smith, E. G., McCarthy, M. E., & Dineen, M. (2014). Income inequality and child maltreatment in the United States. *Pediatrics*, 133, 454–461.

Eitington, M. (1923). Report of the Berlin psycho-analytical policlinic. *Bulletin of the International Psycho-Analytic Association*, 4, 254–269.

Eros, F. (1990). Technique as politics: Sandor Ferenczi's contribution to analytical social psychology. Presented at the Second Congress of the International Association for the History of Psychoanalysis, London, July 20–22.

———. (2014). Freedom and authority in the *Clinical Diary*. *The American Journal of Psychoanalysis*. *74*, 367–380.

Facchinetti, C., & Dias De Castro, R. (2015). The historiography of psychoanalysis in Brazil: The case of Rio de Janeiro. *Dynamis*, 35, 13–34.

Fania All-Stars. (1971). Quitate tu pa ponerme yo. On *Our Latin Thing/Nuestra Cosa* [Album]. New York: Fania Records.

Fanon, F. (1952/2008). *Black skin, white masks*. London: Pluto Press.

———. (1963). *The wretched of the earth* (R. Philcox, Trans). New York: Grove Press.

———. (1964). *Toward the African revolution: Political essays* (H. Chevalier, Trans.). New York: Grove Press.

Fanon, F., & Geronimi, C. (1959). Day hospitalization in psychiatry: Value and limits. Part two: doctrinal considerations. In J. Khalfa & R. Young (eds.), *Alienation and freedom* (S. Corcoran, Trans; pp. 495–509). London, UK: Bloomsbury Academic.

Fenichel, O. (1940). Psychoanalysis of antisemitism. *American Imago*, *1*, 24–39.

———. (1945). *The psychoanalytic theory of neurosis*. New York: W. W. Norton & Company.

———. (1946). Psychoanalysis of antisemitism. In Ernst Simmel (ed.), *Anti-semitism: A social disease* (pp. 11–32). New York: International Universities Press.

———. (1967). Psychoanalysis as the nucleus of a future dialectical-materialistic psychology. *American Imago*, *24*, 290–311.

Ferenczi, S. (1908). Psycho-analysis and education. In M. Baking (ed.), *Final contributions to the problems and methods of psycho-analysis* (pp. 280–290). London: Karnac Press.

———. (1910). Letter from Sandor Ferenczi to Sigmund Freud, March 22, 1910. *The correspondence of Sigmund Freud and Sandor Ferenczi, volume 1, 1908–1914* (pp. 153–154).

———. (1922a). The "family romance" of a lowered social position. In J. Rickman (ed.), *Further contributions to the theory and technique of psycho-analysis by Sandor Ferenczi* (pp. 413–416). London: Hogarth Press.

———. (1922b). Mental disturbance as a result of social advancement. In J. Rickman (ed.), *Further contributions to the theory and technique of psycho-analysis by Sandor Ferenczi* (pp. 417–418). London: Hogarth Press.

———. (1922c). Freud's "group psychology and the analysis of the ego": Progress in individual psychology. In M. Balint (Ed.), *Final contributions to the problems and methods of psycho-analysis by Sándor Ferenczi* (pp. 371–376). London: Hogart Press.

———. (1923). The sons of the "tailor." In J. Rickman (Ed.), *Further contributions to the theory and technique of psycho-analysis by Sandor Ferenczi* (pp. 418–419). London: Hogarth Press.

———. (1932/1988). *The clinical diary* (J. Dupont, Ed.; M. Balint & N. Z. Jackson, Trans.). Cambridge, MA: Harvard University Press.

———. (1929/1994). The principle of relaxation and neo-catharsis. In *Final contributions to the problems and methods of psycho-analysis* (pp. 108–125). New York: Karnac Books.

———. (1933/1994). Confusion of tongues. In *Final contributions to the problems and methods of psycho-analysis* (pp. 156–167). New York: Karnac Books.

Fikes Jr., R., & Cargille, D. A. (1986). The extraordinary career of Juliano Moreira: Afro-Brazilian psychiatrist. *Journal of the National Medical Association, 78*, 679–683.

Fonagy P. Luyten, P., Allison, E., & Campbell, C. (2017). What we have changed our minds about: Part 2. Borderline personality disorder, epistemic trust and the developmental significance of social communication. *Borderline Personality Disorder and Emotional Dysregulation, 4*, 9–21.

Ferenczi, S., & Rank, O. (1925). *The development of psychoanalysis*. Madison, CT: International Universities Press.

Freire, A. M. A., & Vittoria, P. (2007). Dialogue on Paulo Freire. *Revista Interamericana de Educacion para la Democracia, 1*, 97–117.

Freire, P. (1972). *Pedagogy of the oppressed*. New York: Continuum.

———. (1973). *Education for critical consciousness*. New York: The Seabury Press.

———. (1996). *Letters to Cristina: Reflections on my life and work* (D. Macedo, Q. Macedo, & A. Oliveira, Trans). New York: Routledge.

———. (2010). Paulo Freire, Karl Marx, e Jesucristo. Retrieved from https://m.youtube.com/watch?v=MF9–tZMwqjE on February 2, 2019.

Freire, P., & Faundez, A. (1989). *Learning to question: A pedagogy of liberation*. Geneva: World Council of Churches Publications.

Freud, S. (1900). Letter from Freud to Fliess, February 1, 1900. *The complete letters of Sigmund Freud to Wilhelm Fliess, 1887–1904*, 397–398.

———. (1905). Jokes and their relation to the unconscious. In J. Strachey (ed.), *The standard edition of the complete psychological works of Sigmund Freud, volume VIII (1905): Jokes and their relation to the unconscious* (pp. 1–247). London: Hogarth Press.

———. (1909). Letter to Putnam. In N. G. Hale Jr. (Ed.) (1971), *James Jackson Putnam and psychoanalysis*. Cambridge, MA: Harvard University Press.

———. (1913). Totem and Taboo. In J. Strachey (ed.),*The standard edition of the complete psychological works of Sigmund Freud, volume XIII (1913–1914): Totem and taboo and other works* (pp. vi–162). London: Hogarth Press.

———. (1914). The Moses of Michaelangelo. In J. Strachey (ed.), *The standard edition of the complete psychological works of Sigmund Freud, volume XIII (1913–1914): Totem and taboo and other works* (pp. 209–238). London: Hogarth Press.

———. (1916). Those wrecked by success. In J. Strachey (ed.), *The standard edition of the complete psychological works of Sigmund Freud, volume XIV (1914–1916): On the history of the psycho-analytic movement, papers on metapsychology and other works. ii–viii* (pp. 316–331). London: Hogarth Press.

———. (1917). Mourning and melancholia. In J. Strachey (ed.), *The standard edition of the complete psychological works of Sigmund Freud, volume XIV* (1914–1916*): On the history of the psycho-analytic movement, papers on metapsychology and other works* (pp. 237–258). London: Hogarth Press.

———. (1921). *Group psychology and the analysis of the ego*. New York: W.W. Norton & Company.

———. (1925). An autobiographical study. In J. Strachey (ed.), *The standard edition of the complete psychological works of Sigmund Freud, volume XX (1925–1926): An autobiographical study, inhibitions, symptoms, and anxiety, the question of lay analysis and other works, 1–292* (1–74). London: Hogarth Press.

———. (1927). The future of an illusion. In J. Strachey (ed.), *The standard edition of the complete psychological works of Sigmund Freud, volume XXI (1927–1931): The future of an illusion, civilization and its discontents, and other works* (pp. 1–56). London: Hogarth Press.

———. (1930). Civilization and its Discontents. In J. Strachey (ed.), *The standard edition of the complete psychological works of Sigmund Freud, volume XXI (1927–1931): The future of an illusion, civilization and its discontents, and other works* (pp. 57–146). London: Hogarth Press.

———. (1939). *Moses and monotheism*. New York: Knopf.

———. (1955a). Lines of advance in psychoanalytic therapy. In L. Strachey (ed. & trans.), *The standard edition of the complete psychological works of Sigmund Freud* (Vol. 17, pp. 157–168). London: Hogarth Press. (Originally published in 1919.)

———. (1955b). Dr. Anton von Freund. In L. Strachey (ed. & trans.), *The standard edition of the complete psychological works of Sigmund Freud* (Vol. 18, pp. 267–268). London: Hogarth Press. (Originally published in 1920.)

Freud, E. L (ed.). (1968). *The correspondence between Sigmund Freud and Arnold Zweig*. Frankfurt: S. Fischer.

Fromm, E. (1941). *Escape from freedom*. New York: Avon Books.

———. (1958). Psychoanalysis—science or party line? In E. Fromm, *The dogma of Christ and other essays on religion, psychology and culture* (pp. 131–144). New York: Holt, Rinehart and Winston.

———. (1959). *Sigmund Freud's mission*. New York: Grove Press, 1963.

Frosh, S. (2005). *Hate and the "Jewish science": Anti-Semitism, Nazism and psychoanalysis*. New York: Palgrave McMillan.

———. (2008). Freud and Jewish Identity. *Theory & Psychology, 18*, 167–178.

Gadotti, M. (1994). *Reading Paulo Freire: His life and work*. New York: State University of New York Press.

Garcia, J. E. (2014). Entre la aceptacion y el rechazo: Emilio Mira y Lopez y el psicoanálisis. *Revista de Historia de la Psicología, 35*, 99–128.

Garcia Siso, A. (1993). El Dr. Francesc Tosquelles i Llaurado: Posicion del autor dentro de la Psiquiatría catalana anterior a la Guerra Civil y la proyeccion de esta posición en su obra posterior. *Revista de la Asociacion Española de Neuropsiquiatria, 13*, 195–202.

Gates, H. L., & Appiah, K. W. (eds). (2005). *Africana: The encyclopedia of the African and African-American experience, second edition, vol. 5.* (p. 67). New York: Perseus Books.

Gay, P. (1988). *Freud: A life for our time*. London, UK: J.M. Dent & Sons.

Gaztambide, D. (2012). "A psychotherapy for the people": Freud, Ferenczi, and psychoanalytic work with the underprivileged. *Contemporary Psychoanalysis, 48*, 141–165.

———. (2015). A preferential option for the repressed: Psychoanalysis through the eyes of liberation theology. *Psychoanalytic Dialogues, 25*, 700–713.

———. (2017). A "psychoanalysis for liberation": Reading Freire as an act of love. *Psychoanalysis, Culture, & Society, 22*, 193–211.

Geehr, R. S. (1990). *Karl Lueger: Mayor of fin de siecle Vienna*. Detroit: Wayne State University Press.

Geller, Jay. (2007). *On Freud's Jewish body: Mitigating circumcisions*. New York: Fordham University Press.

Gherovici, P. (2003). *The Puerto Rican syndrome*. New York: Other Press.

Gibson, N.C., & Beneduce, R. (2017). *Frantz Fanon, Psychiatry, and Politics*. London: Rowman & Littlefield.

Gilman, S. L. (1991). *The Jew's body*. New York: Routledge.

———. (1993a). *The Case of Sigmund Freud: Medicine and identity at the fin de siecle*. London: The John Hopkins University Press.

———. (1993b). *Freud, race, and gender*. Princeton, NJ: Princeton University Press.

Ginsburg, L. M. (1999). Sigmund Freud's racial vocabulary and related fragments from the analyses of Clarence P. Oberndorf and Smiley Blanton. *International Forum of Psychoanalysis, 8*, 243–248.

———. (2015). An elegy for Clarence P. Oberndorf, M. D. (1882–1954). Posted on internationalpsychoanalysis.net, October 22, 2015. Retrieved on May 20, 2018.

Gonzalez-Monteagudo, J. (2014). Criticism and meaning of the criticism in Paulo Freire. *Practiques de Formation, 8*, 49–65.

Guimaraes, A. (2008). Africanism and racial democracy: The correspondence between Herskovits and Arthur Ramos (1935–1949). *Estudios Interdisciplinarios de America Latina y el Caribe, 19*, 53–79.

Gurin-Sands, C., Gurin, P., Nagda, B. A., & Osuna, S. (2012). Fostering a commitment to social action: How talking, thinking, and feeling make a difference in intergroup dialogue. *Equity & Excellence in Education, 45*, 60–79.

Gutierrez, G. 1988. *A theology of liberation*. New York: Orbis Books.

Haider, A. (2018). *Mistaken Identity: Race and Class in the Age of Trump* [Kindle version]. New York: Verso.

Haney Lopez, I. (2019). *Merge left: Fusing race and class, winning elections, and saving America*. New York: The New Press.

Harper, E. (2012). Homelessness and violence: Freud, Fanon and Foucault and the shadow of the Afrikan sex worker (Unpublished doctoral dissertation). Retrieved from www.Academia.edu on January 20, 2019.

Harris, B., & Brock, A. (1991). Otto Fenichel and the left opposition in psychoanalysis. *Journal of the History of the Behavioral Sciences, 27*, 157–164.

Haynal, A. (1993). Ferenczi and the origins of psychoanalytic technique. In L. Aron & S. Harris (eds.), *The legacy of Sándor Ferenczi* (pp. 53–74). Hillsdale, NJ: Analytic Press.

Herzog, D. (2017). *Cold War Freud: Psychoanalysis in an age of catastrophes*. Cambridge, MA: Cambridge University Press.

Hoffman, D. (2003). Sandor Ferenczi and the origins of humanistic psychology. *Journal of Humanistic Psychology, 43*, 59–86.

Hollander, N. C. (1997). *Love in a time of hate: Liberation psychology in Latin America*. New Brunswick, NJ: Rutgers University Press.

———. (2010). *Uprooted minds: Surviving the politics of terror in the Americas*. New York: Taylor & Francis Group.

Holloway, R. (1978). The limits of education: Siegfried Bernfeld on psychology, political theory, and education. *Interchange, 9*, 72–92.

Horton, M., & Freire, P. (1990). *We make the road by walking: Conversations on education and social change*. Philadelphia, PA: Temple University Press.

Inclan, J. (1985). Variations in value orientations in mental health work with Puerto Ricans. *Psychotherapy: Theory, Research, Practice, Training, 22*, 324–334.

Interian, A., & Diaz-Martinez, A. (2007). Considerations for culturally competent cognitive-behavioral therapy for depression with Hispanic patients. *Cognitive and Behavioral Practice, 14*, 84–97.

Ignatin, N., & Allen, T. (1967). White blindspot. In T. Allen et al. (eds.). *Understanding and fighting White supremacy: A collection* (pp. 26–33). Chicago: Sojourner Truth Organization.

Ivey, A. E. (1995). Psychotherapy as liberation: Toward specific skills and strategies in multicultural counseling and therapy. In J. G. Ponterotto, J. M. Casas, L. A. Suzuki, & C. M. Alexander (eds.), *Handbook of multicultural counseling* (pp. 53–72). Thousand Oaks, CA: Sage Publications.

Ivey, A. E., & Collins, N. M. (2003). Social justice: A long-term challenge for counseling psychology. *The Counseling Psychologist*, *31*, 290–298.
Jacoby, R. (1986). *The repression of psychoanalysis: Otto Fenichel and the political Freudians*. Chicago: University of Chicago Press.
Jeannot, T. (2007). Marx, capitalism, and race. *Radical Philosophy Today*, *5*, 69–92.
Jones, J. W. (2008). *Blood that cries from the earth*. Oxford: Oxford University Press.
Jonte-Pace, D. (2006). Psychoanalysis, colonialism, and modernity: Reflections on Brickman's aboriginal populations in the mind. *Religious Studies Review*, *32*, 1–4.
Judson, P. M. (2016). *The Habsburg empire: A new history*. Cambridge, MA: Harvard University Press.
Krauthamer, B. (2013). *Black slaves, Indian masters: Slavery, emancipation, and citizenship in the Native American South*. Chapel Hill: The University of North Carolina Press.
Kebede, M. (2001). The rehabilitation of violence and the violence of rehabilitation: Fanon and Colonialism. *Journal of Black Studies*, *31*, 539–562.
Khalfa, J., & Young, R. (eds). (2018). *Alienation and freedom* (S. Corcoran, Trans.). London, UK: Bloomsbury Academic.
Kim, S., & Rutherford, A. (2015). From seduction to sexism: Feminists challenge the ethics of therapist-client sexual relations in 1970s America. *History of Psychology*, *18*, 283–296.
Klein, D. B. (1985). *Jewish origins of the psychoanalytical movement*. Chicago: Chicago University Press.
Lake, R., & Dagostino, V. (2013). Converging self/other awareness: Erich Fromm and Paulo Freire on transcending the fear of freedom. In Robert Lake & Tricia Kris's (eds.), *Paulo Freire's intellectual roots: Toward historicity in praxis* (pp. 101–126). London, UK: Bloomsbury Publishing Inc.
Lange, B. (2008). Importing Freud and Lamarck to the tropics: Arthur Ramos and the transformation of Brazilian racial thought, 1926–1939. *The Americas*, *65*, 9–34.
Langer, M. (1978). Vicissitudes of the Argentinian psychoanalytic movement. In Franco Basaglia et al. (ed.), *Razón, Locura, y Sociedad* (pp. 56–84). Buenos Aires, Argentina: Siglo XXI Editores. Reprinted in 2006.
Layton, L. (2006). Racial identities, racial enactments, and normative unconscious processes. *Psychoanalytic Quarterly*, *75*, 237–269.
Sanchez Lazaro, J. (1986). El psicoanálisis de Freud en la obra de Emilio Mira y Lopez (1921–1936). *Revista de la Asociation Española de Neuropsiquiatria*, *VI*, 636–649.
Levinas, E. (1989). *The Levinas Reader*. Edited by Sean Hand. Cambridge, MA: Basil Blackwell.
Lorenzini, N., Campbell, C., & Fonagy, P. (2018). Mentalization and its role in processing trauma. In B. Huppertz (ed.), *Approaches to psychic trauma: Theory and practice* (pp. 403–422). Lanham, MD: Rowman & Littlefield.
Macey, D. (2012). *Frantz Fanon: A biography*. New York: Verso.
Maguire, D. (2005). *A moral creed for all Christians*. Minneapolis, MN: Fortress Press.
Maia, J. M. (2014). History of sociology and the quest for intellectual autonomy in the global South: The cases of Alberto Guerreiro Ramos and Syed Hussein Alatas. *Current Sociology*, *62*, 1–19.
Maio, M. C. (2015). Guerreiro Ramos interpela a UNESCO: ciências sociais, militância e antirracismo. *Caderno, CRH, Salvador*, *28*, 77–89.
Makari, G. (2008). *Revolution in mind*. New York: HarperCollins.
Martín-Baró, I. (1971). Recensión a la obra de Arroyo Lasa, Jesus: *Reflexiones sobre psicología social*. *Estudios Centroamericanos*, *26*, 211–212.
———. (1976). La verdad de la mentira. *Alternativa*, *1*, 1.
———. (1994). *Writings for a liberation psychology* (A. Aron & S. Corne, Trans.). Cambridge, MA: Harvard University Press.
———. (1995). Procesos psíquicos y poder. *Psicología de la acción política*, 205-233.
Marx, K. ([1867–1875] 1976). *Capital, vol. 1* (B. Fowkes, Trans.). New York: Vintage Books.
Mayo, P. (1993). When does it work? Freire's pedagogy in context. *Studies in the Education of Adults*, *25*, 11–31.

McGoldrick, M., Giordano, J., & Garcia Preto, N. (2005). *Ethnicity and family therapy, 3rd ed.* New York: Guilford Press.

McWilliams, C. (1948). *A mask for privilege: Anti-Semitism in America*. New Brunswick, NJ: Transaction Publishers.

MECW: Marx, K., & Engels, F. (1975–2004) Collected Works, 50 vols. New York: International Publishers.

Meszaros, J. (1993). Ferenczi's preanalytic period embedded in the cultural streams of the fin de siécle. In L. Aron & S. Harris (eds.), *The legacy of Sándor Ferenczi* (pp. 41–51). Hillsdale, NJ: Analytic Press.

———. (2012). Effect of dictatorial regimes on the psychoanalytic movement in Hungary before and after World War II. In J. Damousi & M. B. Plotkin (eds.), *Psychoanalysis and Politics: Histories of Psychoanalysis under Conditions of Restricted Political Freedom* (pp. 79–108). Oxford: Oxford University Press.

Meyer, William S. (2005). The "Mother' Returns to Psychoanalysis." *Smith College Studies in Social Work, 75*, 15–31.

Millán, S. (2000). The legacy of Fromm in México. *International Forum of Psychoanalysis, 9,* 207–215.

Mira y Lopez, E. (1937). El rol de las condiciones sociales en la génesis de los disturbios mentales. *Actas del Segundo Congreso Internacional de Higiene Mental, Paris* (pp. 405–420). Paris, FR: Imp. Coueslant.

Mitchell, J. (1974/2000). *Psychoanalysis and feminism: A radical reassessment of Freudian psychoanalysis*. New Edition. New York: Basic Books.

Moreau-Ricaud, M. (1996). The founding of the Budapest School. In P. L. Rudnytsky, A. Bokay, & P. Giampieri-Deutsch (Eds.), *Ferenczi's turn in psychoanalysis* (pp. 41–59). New York: New York University Press.

Muller, J. T., & Miles, J. R. (2017). Intergroup dialogue in undergraduate multicultural psychology education: Group climate development and outcomes. *Journal of Diversity in Higher Education, 10*, 52–71.

Nagel, J. (2000). Ethnicity and sexuality. *Annual Review of Sociology, 26*, 107–133.

Nakagawa, S. (2012). Blackness is the fulcrum. Retrieved from https://www.racefiles.com/2012/05/04/blackness-is-the-fulcrum/ on February 8, 2018.

Nicholls, T. (2015). "Frantz Fanon (1925–1961)" in Internet Encyclopedia of Philosophy, The University of Tennessee Martin. Retrieved from http://www.iep.utm.edu/fanon on January 13, 2019.

Payne, S. G. (1987). *The Franco Regime 1936–1975*. Madison: The University of Wisconsin Press.

Perez-Foster, R. M., Moskowits, M., & Javier, R. A. (1996). *Reaching across boundaries of culture and class: Widening the scope of psychotherapy*. New York: Jason Aronson.

Pettigrew, T. F., & Tropp, L. R. (2008). How does contact reduce prejudice? A meta-analytic test of three mediators. *European Journal of Social Psychology, 38*, 922–934.

Pickett, K., & Wilkinson, R. G. (2015). Income inequality and health: A causal review. *Social Science & Medicine, 128*, 316–326.

Plotkin, M. (2018). Freud and the Latin Americans: A forgotten relationship. In P. Gherovici & C. Christian (eds.), *Psychoanalysis in the Barrios: Race, class, and the unconscious* (pp. 21–37). New York: Routledge Publishers.

Plotkin, M., & Honorato, M. (2017). *Estimado Doctor Freud*. Buenos Aires, AR: Edhasa.

Portillo, N. (2012). The life of Ignacio Martín-Baró: A narrative account of a personal biographical journey. *Peace and Conflict: Journal of Peace Psychology, 18*, 77–87.

Preston, P. (2006). *The Spanish Civil War: Reaction, revolution, and revenge*. New York: Harpercollins

———. (2013). *The Spanish holocaust: Inquisition and extermination in twentieth-century Spain*. New York: W.W. Norton & Company.

Rachman, A. W. (1993). Ferenczi and sexuality. In L. Aron & S. Harris (eds.), *The legacy of Sándor Ferenczi* (pp. 81–100). Hillsdale, NJ: Analytic Press.

———. (1998). Ferenczi's relaxation principle and the issue of therapeutic responsiveness. *The American Journal of Psychoanalysis, 58*, 63–81.

———. (2007). Sándor Ferenczi's contributions to the evolution of psychoanalysis. *Psychoanalytic Psychology, 24* (1), 74–96.
Rampersad, A. (2007). *Ralph Ellison: A biography*. New York: Vintage Books.
Reijzer, H., & Ringold, J. K. (trans). (2011). *A dangerous legacy: Judaism and the psychoanalytic movement*. Uitgeverij, Nederlands: Karnac Books.
Ricoeur, P. (1970). *Freud and philosophy: An essay on interpretation*. New Haven, CT: Yale University Press.
Roediger, D. R. (2007). *The wages of Whiteness: Race and the making of the American working class, revised edition*. New York: Verson.
Rose, J. (2003). Response to Edward Said. In E. Said (ed.), *Freud and the non-European* (pp. 63–80). London: Verson.
———. (2017). *The last resistance*. Brooklyn, NY: Verso Books.
Rothman, S., & Isenberg, P. (1974). Sigmund Freud and the politics of marginality. *Central European History, 7*, 58–78.
Rubin, A., Mandelbaum, B., & Frosh, S. (2016). "No memory, no desire": Psychoanalysis in Brazil during repressive times. *Psychoanalysis and History, 18*, 93–118.
Rubin, G. (1997). The traffic in women: Notes on the "political economy" of sex. In L. Nicholson (ed.), *The second wave: A reader in feminist theory* (pp. 27–62). New York: Routledge.
Rudnytsky, P. (2015). Freud, Ferenczi, Fromm: The authoritarian character as magic helper. First published in *Fromm Forum* (English Edition), *19*, 5–10.
———. (2016). The indispensability of Erich Fromm: The rehabilitation of a "forgotten" psychoanalyst. Erich Fromm Lecture delivered at the International Psychoanalytic University, Berlin, October 13, 2016. Cited with permission from the author.
Ruiz, J. (2012). *The "Red Terror" and the Spanish Civil War: Revolutionary violence in Madrid*. New York: Cambridge University Press.
Russo, J. A. (2014). Psychoanalysis in Brazil—institutionalization and dissemination among the lay public. *Estudios Interdisciplinarios de America Latina y el Caribe, 18*, 63–80.
Safran, J. D., & Muran, J. C. (2000). *Negotiating the therapeutic alliance: A relational treatment guide*. New York: Guilford Press.
Said, E. (2003). *Freud and the non-European*. New York: Verso Books.
Salberg, Jill. (2007). "Hidden in Plain Sight: Freud's Jewish Identity Revisited." *Psychoanalytic Dialogues, 17*, pp. 197–217.
Sand, S. (2017). How contemporary psychoanalysis contributes to LGBT psychology: Examining and addressing gender fluidity and diversity as we slide toward 21st-century transformations. In R. Ruth & E. Santacruz (eds.), *LGBT psychology and mental health: Emerging research and advances* (pp. 69–85). Santa Barbara, CA: Praeger Publishers.
Schorske, C. E. (1981). *Fin-de-Siegel Vienna: Politics and culture*. New York: Vintage Books.
Siassi, I., & Messer, S. (1976). Psychotherapy with patients from lower socioeconomic groups. *The American Journal of Psychotherapy, 30*, 29–40.
Simmel, E. (1946a). *Anti-Semitism: A social disease*. New York: International Universities Press.
———. (1946b). Otto Fenichel. *International Journal of Psychoanalysis, 27*, 67–71.
Simpson, D. J., & McMillan, S. (2008). Is it time to shelve Paulo Freire? *Journal of Thought, 43*, 1–6.
Singh, N. P. (2016). On race, violence, and so-called primitive accumulation. *Social Text, 34*, 27–50.
Skidmore, T. E. (1993). *Black into White: Race and nationality in Brazilian thought*. Durham, NC: Duke University Press.
Stephan, W. G. (2014). Intergroup anxiety: Theory, research, and practice. *Personality and Social Psychology Review, 18*, 239–255.
Sue, D. W. (2001). Multidimensional facets of cultural competence. *The Counseling Psychologist, 29*, 790–821.
Sue, D. W., & Sue, D. (1977). Barriers to effective cross-cultural counseling. *Journal of Counseling Psychology, 24*, 420–429.

———. (2015). *Counseling the culturally diverse: Theory & practice, 7th ed.* New York: Wiley Publishers.

Sue, S., & Zane, N. (1987). The role of culture and cultural techniques in psychotherapy: A critique and reformulation. *American Psychologist, 42*, 37–45.

———. (2009). The role of culture and cultural techniques in psychotherapy: A critique and reformulation. *Asian American Journal of Psychology, S*, 3–14.

Sullivan, H. S. (1940). Discussion of the case of Warren Wall. In E. Franklin Frazier (ed.), *Negro youth at the crossroads: Their development in the middle states* (pp. 228–234). Washington, DC: American Council on Education.

———. (1941). Memorandum on a psychiatric reconnaissance. In Charles Johnson (ed), *Growing up in the black belt: Negro youth in the rural south* (pp. 328–333). Washington, DC: American Council on Education.

Sziklai, A. (2016). The Jewish theme in the relationship of Sigmund Freud and Sándor Ferenczi: Between the state and the public sphere. Instituto de Desarrollo Psicológico. INDEPSI. LTDA. ALSF-CHILE. Retrieved January 9, 2018, from https://pdfs.semanticscholar.org/f46e/c78c0ba8e9acdd7ccadbd53a832ae5295136.pdf.

Tampa, M., Sarbu, I., Matei, C., Benea, V., & Georgescu, S. R. (2014). Brief history of syphilis. *Journal of Medicine and Life, 7*, 4–10.

Tate, C. (1996). Freud and his "negro": Psychoanalysis as ally and enemy of African Americans. *Journal for the Psychoanalysis of Culture and Society, 1*, 53–62.

Tate, K., Rivera, E., & Edwards, L. (2015). Colonialism and multicultural counseling competence research: A liberatory analysis. In R. Goodman & P. Gotski (eds.), *Decolonizing "multicultural" counseling through social justice*. New York: Springer.

Taylor, K. (ed.). (2017). *How we get free: Black feminism and the Combahee River Collective*. Chicago: Haymarket Books.

Technique, I. (2008). Harlem Renaissance. On *The 3rd world* [Album]. New York: Viper Records.

Theiss-Abendroth, P. (2013). Sigmund Freud in the tropics. The first psychoanalytic dissertation in the Portuguese-speaking world (1914). *Archives of Clinical Psychiatry* (São Paulo), *40*, 81.

Tosquelles, F. (1975/2017). Frantz Fanon en Saint-Alban. *Teoría y Crítica de la Psicologia, 9*, 223–229.

Tuhkanen, M. (2009). *The American optic: Psychoanalysis, critical race theory, and Richard Wright*. Albany: State University of New York Press.

Tummala-Narra, P. (2016). *Psychoanalytic theory and cultural competence in psychotherapy*. Washington, DC: American Psychological Association.

Valladares De Oliveira, C. L. M. (2012). Psychoanalysis in Brazil during Vargas' time. In J. Damousi & M. B. Plotkin (eds.), *Psychoanalysis and politics: Histories of psychoanalysis under conditions of restricted political freedom* (pp. 113–133). Oxford: Oxford University Press.

Vera, E. M., & Speight, S. L. (2003). Multicultural competence, social justice, and counseling psychology: Expanding our roles. *The Counseling Psychologist, 31*, 253–272.

Wachtel, P. L. (2002). Psychoanalysis and the disenfranchised: From therapy to justice. *Psychoanalytic Psychology, 19*, 199–215.

Walzer, M. (1985). *Exodus and revolution*. New York: Basic Books.

Watkins, M., & Shulman, H. (2008). *Toward psychologies of liberation*. New York: Palgrave McMillan.

Wertham, F. (1955). *The circle of guilt*. Jackson: University Press of Mississippi.

———. (1966). *A sign for Cain: An exploration of human violence*. New York: MacMillan Publishing Company.

Wilkinson, R. G., & Pickett, K. (2009). *The spirit level: Why greater equality makes societies stronger*. New York: Bloomsbury Press.

———. (2019). *The inner level: How more equal societies reduce stress, restore sanity and improve everyone's well-being*. New York: Penguin Press.

Wistrich, R.S. (1983). Karl Lueger and the ambiguities of Viennese anti-Semitism. *Jewish Social Studies, 45*, 251–262.

Wright, R. (1946). Psychiatry comes to Harlem. *Free World*, September, 49–51.
Yang, C. (2014). Encounters between the "oppressed" and the "oppressor": Rethinking Paulo Freire in anti-racist feminist education in Sweden. *Race, Ethnicity, and Education, 19*, 835–855.
Yeomans, F. E., Clarkin, J. F., & Kernberg, O. F. (2015). *Transference-focused psychotherapy for borderline personality disorder: A clinical guide*. Washington, DC: American Psychiatric Publishing.
Yerushalmi, Y. H. (1991). *Freud's Moses: Judaism terminable and interminable*. New Haven: Yale University Press.
Zaretsky, E. (2004). *Secrets of the soul: A social and cultural history of psychoanalysis*. New York: A. A. Knopf.
———. (2015). *Political Freud*. New York: Columbia University Press.
Zeilig, L. (2016). *Frantz Fanon: The militant philosopher of third world revolution*. London, UK: I.B. Tauris.
Zinn, Howard. (2005). *A people's history of the United States, 1492–present*. New York: Harper Perennial Modern Classics.
Zizek, S. (2006). *The parallax view*. Cambridge, MA: MIT Press.

Index

About the Author

Daniel José Gaztambide, PsyD, is an assistant professor in the Department of Psychology at the New School for Social Research, and a voluntary faculty member at the Mt. Sinai St. Luke's Hospital. He has served in various roles within the American Psychological Association, including as liaison of the Division of Psychoanalysis and Psychoanalytic Psychology (39) to the Committee of Ethnic Minority Affairs, and chair of the Professional Practice Committee of the Division for the Advancement of Psychotherapy (29). Dr. Gaztambide has written numerous articles and book chapters on cultural competency, social justice and psychodynamic practice, race and class in the treatment of borderline personality disorder, and the psychology of religion. He is a clinical psychologist in private practice and is currently an analytic candidate at the NYU Postdoctoral Program in Psychotherapy and Psychoanalysis. Aside from his advocacy, scholarship, and practice as a psychologist, Dr. Gaztambide is also an artist, storyteller, and performer in New York City. He is a member of the Puerto Rican poetry troupe The Títere Poets, and a cohost of the podcast *Pan con Títeres*, which addresses the intersection of poetry, trauma, mental health, and Puerto Rican identity.

Milton Keynes UK
Ingram Content Group UK Ltd.
UKHW041400120324
439387UK00004B/20

9 781498 565745